PENGUIN  CLASSICS

THE PENGUIN BOOK OF THE UNDEAD

SCOTT G. BRUCE is a professor of medieval history and the director of the Center for Medieval and Early Modern Studies at the University of Colorado at Boulder. An expert on medieval monasticism, he has written two books about the monks of the abbey of Cluny: *Silence and Sign Language in Medieval Monasticism: The Cluniac Tradition, c. 900–1200* (2007) and *Cluny and the Muslims of La Garde-Freinet: Hagiography and the Problem of Islam in Medieval Europe* (2015). A coeditor of *The Medieval Review* and an active member of The Medieval Academy of America, he has lectured in Israel and throughout the United States, Canada, and Europe and has held visiting research appointments at the Technische Universität Dresden, in Germany; the Universiteit Gent, in Belgium; and Emmanuel College, University of Cambridge. He worked his way through college as a grave digger.

T0000269

The Penguin Book of the Undead

FIFTEEN HUNDRED YEARS
OF SUPERNATURAL ENCOUNTERS

Edited by SCOTT G. BRUCE

PENGUIN BOOKS

PENGUIN BOOKS

An imprint of Penguin Random House LLC
375 Hudson Street
New York, New York 10014
penguin.com

Translations and renderings into modern English by Scott G. Bruce, unless otherwise indicated.

Grateful acknowledgment is made for permission to use the following copyrighted works:
"Odyssesus in the House of Death" (Book 11: The Kingdom of the Dead) from *The Odyssey* by Homer,
translated by Robert Fagles. Translation copyright © 1996 by Robert Fagles. Used by permission of Viking Penguin, an imprint of Penguin Publishing Group, a division of Penguin Random House LLC.
"Pliny Contemplates the Existence of Ghosts" from *The Letters of the Younger Pliny*, translated with
an introduction by Betty Radice (Penguin Classics, 1963, reprinted 1969). Copyright © Betty Radice,
1963, 1969.
"A Mistress of the Graves" from *Civil War* by Lucan, translated by Matthew Fox. Translation copyright © 2012 by Matthew Fox. Used by permission of Penguin Books, an imprint of Penguin Publishing
Group, a division of Penguin Random House LLC.
"An Army White As Snow" from *Relatio de duobus ducibus*, translated by Christopher A. Jones. Used
by permission of Christopher A. Jones.
"The Ravenous Dead" from *Seven Viking Romances: Arrow-Odd, King Gautrek, Halfdan Eysteins-
son, Bosi and Herraud, Egil and Asmund, Thorstein Mansion-Might, Helgi Thorisson*, translated by
Hermann Palsson and Paul Edwards (Penguin Classics, 1985). Copyright © Hermann Palsson and Paul
Edwards, 1985.
"Old Ghosts, New Laws" from *Eyrbyggja Saga*, translated with an introduction and notes by Hermann
Palsson and Paul Edwards (Penguin Classics, 1989). Translation copyright © Hermann Palsson and
Paul Edwards, 1972, 1989.
"The Torments of Tantalus" from *Phaedra and Other Plays* by Seneca (Penguin Classics, 2011). Trans-
lation copyright © R. Scott Smith, 2011. All rights reserved.
"When Night Draws Swiftly Darkling On" from *A Treatise of Ghosts* by Noel Taillepied, translated by
Montague Summers (London, Fortune Press, 1933).

LIBRARY OF CONGRESS CATALOGING-IN-PUBLICATION DATA
Names: Bruce, Scott G. (Scott Gordon), 1967– editor.
Title: The Penguin book of the undead: fifteen hundred years of supernatural encounters /
edited by Scott G. Bruce.
Description: New York: Penguin Books, 2016. | Includes bibliographical references and index.
Identifiers: LCCN 2016012232 (print) | LCCN 2016023478 (ebook) | ISBN 9780143107682 |
ISBN 9780698406605 ()
Subjects: LCSH: Ghosts. | Vampires. | Zombies.
Classification: LCC BF1461 .P4345 2016 (print) | LCC BF1461 (ebook) | DDC 133.1—dc23

Printed in the United States of America

Stuart Robert Bruce (1959–1989) haunts me still

I see a repose that neither earth nor hell can break, and I feel an assurance of the endless and shadowless hereafter.
—Emily Brontë, *Wuthering Heights* (1847)

They say miracles are past; and we have our
philosophical persons, to make modern and familiar,
things supernatural and causeless. Hence is it that
we make trifles of terrors, ensconcing ourselves
into seeming knowledge, when we should submit
ourselves to an unknown fear.

—WILLIAM SHAKESPEARE,
ALL'S WELL THAT ENDS WELL (ACT 3, SCENE 3)

The throat is deep and the mouth is wide
Saw some things on the other side
Made me promise to never tell
But you know me, I can't help myself

—TRENT REZNOR, "CAME BACK HAUNTED"

Contents

THE PENGUIN BOOK OF THE UNDEAD

Ancient Apparitions

The Autopsy of Souls in Late Ancient Thought

Northern Horrors

Strange Tales of Mystery and Terror

The Reformation of the Wraiths

Haunting the Wings

Introduction

The word *undead* first appeared in the tenth century, when a Christian preacher named Aelfric of Eynsham (c. 955–c. 1010) employed its Old English ancestor—the adjective *undeadlic*—to describe the immortality, the undyingness, of God. The term has undergone an ironic reversal in modern English, where it now denotes dead people who have been reanimated by a supernatural force. This change reflects the intense interest in tales of the living dead that have become ubiquitous in modern societies. The revival of Gothic horror stories like Mary Shelley's *Frankenstein* (1818) and Bram Stoker's *Dracula* (1897) in movie theaters in the 1930s sparked a popular interest in the undead that persists to the present day. Between the release of cult films like *Night of the Living Dead* (1968) and the airing of Joss Whedon's wildly popular television series *Buffy the Vampire Slayer* (1997–2003), stories about the risen dead have saturated the modern imagination. The past decade alone has witnessed the release of dozens of feature-length films about the so-called zombie apocalypse, the catastrophic breakdown of modern society due to an epidemic of living corpses. While similarly restless, ghosts and their kindred spirits have followed a different trajectory in modern media. The psychological trauma of an encounter with a ghost, depicted so vividly in the stories of M. R. James (1862–1936) and his imitators, has receded in the wake of more sentimental treatments. Unlike marauding zombies, whose malevolent intention is never in doubt, the appearance of a dead soul could evoke pity or sadness or regret in the living, especially when it is recognized as a loved one now lost.

This ambivalent relationship between the living and the returning dead is not new; it has been a persistent theme in Western literature for almost three thousand years. This collection of stories about premodern encounters with ghosts and animated corpses spans fifteen centuries from the height of the Roman Empire in the first century CE to the reign of Queen Elizabeth I (1558–1603). Ancient, medieval, and early modern authors related stories and ideas about supernatural events involving the dead in a wide variety of genres, including epic poetry, histories, hagiography, personal letters, theological and polemical treatises, sagas, plays, and collections of miracles and marvels. The persistence of these stories over such a long span of time speaks to the abiding interest among the living in the fate of the dead, who remained a much stronger presence in the face-to-face communities of premodern Europe than they do in the antiseptic anonymity of most modern societies.

Stories about the dead have an ancient pedigree. In the classical period, from the Trojan War to the ascendancy of Rome in the Mediterranean Sea, the spirits of the recently deceased appeared often to the living to plead for proper burial and commemoration, the obligations owed but not always granted to the dead. Professional necromancers animated the corpses of the slain and compelled them in rituals of divination to share the information that only the dead can know. Even with the religious revolution of late antiquity, during which the Christian church triumphed over Greek and Roman paganism, this commerce with the dead persisted, though with new mediators. As early Christian theologians developed the notion that souls underwent a cleansing in fire in preparation for their entry into heaven, stories about the returning dead became an important medium for asserting the benefits of praying and giving alms on behalf of the faithful departed to speed their way to paradise. By the eleventh century, Christian monks had effectively domesticated the ghost story as a tool to teach the faithful about the economy of the afterlife. The stain of unavoidable sins imperiled every soul, but the prayers of the monks, whose denial of the world made them powerful intercessors before God, could wipe those stains away and gain for the soul a much quicker release from purgatorial flames. Donations of revenue-producing land to cloistered communities in this world would secure their prayerful assistance for the souls of faithful donors and their families in the afterlife.

As Christianity pushed inexorably northward into Scandinavia and Iceland around the first millennium, it collided with indigenous non-Christian beliefs about the living dead. From the eleventh century onward, Christian authors on the northern frontiers began to relate stories about unruly corpses that broke loose from the confines of their tombs to plague their communities with acts of violence and their disease-bearing breath. While monastic ghost stories emphasized the empathy of the living in response to the suffering of the dead, these tales of rampaging revenants left Christian authors in doubt about the moral of the stories they were telling. In most cases, only the most wicked individuals rose from the grave as living corpses, animated by the power of the Devil to wreak havoc among their family and friends until put to rest by the equally violent intervention of brave monks and stalwart young men. These events were wonders; their cause and purpose were known only to God.

In the sixteenth century, these age-old relationships between the living and the dead were called into doubt, when Protestant reformers attacked the Catholic doctrine of purgatory as an invention of the papacy and denied that apparitions were genuine manifestations of the souls of the dead. To be sure, Protestants believed that ghostly spirits frequently appeared to human beings, but these spirits were either angels in disguise or, more likely, devils in human form intent on deception and ruin. For their part, Catholic theologians held firm to the medieval doctrine of purgatory. While the Protestants maintained that the inscrutable judgment of God sent souls directly to heaven or hell after death, the Catholics placed their hope in the cleansing fire that prepared all but the most utterly wicked for entry into paradise.

In the premodern imagination, the restless dead appeared in many forms. In this book, the reader will find a macabre menagerie of agitated souls and unquiet corpses: moaning phantoms haunting deserted ruins; dead souls appearing to their loved ones in dreams; the ghosts of sinful monks returning to beseech the prayerful assistance of their brethren to escape the fires of purgatory; great armies of spirits clad in white armor and marshaled for battle; hordes of tormented souls doomed to never-ending nocturnal marches through desolate hinterlands; bloated corpses shambling from their graves to sicken the living with their deathly breath; spectral crows and dogs and cattle encountered on lonely moors; and, perhaps most strangely of all, the tiny ghost of a miscarried fetus rolled up in a sock. To be sure, medieval Europeans lived in a world very different from our own, but, as this volume shows, their stories of supernatural encounters with the dead are no less capable of evoking anguish or pity or even genuine fear in the modern reader.

SCOTT G. BRUCE

Suggestions for Further Reading

Bartlett, Robert. *The Natural and the Supernatural in the Middle Ages.* Cambridge: Cambridge University Press, 2008.

Caciola, Nancy Mandeville. *Afterlives: The Return of the Dead in the Middle Ages.* Ithaca and London: Cornell University Press, 2016.

Felton, D. *Haunted Greece and Rome: Ghost Stories from Classical Antiquity.* Austin: University of Texas Press, 1999.

Greenblatt, Stephen. *Hamlet in Purgatory.* Princeton: Princeton University Press, 2001.

Laqueur, Thomas W. *The Work of the Dead: A Cultural History of Mortal Remains.* Princeton: Princeton University Press, 2015.

Le Goff, Jacques. *The Birth of Purgatory.* Translated by Arthur Goldhammer. Chicago and London: University of Chicago Press, 1984.

Marshall, Peter. *Beliefs and the Dead in Reformation England.* Oxford: Oxford University Press, 2002.

Ogden, Daniel. *Greek and Roman Necromancy.* Princeton: Princeton University Press, 2004.

Schmitt, Jean-Claude. *Ghosts in the Middle Ages: The Living and the Dead in Medieval Society.* Translated by Teresa Lavender Fagan. Chicago and London: University of Chicago Press, 1998.

Watkins, C. S. *History and the Supernatural in Medieval England.* Cambridge: Cambridge University Press, 2007.

Acknowledgments

The book began in conversation with my editor John Siciliano, whose patience and feedback have been invaluable. The conversation would not have begun at all without the kindness of Jay Rubenstein. Most of the research for this book took place in the spring and summer of 2015 while I held the Derek Brewer Visiting Fellowship at Emmanuel College at the University of Cambridge, UK. I am profoundly grateful to Professor Elisabeth Van Houts and Master Fiona Reynolds for making this fellowship possible and for providing such a warm welcome to me and my family. It was an exquisite pleasure to complete a book about medieval ghosts in the former haunts of M. R. James.

Throughout this process I received guidance and support from numerous friends and scholars in Cambridge and elsewhere. Many thanks to John Arnold, Julie Barrau, Nora Berend, Nancy Mandeville Caciola, Matthew Champion, Caroline Goodson, Tom Johnson, Miri Rubin, Carl Watkins, and, of course, Anne E. Lester. I am especially grateful to Drew Jones, who kindly translated one of the texts in chapter 6. His virtuosity in medieval Latin is surpassed only by his generosity as a scholar and a friend. My thanks to the students who enrolled in History 4803: Ghosts in the Western Tradition, and Latin 5014: Topics in Latin Prose: Medieval Ghost Stories, which I taught at the University of Colorado at Boulder during the 2015/2016 academic year. They read many of these texts with me and shared their insights about the depiction and function of ghosts in the premodern world. A special thank you to Sean Babbs, Jordan Becker, Amanda Racine, and Manon Williams, who read the entire manuscript. I am richer for their industry and enthusiasm.

Medieval Latin is a difficult language to translate in the best of circumstances. While the translations in this volume are my own (unless stated otherwise), I would like to acknowledge my debt to the scholars who translated them before me, particularly the editors of the works by Gervase of Tilbury, Walter Map, Geoffrey of Burton, Saxo Grammaticus, Bede, and Orderic Vitalis published in the Oxford Medieval Texts series. Because I worked with these translations at hand, my wording is at times very close to theirs.

The Penguin Book of the Undead

ANCIENT
APPARITIONS

I. GREEK AND ROMAN REMAINS

The relationship between the living and the dead has been an important aspect of human society since the beginning of recorded history. In ancient times, supernatural encounters with the dead occurred most often when the living failed in their duties to the deceased by neglecting their proper burial or refusing to visit their tombs. Negligence of this kind could prompt a haunting. The living could also summon the spirits of the dead with magical spells in order to learn information that only the deceased could know, a practice known as "necromancy," a Greek term that means "divination by means of communication with the spirits of the dead."

Ghosts appear in some of the earliest works of European literature, dating back to Homer's epic poem The Odyssey (c. 700 BCE). The descriptions of the restless dead in the oldest Greek sources provided the template for depictions of them for centuries to come. The ancients described ghosts as shadows in human form or as insubstantial corpses, stained with the blood of the wounds that killed them. Some were as black as the night; others were pallid from their loss of blood and the lack of sunlight in the underworld. Ancient apparitions swarmed like bees and flocked like night-birds near the caves and riverbanks that provided entrance to the realm of the dead. Their voices ranged from low groans and baleful mutterings to high-pitched squeaks and gibbering.

In most cases, the souls of the recently deceased made the journey to their subterranean realm (Hades) without any *trouble, but certain kinds of death agitated the soul, causing it to linger on the threshold of the world of the living as a ghost. These restless souls included people who had died before their time, primarily infants, but also men and women who had died before marriage. The souls of those killed by violence tarried among the living as well, especially suicides and warriors who were slain in combat. Lastly, those whose corpses remained unburied were also exiled among the living. Among them were those unfortunate souls who died in shipwrecks, for their bodies could find no rest in the storm-tossed sea.*

The restless dead were particularly susceptible to the power of necromancers, who worked spells to summon souls, bind them to their will, and exploit them for information. Many ghosts in ancient literature appeared in a necromantic context. Rites for the summoning of restless souls involved a ceremony of evocation, first described in Homer's Odyssey *(see below) and elaborated in later literature. The summoner dug a shallow pit, into which he or she poured libations of honey-sweetened milk, wine, and water, and made offerings of barley and blood. There followed a burnt sacrifice and prayers to the gods of the dead, including Hades and Persephone.*

The response of ghosts to necromantic binding varied considerably. Some were eager to return to the world of the living for conversation, even briefly. Others were reluctant to speak. Bitter that their otherworldly peace had been disturbed, only the proper spells could compel them to converse. Ghosts also appeared to necromancers in their dreams. In these cases, it is unclear if the rituals of summoning were performed prior to sleep or if they took place in the dream sequence that culminated in the appearance of an apparition.

What could be gained by summoning a ghost? A necromantic encounter was a useful way to learn the cause of a haunting and to put a stop to it. Ghosts liked nothing more than to talk about the circumstances of their own deaths and often aided in laying their own spirits to rest by revealing the identity of their murderers or the location of their unburied bodies. The restless dead tended to hover near the location of their mortal remains, whether it was in a tomb or not, and therefore knew what went on in the vicinity of their corpses. It was also believed that ghosts had access to important information shared by the spirits of the recently slain, with whom they had conversed in the underworld. In some cases, however, necromancers summoned the spirits of the dead to exploit important skills that the deceased had in life, especially the power of prophecy.

ODYSSEUS IN THE HOUSE OF DEATH[1]

Homer's Odyssey *tells the story of Odysseus, a veteran of the Trojan War, and his decade-long voyage back to the island of Ithaca. Odysseus's journey home was fraught with peril because he and his crew offended the sea god Poseidon by blinding his son, the Cyclops Polyphemos. On the advice of the enchantress Circe, Odysseus traveled to the threshold of the underworld to ask the ghost of Tiresias of Thebes, a renowned prophet, to peer into the future and provide advice about his best course back to Ithaca.*

The summoning of Tiresias takes place in book eleven of The Odyssey, *which provided a description of the underworld and its inhabitants that subsequently had a profound influence on their depiction in Western literature from Virgil's* Aeneid *to Dante's* Divine Comedy. *The land of the dead is a somber place in Homer's imagination, a dark and comfortless realm. The hardships of Odysseus's travels often led him to thoughts of suicide, but once he visited the House of Death, he came to realize that living is much better than dying. The ghost of Achilles warned Odysseus directly not to glorify the condition of death: "No winning words about death to me, shining Odysseus! By god, I'd rather slave on earth for another man—some dirt-poor tenant farmer who scrapes to keep alive—than rule down here over all the breathless dead." (*The Odyssey *11.488–491). While Odysseus performed his necromantic ritual specifically to speak to Tiresias, he was unprepared for the great number of ghosts that responded to his summons—"hordes of them, thousands raising unearthly cries" (*The Odyssey *11.724)—among*

them his recently deceased companion Elpenor and his beloved
mother Anticlea, who had died of grief in his long absence.
Their heartbreaking conversation provided a brief respite from
the otherworldly horrors that surrounded them.

And [our ship] made the outer limits, the Ocean River's
bounds, where Cimmerian people have their homes—their
realm and city shrouded in mist and cloud. The eye of the Sun
can never flash his rays through the dark and bring them light,
not when he climbs the starry skies or when he wheels back
down from the heights to touch the earth once more—an endless, deadly night overhangs those wretched men. There, gain-
ing that point, we beached our craft and bearing out the sheep,
we picked our way by the Ocean's banks until we gained the
place that Circe made our goal.

Here at the spot Perimedes and Eurylochus held the victims
fast, and I, drawing my sharp sword from beside my hip, dug
a trench of about a forearm's depth and length, and around it
poured libations out to all the dead, first with milk and honey,
and then with mellow wine, then water third and last, and
sprinkled glistening barley over it all, and time and again I
vowed to all the dead, to the drifting, listless spirits of their
ghosts, that once I returned to Ithaca I would slaughter a barren heifer in my halls, the best I had, and load a pyre with
treasures—and to Tiresias, alone, apart, I would offer a sleek
black ram, the pride of all my herds. And once my vows and
prayers had invoked the nations of the dead, I took the victims, over the trench I cut their throats and the dark blood
flowed in—and up out of Erebus they came, flocking toward
me now, the ghosts of the dead and gone: brides and unwed
youths and old men who had suffered much and girls with
their tender hearts freshly scarred by sorrow and great armies
of battle dead, stabbed by bronze spears, men of war still
wrapped in bloody armor—thousands swarming around the
trench from every side—unearthly cries—blanching terror
gripped me![2] I ordered the men at once to flay the sheep that
lay before us, killed by my ruthless blade, and burn them both,

and then say prayers to the gods, to the almighty god of death
and dread Persephone.[3] But I, the sharp sword drawn from beside my hip, sat down on alert there and never let the ghosts of
the shambling, shiftless dead come near that blood till I had
questioned Tiresias myself.

But first the ghost of Elpenor, my companion, came toward
me. He'd not been buried under the wide ways of earth, not
yet, we'd left his body in Circe's house, unwept, unburied—
this other labor pressed us. But I wept to see him now, pity
touched my heart and I called out a winged word to him there:
"Elpenor, how did you travel down to the world of darkness?
Faster on foot, I see, than I in my black ship."

My comrade groaned as he offered me an answer: "Royal son
of Laertes, Odysseus, old campaigner, the doom of an angry
god, and god knows how much wine—they were my ruin, cap-
tain. I'd bedded down on the roof of Circe's house but never
thought to climb back down again by the long ladder—headfirst
from the roof I plunged, my neck snapped from the backbone,
my soul flew down to Death. Now, I beg you by those you left
behind, so far from here, your wife, your father who bred and
reared you as a boy, and Telemachus, left at home in your halls,
your only son. Well I know when you leave this lodging of the
dead that you and your ship will put ashore again at the island of
Aeaea—then and there, my lord, remember me, I beg you![4] Don't
sail off and desert me, left behind unwept, unburied, don't, or
my curse may draw god's fury on your head. No, burn me in full
armor, all my harness, heap my mound by the churning gray
surf—a man whose luck ran out—so even men to come will
learn my story. Perform my rites and plant on my tomb that oar
I swung with mates when I rowed among the living."

"All this, my unlucky friend," I reassured him, "I will do for
you. I won't forget a thing." So we sat and faced each other,
holding my sword above the blood, he across from me there,
my comrade's phantom dragging out his story.

But look, the ghost of my mother came, my mother,
dead and gone now. Anticlea—daughter of that great heart
Autolycus—whom I had left alive when I sailed for sacred
Troy. I broke into tears to see her here, but filled with pity,

even throbbing with grief, I would not let her ghost approach
till I had questioned Tiresias myself.

At last he came. The shade of the famous Theban prophet,
holding a golden scepter, knew me at once and hailed me:
"Royal son of Laertes, Odysseus, master of exploits, man of
pain, what now, what brings you here, forsaking the light of
day to see this joyless kingdom of the dead? Stand back from
the trench—put up your sharp sword so I can drink the blood
and tell you the truth."

Moving back, I thrust my silver-studded sword deep in its
sheath, and once he had drunk the dark blood the words came
ringing from the prophet in his power: "A sweet smooth journey
home, renowned Odysseus, that is what you seek, but a god will
make it hard for you—I know—you will never escape the one
who shakes the earth, quaking with anger at you still, still enraged because you blinded the Cyclops, his dear son. Even so, you
and your crew may still reach home, suffering all the way, if you
only have the power to curb their wild desire and curb your own,
what's more, from the day your good trim vessel first puts in at
Thrinacia Island, flees the cruel blue sea. There you will find them
grazing, herds and fat flocks, the cattle of Helios, god of the sun
who sees all, hears all things. Leave the beasts unharmed, your
mind set on home, and you *all* may still reach Ithaca—bent with
hardship, true—but harm them in any way, and I can see it now:
your ship destroyed, your men destroyed as well. And even if you
escape, you'll come home late and come a broken man—all ship-
mates lost, alone in a stranger's ship—and you will find a world of
pain at home, crude, arrogant men devouring all your goods,
courting your noble wife, offering gifts to win her. No doubt you
will pay them back in blood when you come home! But once you
have killed those suitors in your halls—by stealth or in open fight
with slashing bronze—go forth once more, you must. Carry your
well-planed oar until you come to a race of people who know
nothing of the sea, whose food is never seasoned with salt, strangers all to ships with their crimson prows and long slim oars, wings
that make ships fly. And here is your sign—unmistakable, clear,
so clear you cannot miss it: When another traveler falls in with
you and calls that weight across your shoulder a fan to winnow

grain, then plant your bladed, balanced oar in the earth and sacrifice fine beasts to the lord god of the sea, Poseidon—a ram, a bull,
and a ramping wild boar—then journey home and render noble
offerings up to the deathless gods who rule the vaulting skies, to
all the gods in order. And at last your own death will steal upon
you, a gentle, painless death, far from the sea it comes to take you
down, borne down with the years in ripe old age with all your
people there in blessed peace around you. All that I have told you
will come true."

"Oh Tiresias," I replied as the prophet finished, "surely the
gods have spun this out as fate, the gods themselves. But tell me
one thing more, and tell me clearly. I see the ghost of my long-
lost mother here before me. Dead, crouching close to the blood
in silence, she cannot bear to look me in the eyes—her own
son—or speak to me. How, lord, can I make her know me for
the man I am?"

"One rule there is," the famous seer explained, "and simple
for me to say and you to learn. Any one of the ghosts you let
approach the blood will speak the truth to you. Anyone you
refuse will turn and fade away."

And with those words, now that his prophecies had closed,
the awesome shade of lord Tiresias strode back to the House
of Death. But I kept watch there, steadfast till my mother approached and drank the dark, clouding blood. She knew me at
once and wailed out in grief and her words came winging
toward me, flying home: "Oh my son! What brings you down
to the world of death and darkness? You are still alive! It's
hard for the living to catch a glimpse of this. Great rivers flow
between us, terrible waters, the Ocean first of all—no one
could ever ford that stream on foot, only aboard some sturdy
craft. Have you just come from Troy, wandering long years
with your men and ship? Not yet returned to Ithaca? You've
still not seen your wife inside your halls?"

"Mother," I replied, "I had to venture down to the House of
Death to consult the shade of Tiresias, seer of Thebes. Never
yet have I neared Achaea, never once set foot on native ground,
always wandering—endless hardship from that day I first set
sail with King Agamemnon bound for Troy, the stallion-land,

to fight the Trojans there. But tell me about yourself and spare me nothing. What form of death overcame you, what laid you low, some long, slow illness? Or did Artemis showering arrows come with her painless shafts and bring you down? Tell me of Father, tell of the son I left behind: do my royal rights still lie in their safekeeping? Or does some stranger hold the throne by now because men think that I'll come home no more? Please, tell me about my wife, her turn of mind, her thoughts. Still standing fast beside our son, still guarding our great estates, secure as ever now? Or has she wed some other countryman at last, the finest prince among them?"

"Surely, surely," my noble mother answered quickly, "she's still waiting there in your halls, poor woman, suffering so, her life an endless hardship like your own. Wasting away the nights, weeping away the days. No one has taken over your royal rights, not yet. Telemachus still holds your great estates in peace, he attends the public banquets shared with all, the feasts a man of justice should enjoy, for every lord invites him. As for your father, he keeps to his own farm—he never goes to town—with no bed for him there, no blankets, no glossy throws; all winter long he sleeps in the lodge with servants, in the ashes by the fire, his body wrapped in rags. But when summer comes and the bumper crops of harvest, any spot on the rising ground of his vineyard rows he makes his bed, heaped high with fallen leaves, and here he lies in anguish, with his old age bearing hard upon him, too, and his grief grows as he longs for your return. And I with the same grief, I died and met my fate. No sharp-eyed huntress showering arrows through the halls approached and brought me down with painless shafts, nor did some hateful illness strike me, that so often devastates the body, drains our limbs of power. No, it was my longing for *you*, my shining Odysseus—you and your quickness, you and your gentle ways—that tore away my life that had been sweet."

And I, my mind in turmoil, how I longed to embrace my mother's spirit, dead as she was! Three times I rushed toward her, desperate to hold her, three times she fluttered through my fingers, sifting away like a shadow, dissolving like a dream, and each time the grief cut to the heart, sharper, yes, and I, I cried out to her, words winging into the darkness: "Mother, why not wait for me? How I long to hold you! So even here, in the House of Death, we can fling our loving arms around each other, take some joy in the tears that numb the heart. Or is this just some wraith that great Persephone sends my way to make me ache with sorrow all the more?"

My noble mother answered me at once: "My son, my son, the unluckiest man alive! This is no deception sent by Queen Persephone, this is just the way of mortals when we die. Sinews no longer bind the flesh and bones together—the fire in all its fury burns the body down to ashes once life slips from the white bones, and the spirit, rustling, flitters away, flown like a dream. But you must long for the daylight. Go, quickly. Remember all these things so one day you can tell them to your wife."

PLINY CONTEMPLATES THE EXISTENCE OF GHOSTS[1]

Pliny the Younger (c. 61–113) was a Roman provincial governor who served under Emperor Trajan (98–117). He was the author of hundreds of letters on a wide range of topics from politics and family affairs to the eruption of Mount Vesuvius and the local troubles caused by early Christians. In a letter to his friend Lucius Licinius Sura, he contemplated the existence of ghosts. This letter includes three stories about the appearance of apparitions and their possible meanings. In the first story, a larger-than-life woman appeared to a Roman nobleman named Curtius Rufus. Claiming to be "the spirit of Africa," she foretold his future as governor of Africa. In the second story, a philosopher named Athenodorus stayed in a haunted house in Athens. There he confronted a restless ghost who rattled chains in the night, kept his cool despite its frightening demeanor, and helped lay it to rest. The third and final story happened in Pliny's very own household: his slaves complained about figures in white who came into their dormitory at night and cut their hair with scissors. Pliny offered an interpretation of this spectral visitation as a sign that he would escape the plots made against him by a political enemy named Carus. These stories contained elements inherited from the Greek tradition of ghost stories: apparitions can provide useful information to the living, both directly and indirectly; and spirits of the dead cannot find rest until their bodies receive proper burial.

To Licinius Sura,

Our leisure gives me the chance to learn and you to teach me; so I should very much like to know whether you think that ghosts exist, and have a form of their own and some sort of supernatural power, or whether they lack substance and reality and take shape only from our fears. I personally am encouraged to believe in their existence largely from what I have heard of the experience of Curtius Rufus.[2] While he was still obscure and unknown he was attached to the suite of a new governor of Africa. One afternoon he was walking up and down in the colonnade of his house when there appeared to him the figure of a woman, of superhuman size and beauty. To allay his fears she told him that she was the spirit of Africa, come to foretell his future: he would return to Rome and hold office, and then return with supreme authority to the same province, where he would die. Everything came true.[3] Moreover, the story goes on to say that as he left the boat on his arrival at Carthage the same figure met him on the shore. It is at least certain that when he fell ill he interpreted his future by the past and his misfortune by his previous success, and gave up all hope of recovery although none of his people despaired of his life.

Now consider whether the following story, which I will tell just as it was told to me, is not just as remarkable and even more terrifying. In Athens there was a large and spacious mansion with the bad reputation of being dangerous to its occupants. In the dead of night the clanking of iron and, if you listened carefully, the rattle of chains could be heard, some way off at first, and then close at hand. Then there appeared the specter of an old man, emaciated and filthy, with a long flowing beard and hair on end, wearing fetters on his legs and shaking the chains on his wrists. The wretched occupants would spend fearful nights awake in terror; lack of sleep led to illness and then death as their dread increased, for even during the day, when the apparition had vanished, the memory of it was in their mind's eye, so that their terror remained after the cause of it had gone. The house was therefore deserted, condemned to stand empty and wholly abandoned to the specter; but it was advertised as being for rent or for sale in case someone was found who knew nothing of its evil reputation.

The philosopher Athenodorus came to Athens and read the notice. His suspicions were aroused when he heard the low price, and the whole story came out on inquiry; but he was nonetheless, in fact all the more, eager to rent the house. When darkness fell, he gave orders that a couch was to be made up for him in the front part of the house and asked for his notebooks, a pen, and a lamp. He sent all his servants to the inner rooms, and concentrated his thoughts, eyes, and hand on his writing, so that his mind would be occupied and not conjure up the phantom he had heard about nor other imaginary fears. At first there was nothing but the general silence of night; then came the clanking of iron and dragging of chains. He did not look up or stop writing, but steeled his mind to shut out the sounds. Then the noise grew louder, came nearer, was heard in the doorway, and then inside the room. He looked around, saw, and recognized the ghost described to him. It stood and beckoned, as if summoning him. Athenodorus in his turn signaled to it to wait a little, and again bent over his notes and pen, while it stood rattling its chains over his head as he wrote. He looked around again and saw it beckoning as before, so without further delay he picked up his lamp and followed. It moved slowly, as if weighed down with chains, and when it turned off into the courtyard of the house it suddenly vanished, leaving him alone. He then picked some grass and leaves and marked the spot. The following day he approached the magistrates and advised them to give orders for the place to be dug up. There they found bones, twisted around with chains, which were left bare and corroded by the fetters when time and the action of the soil had rotted away the flesh. The bones were collected and given a public burial, and after the shades had been duly laid to rest the house saw them no more.

For these details I rely on the evidence of others, but here is a story I can vouch for myself. One of my freedmen, a man of some education, was sleeping in the same bed as his younger brother when he dreamed that he saw someone sitting on the bed and putting scissors to his hair, even cutting some off the top of his head. When day dawned he found his head shorn and the hair lying on the floor. A short time elapsed and then another similar occurrence confirmed the earlier one. A slave boy was sleeping with several others in the young slaves' quarters. His story was that two men clad in white came in through the window, cut his hair as he lay in bed, and departed the way they had come. Daylight revealed that his head had also been shorn and the hair was scattered about. Nothing remarkable followed, except perhaps the fact that I was not brought to trial, as I should have been if Domitian (the emperor under whom all this happened) had lived longer.[4] For among the papers in his desk was found information laid against me by Carus, from which, in view of the custom for accused persons to let their hair grow long, one may interpret the cutting of my slaves' hair as a sign that the danger threatening me was averted.

So please apply your learned mind to this question; it deserves your long and careful consideration, nor can I be called undeserving as a recipient of your informed opinion. You may argue both sides of the case as you always do, but lay your emphasis on one side or the other and do not leave me in suspense and uncertainty; my reason for asking your opinion was to put an end to my doubts.

A MISTRESS OF THE GRAVES[1]

Ancient necromancers were typically male, but in the Roman literary tradition it became common to associate the practice of summoning the dead with women. Homer's depiction of the central role played by the enchantress Circe in Odysseus's consultation with Tiresias was an important precedent. Why did this change take place? By assigning necromantic agency to women, Roman authors simultaneously expressed their disdain for this ancient practice and distanced themselves from rites that were increasingly viewed as unsavory and suspicious in their culture. The most vivid Roman portrait of a necromancer at work appears in Lucan's Pharsalia, *an epic poem about the civil war between Julius Caesar and Pompey in the twilight of the Roman Republic written a century later (c. 61–65) toward the end of Emperor Nero's reign. On the eve of a battle in Greece, Sextus, the son of Pompey, sought out a powerful witch named Erictho to divine the outcome of the war. At the culmination of a ghastly ritual, Erictho summoned the ghost of a recently slain soldier, compelling it to reanimate its own corpse and binding it with spells to reveal the future. The reluctant ghost then foretold both the defeat of Pompey and the assassination of victorius Caesar.*

These wicked rites and crimes of a dire race would be damned as still too pious by savage Erictho, who had applied her polluted art to novel rites. To submit her funereal head to a city's roof or to household gods is an unthinkable deed. She haunts deserted graves and lurks in sepulchers from which ghosts have been driven, a welcome friend to the gods of Erebus. To hear the gatherings of the silent dead and know the Stygian halls and buried secrets of Dis, neither the gods above nor being alive prevents her.[2] Her ill-omened face is thin and filthy from neglect, her features frighten with Stygian pallor, never knowing the light of day; her head droops heavy with matted, knotted hair. Whenever black storm clouds conceal the stars, Thessaly's witch emerges from her empty tombs and hunts down the nightly bolts of lightning. Her tread has burned up seeds of fertile grain and her breath alone has turned fresh air deadly. She doesn't pray to gods above, or know the ways to offer entrails and receive auspicious omens. She loves to light altars with funereal flames and burn incense she's snatched from blazing pyres. At the merest hint of her praying voice, the gods grant her any outrage, afraid to hear her second song. She has buried souls alive, still in control of their bodies, against their will death comes with fate still owing them years. In a backward march she has brought the dead back from the grave and lifeless corpses have fled death. The smoking cinders and burning bones of youths she'll take straight from the pyre, along with the torch, ripped from their parents' grip, and the fragments of the funeral couch with smoke still wafting black, and the robes turning to ashes and the coals that reek of their limbs.

But when dead bodies are preserved in stone, which absorbs their inner moisture, and they stiffen as the decaying marrow is drawn off, then she hungrily ravages every single joint, sinks her fingers in the eyes and relishes it as she digs the frozen orbs out, and gnaws the pallid, wasting nails from desiccated hands. With her own mouth she cuts the fatal knotted noose, plucks down hanging bodies, and scours crosses ripping at guts the rains have pounded and innards exposed to the sun and cooked. She takes the nails piercing the hands and the black decaying poison and coagulated slime oozing through the joints. If a tendon resists her bite, she throws her weight into it. Whatever corpses lie out on the naked ground she seizes before the beasts and birds; not wanting to pick the bones with iron or her own hands, she waits and snatches pieces from the thirsty jaws of wolves.

Her hands don't flinch from slaughter either, if she needs fresh blood, first gushing from an opened throat, if her grave-yard feasts demand still-throbbing entrails. So, too, from a belly's wound, not as nature would do it, a fetus is removed and placed on blazing altars. And every time she needs force-ful savage shades, she makes the ghost herself. She finds a use for the death of every man.

She plucks from a youthful body the blossom on its cheek, and her left hand shears off the lock from a dying teen. And at a rela-tive's funeral the dire Thessalian often bends down over the body and feigning kisses she mutilates the head, opens the clenched mouth with her teeth and, biting the tongue that cleaves in a dry throat, pours her murmurings into the chilly lips, send-ing commands for secret crimes down to the shades of Styx.

Once Pompey's son had heard the country's rumors about *her*, when night was high in heaven—that time the Titan draws midday beneath our earth—he makes his way . . .

His faithful servants, used to crime, wandered about the grave mounds and plundered tombs and spied her afar, seated on a sheer rock cliff where Haemus slopes down reaching Phar-salia's hills.[3] She was trying out words unknown to magicians and their gods, crafting a spell for strange new purposes. For fearing lest fickle Mars go elsewhere in the world and the land of Emathia lose out on so much slaughter, the sorceress had forbidden Philippi to let the wars pass through, polluting the land with charms and strewing her dire poisons, so that she would have so many deaths for her own and she would enjoy the profit from the world's blood.[4] She hopes to mutilate the slaughtered carcasses of kings and to steal the ashes of the Hes-perian nation and the bones of nobles, and to own *so many* souls. Her passion now and final toil is what she'll snatch from Magnus's downcast body, what pieces of Caesar she'll manage to pounce on.

Pompey's worthless offspring addressed her first: "Splendor of Haemonia's ladies, you can reveal people's fates, and deflect things coming from their course. I pray you, let me learn for certain the end that this war's fortune is preparing. I'm not some lowly member of the Roman mob, but a most illustrious

child of Magnus—either the world's master, or heir to a mighty
funeral. My mind quakes, stricken by doubts; nonetheless, I'm
ready for definite horrors. Take away from chance the power to
rush down blind and all of a sudden. Either torment divine spirits with questions or spare them and disclose the truth from
ghosts. Unlock the abodes of Elysium and call forth Death herself, and force her to confess to me which ones of us she's hunting. It's no small task. It's worth *your* trouble, too, to ask what
way this weighty die of fate is leaning and will fall."

The evil Thessalian, thrilled to hear her name was famous
and well known, responded, "If you'd asked of lesser fates,
young man, it would have been easy to rouse unwilling gods
and attain your wish. My art can cause delay when the rays of
stars have marked one death, or even if all constellations would
grant one an old age, we can cut his years in half with magic
herbs. But once a series of causes has descended from the world's
first origin and all fates struggle if you want to change anything,
when the human race is subject to a single blow, then Thessaly's
ilk admits it—Fortune is stronger. But if you're intent on knowing events beforehand, there are many easy paths that open
onto truth. The earth and skies and Chaos, the seas and plains
and crags of Rhodope speak to us.⁵ But it's simple—since there's
plenty of fresh dead—to lift one body from Emanthia's fields, so
that the mouth of a corpse just slain and still warm will speak
with full voice, and not some deathly ghost with sunburned
limbs rasping out things dubious to our ears."

She spoke, and with her craft redoubled the shadows of
night; her dismal head shrouded in squalid mist, she wanders
among slain bodies cast off and denied their burial. Straightaway fled wolves, hungry birds of prey pulled out their talons
and fled, while the Thessalian selects her prophet; probing entrails chilly with death, she finds the fibers of strong, un-
wounded lungs and seeks the voice in a body discharged from
life. Many fates of slain men already hanging there—which
one would she want to call back up to life? If she had tried to
raise up all the ranks and return them to war, the laws of Erebus would have obeyed, and that powerful monster would
have hauled out of Stygian Avernus a people ready to fight.⁶ At

last she picks a body with its throat cut, takes and drags it by
a hook stuck in its fatal noose, a wretched corpse over rocks
and crags, then lays it high up under a mountain's cave, which
gloomy Erictho damned with her sacrifice.

The ground sheers off and sinks down nearly to the blind caverns of Dis; it's hemmed in by a dreary wood with stooping
branches, and a yew, which no sun penetrates nor crown be-
holds the sky, throws shadow over it. Darkness droops inside the
caves and, due to long night, gray mold hangs; no light shines,
except that cast by spells. The air in the jaws of Taenarus doesn't
sit so stagnant—a dismal boundary between the hidden world
and our own, where the rulers of Tartarus wouldn't fear to let
ghosts enter.[7] For though the Thessalian witch can ply the Fates
with force, it's doubtful whether she visits with shades of Styx by
drawing them up or descending to them.

Clad in motley dress like a Fury's mottled robe, she bares
her face and binds her tangled hair up with a crown of vipers.
When she sees the young man's friends are quaking and he
himself is trembling, his fixed eyes staring with the life drained
from his face, she says, "Put off the fears your fretful minds
have conjured. Now new life in its true form will be restored,
so that even the horrified can hear him speaking. If indeed I
show you the swamps of Styx and the shore that roars with
fire, if by my aid you're able to see the Eumenides and Cerberus, shaking his necks that bristle with snakes, and the con-
quered backs of Giants, why should you be scared, you cowards,
to meet with ghosts who are themselves afraid?"[8]

First she fills the chest with boiling blood through new
wounds that she opens, then washes out the bowels of putre-
faction and liberally applies poison from the moon. To this she
adds whatever nature has brought forth in inauspicious birth.
She doesn't leave out froth of dogs afraid of water, nor guts of
lynx nor joint of dread hyena and marrow of a stag that had
fed on serpents; nor *echenais*, which hinders ships although
east winds strain at their ropes, and eyeballs of dragons, and
stones that sound when warmed under a pregnant eagle; nor
Arabia's flying serpent and the Red Sea's viper that guards the
precious oyster, nor the skin that Libya's horned snake sheds

while still alive nor ash the phoenix left on its eastern altar.[9] And once she'd mixed together these common banes with well-known names, she added leaves soaked through with evil spells, and plants her wicked mouth had spat on as they grew, and every other poison she herself gave to the world. Last, her voice—stronger than any plant to bewitch the gods of Lethe—pours forth cacophonous murmurs in great discord with the human tongue. It contained the bark of dogs and howl of wolves, the fearsome eagle owl's and nocturnal tawny owl's laments, the shrieks and cries of beasts, the serpent's hiss, and it expressed the crash of waves that beat upon the rocks, the rustle of forests, and thunder from fractured clouds—one voice held all these things.

The rest she then spelled out in a Haemonian chant, piercing Tartarus with her tongue: "Eumenides, Stygian crime and punishments of the guilty, Chaos, greedy to pour disorder on countless worlds, Ruler of the earth, tortured through long ages by Death, delayed for gods, Styx and Elysium, which no Thessalian witch deserves, Persephone, loathing heaven and her mother, and the third part of our Hecate, through whom commerce between the ghosts and me occurs with quiet tongue, doorman of the open halls who throws our guts to the savage dog, and sisters who will spin out threads anew, and you, O ancient ferryman of the burning river, weary by now from bringing shades back up to me.[10] Pay heed to my prayers!

"If I call on you with a mouth that's sinful and polluted enough, if I never sing these songs while still famishing for human entrails, if I've often bathed a hacked-up breast still full of soul divine and brains still warm, if any infant whose insides and head I've laid upon your platters would have lived if I had not—obey me as I pray!

"We don't want one hiding out in Tartarus's chasm, long accustomed to the darkness, but a soul who has just been exiled from the light and is just now descending, who still clings in the jaws of murky Orcus and will, so long as it pays heed to my drugs, go to the ghosts but once.[11] For the general's son let the shade of this one who is now our solider sing all the Pompeian affairs—if civil wars deserve your gratitude."

With these declarations she lifted her head and frothing mouth and saw stand forth before her the shade of the cast-off corpse, afraid of its lifeless limbs, those hateful confines of its old prison. It dreads to enter that opened chest and guts and innards ruptured by lethal wounds. Poor man, unfairly stripped of death's last gift—to not be able to die!

Erictho is astounded that Fates are so free to linger, and, angry at the dead, she whips the motionless body with a living serpent, and down the gaping fissures in the earth her spells had opened up she barks at the ghosts of the dead, disturbing their kingdom's silence:

"Tisiphone! Indifferent to my voice? Megaera![12] Aren't you driving with your savage lashings through the emptiness of Erebus that hapless soul? Soon I'll conjure you by your real names and then abandon you Stygian dogs in the light above. I'll stand guard, hunt you down through graveyards and burial grounds, expel you from tombs, drive you from every urn. And I will reveal you, Hecate, to the gods in your pale, wasting form when you are used to going before them in a different guise, but I will forbid you from changing the face you wear in Erebus. And I will declare what banquets hold you, lady of Henna, under earth's great weight, by what marriage bond you love night's gloomy king, what pollution you suffered that your mother, Ceres, would not call for your return. And against you, worst of the world's rulers, I'll send the Titan Sun, bursting your caverns open and striking with sudden daylight. Will you obey? Or must I address by name *that* one at whose call the earth never fails to shudder and quake, who openly looks on the Gorgon's face, who tortures the trembling Erinyes with her own scourge and dwells in a Tartarus whose depths your eye can't plumb? To him, *you* are the gods above; he swears, and breaks, his oaths by the waters of Styx."

Just then the cold blood clots warmed and nourished the dark wounds, running into veins and to the ends of every limb; his insides pulse, shaking under his frozen chest, as new life creeps back into unused marrow, mingling with death. Every muscle palpitates, every nerve goes tense—then the body rises from the ground, not slowly, limb by limb, but thrown straight up from the earth all at once. He did not yet look alive, but like someone who was now dying. Still pale and stiff, he stands dumbstruck at being thrust back into the world. But no sound comes from his closed mouth; his voice and tongue are only allowed to answer.

"Speak," said the Thessalian, "at my command and great will be your reward. For if you tell the truth, we promise to make you immune for all ages from Haemonian arts; I will burn your body on such a pyre of logs, with Stygian chants, that your shade will never be summoned by spells of any magicians. Living twice is worth this much! No words or herbs will dare disturb your slumber of long forgetfulness once you've died at my hand! Ambiguous sayings are suited to tripods and seers of the gods. But anyone who bravely comes and seeks true oracles of callous death from the shades should leave with certainty. Don't hold back, I pray—give names to events, give places, and give voice so that the Fates may speak with me." She added a spell that gave the shade the power to know whatever she asked of it.

Dripping with tears, the wretched corpse said: "Well, I did not see the sad threads of the Parcae since I was called back from the edge of the silent bank. But what I happened to learn from all the shades is that brutal discord troubles the Roman spirits and impious arms have disrupted the quiet of hell. Some leaders have left their homes in Elysium, others come up from sad Tartarus; they have made it clear what the Fates are preparing.

"The blessed shades wore sorrowful faces. I saw the Decii, son and father who offered their souls in battle, Camillus weeping, the Curii and Sulla, complaining about you, Fortune. Scipio mourned that his ill-fated offspring would fall in the land of Libya. Carthage's greater enemy, Cato, cried for the fate of his great-grandson who would not be a slave. Only you, Brutus, first to be consul after the kings were expelled, I saw rejoicing among the dutiful shades.

"Suddenly, Catiline the menace, breaking his chains, ran riot, thrilled, with the fierce Marii and Cethegi, their arms bared. I saw delighted demagogues, the Drusi, immoderate legislators, the Gracchi, who dared outrageous deeds. Eternal chains of steel bound their hands applauding in the prisons of Dis—a criminal mob demanding the plains of the pious. The landlord of that idle kingdom is opening his gray estates and sharpening his jagged rocks and solid adamant for fetters, putting in order his punishment for the victor.

"Take this solace with you, young man: the spirits await your father and his house in their peaceful hollow and are reserving a place for Pompey's line in a calm, clear part of that realm. Don't let the glory of this brief life disturb you. The hour comes that will level all the leaders. Rush into death and go down below with pride, magnanimous, even if from lowly tombs, and trample on the shades of the gods of Rome. Which tomb the Nile's waves will wash and which the Tiber's is the only question—for the leaders, this fight is only about a funeral.

"Don't ask about your fate. The Parcae will grant you knowledge where I am silent. A clearer seer will sing you all, your father, Pompey, himself, in Sicily's fields, but he, too, will be unsure where to call you, where to drive you from, which tracts or skies of the world he should order you to shun. Unhappy men, beware of Europe, Libya, Asia—O pitiful house, you will look on nothing in all the world safer than Emathia."

So once he finished the words of fate, he stands with muted face and sad, then asks again for death. She must resort to magic spells and drugs before the corpse will fall, since Fate's law had been used once and could not take the soul back. Then she heaps up a great wood pyre; the dead man approaches the fire. Erictho left the youth lying on the kindled pile and let him die at last.

She accompanied Sextus back to his father's camp as dawn's light drew its colors in the sky; but till they bore their steps safe into their tents, she ordered the night to keep day back; it complied with deep, dark shadows.

II. EARLY CHRISTIAN HAUNTINGS

The earliest Christians inherited a rich tradition of beliefs about interactions between the living and the dead from the Greeks and the Romans, but the texts that comprised the New Testament added surprisingly little to this heritage. Many early Christian authors followed the apostle Paul in believing that the followers of Christ would join him immediately in paradise when they died. In the Gospel accounts of the Passion, Jesus likewise promised the repentant thief who was executed with him that "today you will be with me in paradise." On the other hand, the souls of the sinful dead departed without delay to the dark realm of Hades. The Gospel of Luke contrasted the fates of Lazarus, a destitute man whose soul the angels carried to the bosom of Abraham, and an unnamed rich man, who proceeded directly to Hades where he was tormented for neglecting to give alms to the poor.

While the authors of the New Testament texts took for granted the existence of ghosts, they made no new claims about where they came from or how they behaved. In fact, the geography of the ancient otherworld remained largely unchanged in the imagination of the earliest Christians. The apostles employed the Greek term Hades *alongside Hebrew words like* Sheol *and* Gehenna *to denote the abode of the dead, but they did not contribute to a new understanding of the meaning of these words. The behavior of the restless dead remained the same as well. In early Christian texts, the spirits of the deceased still visited their loved ones in dreams, crowded menacingly around visitors to their domain, and haunted the places where their bodies lay unburied or slain by violence, much like they did in Greek and Roman antiquity.*

These similarities stem in part from a shared funerary culture throughout the ancient Mediterranean world. For several centuries after the death of Jesus Christ, early Christians did not have death rites or burial places separate and distinct from their pagan neighbors. In the Roman Empire, the interment and commemoration of a deceased person was largely a family affair. Many Christians attached a new significance to the day of a person's death, believing it to be the day of their rebirth into a new life with Christ, and some of them sought burial in proximity to the tombs of the martyrs, but it was only in the early Middle Ages that Christian communities developed the preference for burial in the hallowed ground of churchyard cemeteries.

Unlike the Greeks and Romans, however, ancient Christians were strict monotheists who recognized the God of the Hebrews as their own. From the very beginning of the Christian movement, they appropriated the Hebrew scriptures as a foreshadowing of their claims about the meaning of the life and death of Jesus Christ. In doing so, they became the heirs to a long and ambivalent tradition about the practice of necromancy in the ancient Near East. Christian readers found in the Book of Deuteronomy an ancient prohibition against speaking with the dead, a practice outlawed by Moses as an affront to God. In contrast, they also read the story of King Saul's consultation with the witch of Endor, who performed a necromantic ritual to summon the ghost of the prophet Samuel on the king's behalf. Thus, the classical tradition and the Hebrew scriptures each played formative roles in shaping how the early Christians thought about the restless dead. Despite this inheritance, Christians abandoned commerce with professional diviners like Erictho. As these stories show, God granted the authority to communicate with the dead to martyrs and saints for purposes far removed from the unsavory activities of ancient necromancers.

SPEAKING WITH THE DEAD IN THE HEBREW SCRIPTURES

The practice of necromancy is not mentioned very often in the Hebrew scriptures, but it was common enough in the ancient Near East to prompt strict prohibitions against its use in legal and prophetic texts written by the Israelites. Like many other divinatory and magical practices, necromancy was considered to be an insult to God and punishable by death. Despite these condemnations, King Saul's consultation with the witch of Endor clearly shows that speaking to the dead for the purpose of divination persisted for centuries among the Jews. This unusually vivid description of a necromantic ritual was widely read by ancient and medieval Christians, who argued at length about the efficacy of this practice and the identity of the spirit conjured by the witch.

(A) A PROHIBITION AGAINST NECROMANCY[1]

When you have come into the land that the Lord God will give to you, beware that you do not wish to imitate the abominations of the people who already dwell there. Let there not be found among you anyone who sacrifices while leading his son or daughter through fire or anyone who consults fortune-tellers or interprets dreams and omens. Do not become a sorcerer or a conjurer or one who consults with soothsayers or supernatural spirits or one who seeks the truth from the dead. For the Lord hates all of these things and it is because of these evils that He will destroy these people at your coming. You will be perfect and without blemish before the Lord your God. Those peoples, whose land you will possess, pay heed to soothsayers and diviners, but you have been instructed otherwise by the Lord your God.

(B) KING SAUL CONSULTS THE WITCH OF ENDOR[2]

It came to pass in those days that the Philistines gathered their forces in preparation for war against Israel . . . Now Samuel was dead and all Israel mourned him and they buried him in Ramatha, his own city. And Saul exiled magicians and soothsayers from the land. And the Philistines gathered and marched and camped in Sunam. And Saul also marshaled all of Israel and came to Gelboe. And Saul saw the forces of the Philistines and feared and there was a great trembling in his heart. And he consulted the Lord and He did not respond to him, neither through dreams nor through priests nor through prophets. And Saul said to his servants, "Find for me a woman with the power of divination and I will go to her and consult her." And his servants told him that there was a woman with the power of divination at Endor.

So Saul changed his garments and put on different clothes and departed and two men went with him. And they came to the woman by night and he said to her, "Divine for me with a spirit and raise up for me whomever I say." And the woman said to him, "Behold, you know what Saul has done and how he has banished the magicians and fortune-tellers from the land. Why then are you attempting to snare my life and bring about my death?" And Saul swore to her by the Lord, saying, "As the Lord lives, no harm will come upon you because of this act." And the woman said to him, "Whom shall I raise up for you?" He said, "Raise up Samuel for me." But when the woman saw Samuel, she cried out with a great voice and said to Saul, "Why have you tricked me? You are none other than Saul!" The king said to her, "Do not fear. What do you see?" And the woman said to Saul, "I see gods rising up from the earth." And he said to her, "What does he look like?" She

said, "An old man rises and he is shrouded in a cloak." And
Saul knew that it was Samuel and he bowed with his face to
the ground and paid him respect.

Then Samuel said to Saul, "Why have you disturbed me to
raise me up?" And Saul said, "I am in a very tight spot, for the
Philistines wage war against me and God has turned away
from me and does not answer me, neither through the power
of the prophets nor through dreams. Therefore, I have summoned you, so that you may show me what to do." And Samuel said, "What is the use of asking me, when the Lord has
turned away from you and gone over to your rival? For the
Lord has done to you just as he said through my power, and he
has torn your kingdom from your hand and he will give it to
your neighbor David. Because you did not obey the voice of
the Lord and you did not take out the wrath of his anger
against Amalek, for this reason you endure what the Lord has
done to you today. Moreover, the Lord will also give Israel
with you into the hands of the Philistines. Tomorrow you and
your sons will be with me, but the Lord will give the camps of
Israel into the hands of the Philistines."

And immediately Saul fell stretched out on the ground, for
he feared the words of Samuel and there was no strength in
him because he had not eaten any bread that whole day. And
then that woman came to Saul—he was still very shaken—and
said to him, "Behold, your servant obeyed your request and I
have taken my life in my hands and listened to the words that
you spoke to me. Now, therefore, listen to me and heed the
voice of your servant. I will set a small morsel of bread before
you so that you may eat it and recover your strength to get on
your way." He refused and said, "I will not eat it." But his servants and the woman urged him to do so. He heeded their
pleas and got up from the ground and sat upon a bed. Now
that woman had a fattened calf in the house, so she quickly
prepared it for slaughter. And then taking some flour, she
kneaded it and baked unleavened bread and put it before Saul
and his servants. Once they had eaten, they rose and walked
all night back to their camp.

A GHOST UPON THE WATERS[1]

Spirits of the dead are largely absent from the texts that comprise the New Testament. An exception is the Gospel of Matthew (composed 80—90), which recounts how Jesus walked upon the water of a lake to catch up with the followers, who had gone ahead of him in their boats. When the apostles saw the form of a man that seemed to hover over the water in the early morning light, they thought for certain that it was a spirit of the dead and cried out in fear.

And immediately Jesus ordered the disciples to get into the boat and go on ahead of him across the lake, while he dismissed the crowds. After he had dismissed them, Jesus climbed up the mountain by himself to pray. When night fell, he was alone there. The boat was already a good distance away, tossed by the waves because the wind was against it. Just before dawn, Jesus came to them walking upon the lake. And when the disciples saw him walking upon the lake, they were upset, saying "It is a ghost!" and they cried out in fear. Jesus immediately spoke to them, saying "Have faith, it is I. Do not fear." And Peter responding to him said, "Lord, if it is you, command me to come to you upon the waters." And he said, "Come!" And coming down from the boat, Peter walked upon the waters and came to Jesus. But seeing a strong wind, he was afraid, and when he began to sink, he cried out saying "Lord, save me!" Immediately reaching out his hand, Jesus caught him and said to him, "You of little faith, why did you doubt?" And when they climbed up into the boat, the wind died down. And everyone who was in the boat worshipped him saying "Truly you are the son of God!"

DREAMING OF THE DEAD[1]

Before the conversion of Emperor Constantine to Christianity in 312, Roman authorities frequently persecuted Christians for rejecting the rites of worship owed to the pagan gods. During these persecutions, many Christians suffered martyrdom, that is, they died for their faith rather than sacrifice to false deities. One of the most remarkable documents of the early Christian period is a diary kept by a North African woman named Perpetua, who was imprisoned in Carthage in 203 for being a Christian and died in the Roman coliseum. In the days before her death, Perpetua recounted in her diary how the spirit of her brother Dinocrates, who had died a pagan, visited her in her dreams and how her prayers earned for him the refreshment and relief of a Christian afterlife.

A few days later, while we were all praying, suddenly in the midst of a prayer a voice came to me and I spoke the name Dinocrates. I was astonished because he had never before now entered into my mind, and the memory of his misfortune made me sad. And I knew at once that I was worthy and that I should pray for him. So I began to pray for him in earnest and to groan to the Lord. Then, that very night, this vision was shown to me. I saw Dinocrates coming out of a place of shadows, where many others dwelt with him. He was very hot and thirsty, covered in dirt and pale in color, and on his face was the wound that he had when he died. This boy Dinocrates had been my brother in the flesh, but at the age of seven he died horribly due to a cancer of the face and his death filled everyone with loathing. Thus, it was for this boy that I made my prayer. But between me and him there was a wide gulf with the result that neither of us could approach the other. But there was in that place where Dinocrates stood a basin full of water, the lip of which was higher than the height of the boy and Dinocrates was stretching himself toward it as if he were going to drink. I was saddened because that basin held water and yet because of the height of the rim he was not able to drink from it. Then I woke up and I knew that my brother was suffering, but I was sure that I could help him in his trouble and I prayed for him every day until we were transferred to the military prison. For we were to fight in the military games on the birthday of Geta Caesar [March 7, 203]. And I said a prayer for him, groaning and crying night and day, so that this favor might be granted to me.

On the day that we remained in chains, this vision was shown to me. I saw that place that I had seen before and Dinocrates was there, his body cleansed, well-dressed, and refreshed. And where his wound had been, there was a scar, and that basin, which I had seen before, now had its lip lowered to the height of the boy's navel and he could draw water from it without any hindrance. And upon the lip of the basin there was a golden cup full of water and Dinocrates approached and began to drink from it and the cup did not empty. And once he was sated, he began to play in the water joyfully as children do. And then I woke up and I knew that he had been freed from his suffering.

THE DISCERNMENT OF
THE SAINTS

*In the Christian tradition, men and women who died for the
faith or who lived virtuous lives of self-denial were recognized
as saints. Christian authors narrated the stories of these heroic individuals in works of hagiography, a Greek word meaning "writings about the holy." The lives of the saints were not
biographies in the modern sense. They were written to promote the holiness of their subjects by relating how the power
of God allowed them to perform miracles of healing and exor-
cise demons. Two early works of hagiography—the* Life of
Saint Martin *by Sulpicius Severus (written in 396) and the*
Life of Saint Germanus of Auxerre *by Constantius of Lyon
(written around 480)—included stories about hauntings. In
each case, the saint demonstrated his holy power by compelling the spirits of the dead to reveal their identity and the
cause of their unrest. The story about the fifth-century mis-
sionary, Saint Patrick, was written down in the eleventh century, but it derived from a much older oral tradition. Like the
saintly bishops of late antique Gaul, the apostle to Ireland had
the God-given authority to make the dead speak.*

(A) SAINT MARTIN AND THE
BANDIT'S GHOST[1]

There was a place not far from the town [Tours] and near to
the monastery [Marmoutier], which the false belief of men considered to be sacred, as though martyrs had been buried there.
And there was even an altar there, set up by past bishops. But

Martin, not one to believe idly in rumors, sought the name of this martyr and the date of his death from presbyters and priests older than him. He felt considerable doubt because no established tradition had been passed down. For a while he stayed away from that place, neither speaking out against the veneration of the martyr, because he was unsure of his identity, nor lending his authority to the rumor, because he did not wish to strengthen a false belief. Then one day, he went to that place with a few of the brethren. Standing upon the very grave, he prayed to the Lord to reveal who this man was and the reason why he had been buried there. Then turning to the left, he saw standing close at hand a wraith that was ragged and grim. Martin commanded the spirit to speak its name and to explain the reason for its presence there. The wraith shared his name and confessed to a crime. He had been a bandit, who was executed for his wicked deeds only to be venerated by a widely held mistake. He had nothing in common with the martyrs; they had earned glory, while he had only earned punishment. Amazingly, those who had accompanied Martin could hear the voice of someone speaking, but they could not see who it was, so Martin described what he had seen and ordered that the altar be removed from that place and thereby freed the people from the error of their false belief.

(B) SAINT GERMANUS QUIETS A SPECTER[2]

Once when Germanus was on the road in the winter and had passed the entire day in fasting and weariness, he was advised to find shelter somewhere with the approach of evening. There was a little house some distance from the road. Now long abandoned, its roof had partially collapsed and it was covered in foliage due to general neglect, so it seemed almost better to brave the night in the cold of the open air rather than to find shelter in that place of danger and horror, especially since two old men had claimed that this particular house was uninhabited because something terrible dwelt there. When the most

blessed man learned this, he approached the dreadful ruin as
though it was a place of beauty, and among what had once
been many dwellings he found one that just barely retained the
semblance of a living space. There his few companions placed
their light packs and prepared a modest meal, but the bishop
ate nothing at all.

As the night wore on, one of the priests assumed the duty of
reading aloud and Germanus, exhausted by fasting and weariness, was overcome by sleep. Then, suddenly, a dreadful
shadow appeared before the reader and rose little by little in
front of his eyes, while a shower of hail struck the walls. The
terrified reader implored the aid of the bishop. Springing up
immediately, Germanus stared down the image of the fearful
apparition. Once he had invoked the name of Christ, he commanded the ghost to say who he was and what he was doing
there. Putting aside its frightful façade, the ghost replied in a
low voice like a suppliant that he and his companion had been
the perpetrators of many crimes, that they lay unburied and
because of this they disturbed living men, as they were unable
to find rest themselves, and they asked Germanus to petition
the Lord on their behalf so that He might receive them and
grant them eternal rest.

The holy man grieved to hear this story and ordered that the
ghost reveal the place where their bodies lay unburied. Then,
with a candle lighting the way, the shade led the way, and
amid great difficulties caused by the ruins because the night
was stormy, he indicated the place where their bodies had been
thrown. When the day returned once more, the bishop invited
some of the locals and encouraged them to help, while he
stood by to oversee the completion of the work. Heaps of de-
bris that had piled up over time were cleared away with rakes.
The bodies were found strewn about in disarray, the bones
still fastened with iron bindings. According to the law of
burial, a grave was dug, the remains were freed from their
chains and wrapped in linen, earth was thrown upon them,
and the prayer of intercession for the dead was recited. Rest
for the dead was achieved and relief for the living as well, for

after that day the little house, without any hint of its former terror, prospered with new inhabitants.

(C) SAINT PATRICK SPEAKS TO THE DEAD[3]

It was Patrick's custom to make the sign of the cross one hundred times every day and every night. And whether he was in a chariot or on horseback, he would visit every standing cross, sometimes leaving the road to do so, even if it was a thousand feet away, provided that he saw it from a distance or knew that it was there. Once on a certain day Patrick did not visit a standing cross that was on his route. In fact, he did not even realize that it was there. Then at the end of the day, his chariot driver remarked that the saint had passed by a standing cross without stopping to visit it. Hearing this, Patrick abandoned the guesthouse where he was lodged and his dinner to seek out this standing cross.

While Patrick was praying at the cross, he realized that it was a grave and asked, "Who is buried here?" From the depth of the grave, a corpse answered, "I am a wretched pagan. While I was alive, great pain wracked my soul and I died and then I was buried here." Patrick asked, "Why was a cross, the symbol of the Christians, erected on your grave?" "The answer is easy," the corpse said. "A woman who lived in a distant land lost her son in this country and he was buried hereabouts. When she came from her home faraway, she mistook my grave for his and raised this cross upon it. Her grief did not allow her to realize her mistake." "That is why I passed this cross by," said Patrick, "for this is a pagan grave." So Patrick had the cross moved to its rightful place over the grave of the Christian son.

THE AUTOPSY OF
SOULS IN LATE
ANCIENT THOUGHT

The fourth century marked a turning point for the history of the Christian Church. At the beginning of the century, Emperor Constantine declared his allegiance to the god of the Christians and passed legislation protecting Christian believers from imperial persecution. In the decades that followed, many pagans recognized the advantage of being a Christian under the regimes of Constantine and his successors and converted to the Christian faith. By the end of the fourth century, traditional Roman religion was in decline. In 382, Emperor Gratian abandoned the title of high priest (pontifex maximus) of the imperial cult and removed the altar of the goddess Victory from the Roman senate house. A decade later, in 393, Emperor Theodosius the Great outlawed public sacrifice altogether and dismantled the imperial funding that supported pagan priesthoods. Despite ineffectual resistance from stalwart traditionalists, the decades around 400 witnessed the triumph of the Christian church in the Roman Empire.

Augustine of Hippo (354–430) came of age in this period of transition. After dabbling in the mysteries of Manichaeism and pursuing a secular career as a professor of rhetoric in Milan, he underwent a dramatic conversion experience in the summer of 386 at the age of thirty-one and returned to his native North Africa as a committed Christian. He was ordained a priest in 391 and served as bishop of his hometown Hippo Regius (modern Annaba, Algeria) from 395 until his death in 430. Augustine was recognized as one of the most authoritative Christian leaders of his time. As a result, during his three *and a half decades as bishop, he wrote hundreds of letters and sermons, as well as voluminous treatises on all aspects of Christian life and thought.*

Many of Augustine's writings were responses to questions about the faith from fellow bishops. His friends Evodius of Uzalis and Paulinus of Nola were two such petitioners. The nature of the soul and the fate of ordinary believers after death occupied the minds of their anxious parishioners. Unable to find the answers to their questions in the sacred scriptures or in the customs of the church, these bishops turned to Augustine for help. There is an urgency to these inquiries that speaks to the rapid success of the Christian faith in the late Roman Empire. The huge numbers of pragmatic conversions to Christianity that took place over the course of the fourth century created massive congregations of believers all around the rim of the Mediterranean Sea. These converts brought to their new faith a dizzying array of ideas about the ability of the dead to communicate with the living. It would take several centuries for Christian thinkers to work out the obligations of ordinary believers toward the dead and the role of ghosts as intermediaries between this world and the next. An important step in this process was an inquiry into the very nature of the soul itself. Was it material or immaterial? Did it retain its individual identity in the afterlife? And, most important, could the living do anything to help the souls of sinners attain heaven?

EVODIUS'S INQUIRY: GOING FORTH FROM THE BODY, WHO ARE WE?[1]

A firm believer in the reality of ghosts, Bishop Evodius of Uzalis (modern El Alia, Tunisia) was nonetheless confused about the nature of human souls. Around 420, the sudden death of a young notary and his subsequent communication from beyond the grave prompted Evodius to write to Augustine for advice on the matter: "Going forth from the body and leaving behind every burden and nimble sin, who are we?" As this letter makes vividly clear, Evodius's community was crowded with ghosts, who frequently communicated to the living in dreams. In addition to the spirit of the bishop's young notary, whose soul returned to foretell the death of his father, other apparitions appeared as well: in the middle of the night, a drowsy old man saw a mysterious person carrying a laurel branch and an unspecified text, while a virtuous widow spoke in her dreams to the ghost of a deceased deacon who is busy preparing a palace for the notary's soul in heaven. For his part, Augustine denied in no uncertain terms that the soul retained any kind of material shell after death, but otherwise he was reluctant to lend false certainty to an issue that he felt was knowable only to God.

[Bishop Evodius of Uzalis writes to Augustine:] I had a certain young man as my notary, who was the son of the priest Armenius of Melonita. Just as he was coming of age—for he was training as a shorthand writer in the service of the governor—through my humble agency God rescued him. As a youth, he was rash and sometimes restless, but as he advanced in age—for he is now twenty-two years old—a seriousness of manners and a life of virtue adorned him like a watchman, so that just the memory of him delights me. He was nimble in his note taking and very diligent in writing; he had also begun to apply himself so eagerly to reading that he would rouse me from sleep in the middle of the night to read; for sometimes he would read to me at night, when everything was silent, and he would never pass over a passage unless he understood it, and he would repeat it three or four times and not give up until the answer was clear to him. I had begun to hold him not just as a boy and a notary, but as a friend who was indispensable and sweet. His stories did indeed delight me.

He also wished "to depart and to be with Christ" and this was granted to him.[2] For he was sick for sixteen days in his parents' house and, while he was awake, he spoke about the scriptures for almost the entire duration of his illness. But as he began to draw near to the end of his life, he sang for all to hear, "My soul longs for and hastens to the halls of God" and after this he sang once more, "You have anointed my head in oil and drinking from your cup, how good it is!"[3] This was how he passed his time; this was his consolation. Finally, when he had begun to depart from this life, he began to make the sign of the cross on his forehead, then brought his hand down to his mouth, on which he also wished to make the sign of the cross, but by then the person inside, who had been renewed day by day, had left its house of clay. Such a great joy filled me that I thought that he had entered into my mind after he had departed from his own body and there he bestowed upon me the very brightness of his presence. It cannot be stated how overjoyed I felt for his freedom and safety. For I felt no small concern for him; I was fearful on account of his youth. Indeed, I had taken care to ask him, whether perhaps he had been polluted by sexual contact with a woman; he assured me that he was free from that sin, much to our joy. Therefore, he was set free. We celebrated his funeral rites in a manner both very fitting and honorable for such a great soul, for we praised the Lord with hymns for three days around his tomb and on the third day we offered the sacrament of redemption.

But behold two days later a certain honorable widow named Urbica from the town of Figes, who said that she had been widowed twelve years before and was a handmaiden of God, experienced this in a dream. She saw a certain deacon who had died four years earlier, preparing a palace in the company of servants and handmaidens of God, both virgins and widows. It was adorned in such a way that the brightness of the place shone with such intensity that the entire structure could have been made of silver. And when this woman asked the deacon very earnestly for whom they were preparing this palace, he responded that it was being prepared for a young man, the son of a priest, who had been taken from life the day before. And in the same palace there appeared an old man clad in white, who instructed two others who were also clad in white to go and take the body from its tomb and carry it up to heaven. And she said that after the body had been taken from the tomb and carried up to heaven, shoots of virgin roses—for this is what unopened buds are usually called—rose up from the very same tomb.

I have related what took place. Now please lend your ear to my question and explain to me what I am asking. The migration of that young man's soul compels me to make such inquiries . . . While we are in this life, we are weighed down by the needs of the body and yet, as it is written, "We overcome through him, who has loved us," but going forth from the body and leaving behind every burden and nimble sin, who are we?[4] . . . It seems to me that, when placed in the body, as I said, the soul grows strong, it benefits from the vigorous exertion of the mind, and the quicker, more agile, stronger, more active, eager, and intent it is, the more competent and better it becomes. Once the soul has been placed in the body, it relishes its own strength. And when the body is put aside, like a cloud that has blown away, the soul becomes completely bright in a state of tranquility without temptation, seeing what it desires, embracing what it loves, remembering its friends, even recognizing those who it preceded in death and those who followed after it. Perhaps this is true. I do not know; I seek to learn. But it bothers me a great deal to believe that the soul enters a kind of sleep, so that it becomes just like one who is sleeping in the body, just like one buried and living only in hope, but taking no action, knowing nothing, especially if it is not roused by a dream. This idea is really terrifying and suggests that the soul is like something dead.

But I also ask this: if it follows that the soul does have a body, does it lack any of the bodily senses? If it has no need to smell and to taste, as I believe, then it remains doubtful that it has any need to touch, see, and hear. For why is it then that demons are said to hear not through the men who they possess— for that is another question entirely—but indeed when they appear in their own bodies. With regard to seeing, how do they move from place to place if they have a body, when they lack the guidance of the sense of sight? Do you think that human souls are not like that, when they go forth from the body, so that they have some kind of body and yet they lack bodily senses? Why is it that individuals who are awake and restless have seen many dead people entering into houses, as they were accustomed to do, either by day or at night—I have heard this on more than one occasion—and many people also say that the dead are seen at certain hours of the night in the places in which their bodies were buried and especially in the basilicas, where they are known to make noises and say prayers? I remember that I had heard this from more than one person, for a certain holy priest was a witness to this vision. He saw a multitude of the dead leaving the baptistery in luminous bodies and afterward he heard prayers in the middle of the same church. All of these things either support my line of questioning or, if they are nonsense, it is strange and I would like to know more about it, because the dead do seem to come and visit the living and are seen outside of dreams . . .

At the time of his death, the young man in question experienced a vision and in a certain way he followed through on it. For it seemed that in his sleep a fellow student and reader, who had died eight months earlier, came back to him. When he was asked by the young man, to whom he had appeared, why he had come back, this student said, "I have come to lead my friend away from here." And so it happened. And in the same

house there appeared to a certain old man who was half awake
a person carrying a laurel branch and a text. But after this person was seen, we can add that following the death of the boy,
his father, a priest, began to stay in the monastery with the old
man Theasius for the sake of consoling him, but on the third
day after the boy's death, the same boy was seen entering the
monastery and was asked by a certain brother in a dream
whether he knew that he was dead. He replied that he was
aware of it. When asked whether he had been received by God,
he related this with great joy. When asked the reason why he
had come, he then said, "I was sent to summon my father." The
brother to whom these things were shown then woke up and
told this story. It came all the way to the ear of Bishop Theasius, who was alarmed and chastised the brother who told it,
lest the tale come too easily to the ear of the priest and trouble
him. Why go on for so long about it? As it happened, four days
after the visit from the ghost, while he was speaking—for he
had a mild fever and there was no danger at all; the doctor was
not present, but he would have attested that he had no anxiety
about the case—this same priest lay down on a bed and died.
Nor can I be silent that on that very same day when his son
died, he sought from his father the kiss of peace and he asked
for it three times and with every kiss he said to his father, "Let
us give thanks to God together" and he made his father say this
with him as though urging him to depart from his life with
him. Thus between the two deaths there was a space of seven
days. How are we to understand such events? Who will be the
most faithful master to reveal their hidden causes? The emo-
tion of my heart flows out to you in this time of distress. The
divine plan for the death of the boy and his father is clear because two sparrows will not fall to the earth without the will of
the Father.[5] Therefore, this event shows, I think, that the soul
cannot entirely lack a body of its own, because God is the only
one who lacks any kind of body whatsoever.

[Augustine responds:] There were indeed two letters from
you, in which you asked many a deep question. One of them
was somehow lost and though I looked for quite a while I
could not find it; the other, which I did find, provided a very

sweet portrait of a young man who was a good and chaste servant of God, explained how he died, and also how he made
known his heavenly reward by the testimony of visions shown
to the brethren. Then in this context you put forward a very
difficult question about the soul, whether it departs from its
mortal body with some body of its own, which allows it to be
carried to or to be confined in material places. Really though,
the treatment of this topic, if it can be considered clearly by
people like us, requires care and the most attentive kind of
mental exertion and for this a mind completely free from any
distractions. If, however, you wish to hear very briefly how it
seems to me, I simply do not believe that the soul departs from
the body with a body of its own.

AUGUSTINE'S REJECTION
OF GHOSTS[1]

About a year after his correspondence with Evodius (c. 421),
a letter from Bishop Paulinus of Nola (a town in Campania,
Italy) prompted Augustine's longest rumination on the rela-
tionship between the living and the departed in a treatise
called On the Care to Be Taken for the Dead. *Paulinus wanted*
to know if there was any merit to burying a Christian near the
tombs of the saints. Would the soul benefit in the afterlife
from proximity to their holy bodies? Augustine's response
challenged more than a millennium of tradition concerning
the treatment of the dead. It did not matter where the dead
were buried or if they were buried at all, he argued, for God
would raise the faithful back to life at the Last Judgment
irrespective of where their corpses lay, properly interred or
scattered by slaughter. Moreover, against prevailing beliefs,
Augustine flatly denied that the souls of the dead communi-
cated to ordinary people as apparitions or in dreams. Just as
the living do not know when someone dreams about them, the
same holds true for the dead.

Reports of certain visions bring to our discussion a question
that we should not ignore. It is said that some dead people
have appeared to the living in dreams or in some other way,
who did not know where their bodies lay unburied. Once these
places were revealed, the dead people admonished the living to
provide for them the proper burial that they had neglected.
Now if we assert that these stories are false, we will seem to

contradict blatantly the writings of certain faithful men and the perception of those who have affirmed that such things have happened to them. But one must reply that it should not therefore be believed that the dead know these things just because they seem to say them or indicate them or seek them in dreams. For the living often appear to the living while asleep, even though they are not themselves aware of this, and they hear from them in conversation the content of their dreams, that is to say, that they saw them in their dreams doing or saying something. Therefore, it is possible for someone to see me in their dreams indicating to him something that has happened or indeed foretelling something that will happen in the future, while for my part I am completely ignorant of this and do not care whatsoever not only what he is dreaming about, but also whether he is awake while I am sleeping or whether he is asleep while I am awake or whether we are both awake or asleep at one and the same time, when he experiences the dream in which I appear. Why then is it so strange that the dead, without their knowledge and unable to perceive these things, are seen by the living in dreams and say something, which the living know to be true when they wake up?

I might believe that these visions occur due to the intervention of angels, whether it is permitted from on high or otherwise ordained that the dead seem to say something in dreams concerning how their bodies should be buried, when really those souls whose bodies these are have no knowledge of this exchange. This may sometimes happen profitably whether for the solace of the living, to whom the dead are related, whose images appear to them while they sleep, or so that by these reminders to the human race the humanity of the burial of the dead is commended. For, even though burial does not help the dead, one who neglects this duty runs the risk of seeming impious. But men have sometimes been led into serious trouble by false visions, which it would have been better to resist. What if someone should see in their dreams what Aeneas is said, with poetic license, to have seen among the dead and the image of someone who has not been buried should appear to him and should say such things as Palinurus allegedly said to

Aeneas?[2] And when he wakes up, he should find the body there in the place where he heard in his dream that it was lying unburied. And then having been admonished and petitioned to bury the body he has found and because he finds this to be true, he should believe therefore that the dead must be buried so that their souls may pass to those places, from where he dreamed that the souls of the unburied are forbidden by a law of the underworld, would he not, holding this to be true, veer widely from the path of truth?

But human weakness is such that, whenever someone sees a dead person in their dreams, that person believes that he has seen the dead person's soul. When, however, he has dreamed likewise of a living person, he has no doubt that it was not his soul or body that appeared to him, but rather the likeness of the person. This seems to suggest that the images, but not the souls, of dead men appear to sleepers in the same manner without their knowledge. For certain, when we were in Milan, we heard that someone brought forth a bill and demanded payment from the son of a man who had recently died, even though the father had already paid the bill without his son's knowledge. The son was very sad and wondered why his dying father had not informed him what he owed, since he had drawn up a will. Then in a dream the father appeared to his son, who had grown quite distressed, and revealed to him the location of the receipt, which showed that he had in fact paid the bill. And once he had found the bill and presented it as proof of the payment, the young man not only cast off the infamy of the fraudulent debt, but he also recovered the receipt signed by his father, which his father had not received when he had originally paid back the money he owed. In this case, the soul of the father is believed to have provided care for his son and came to him while he was sleeping, so that he might teach him what he did not know and thus free him from a great deal of trouble.

But right around the same time that we heard this anecdote, a similar story reached us in Milan about Eulogius, an expert in rhetoric at Carthage, who has been a student of mine. He related it to me himself after we returned to Africa. When Eulogius was teaching Cicero's rhetorical treatises to his students, he was reviewing the lesson that he was going to teach the next day and came upon a complicated passage. His inability to understand it troubled him so much that he could barely sleep. That very night I appeared to him in a dream and explained the passage he could not understand, well, not me, but my image, for I had no knowledge of it as I was very far away across the sea either doing or dreaming something else and worrying not in the least about his troubles. How such things happen, I do not know, but in whatever way they do. Why do we not believe that they happen in the same way, so that whoever in his sleep sees a dead person, it is the same as when he sees a living person? Neither the living nor the dead know or care when someone dreams of their likenesses nor do they know or care when or where this takes place.

Similar to dreams are the kinds of visions sometimes seen by people who are wide awake, whose senses have been disturbed, like those who are mad or prone to fits of raving. For they talk to themselves as though they were in fact talking to someone who was present. Indeed, they are more likely to converse with people who are not there, whose likeness they can see, whether they are living or dead, rather than those who are actually present. But the ones who are living do not know that they are seen by those who are mad or that they converse with them. They are not really present nor are they really conversing at all, but people with troubled senses suffer from these kinds of imaginary visions. In this manner, those who have departed from this life seem as though they are still present to people thus afflicted, when they are in fact absent and altogether unknowing whether someone sees them in their imagination.

Similar to this is the case when men take leave of the senses of the body more deeply than when they are sleeping and experience these kinds of visions, for images of the living and the dead often appear during their trances. And when they have returned to their senses, they report that they have seen certain people who have died, for they truly believe that they have been with them, but those who hear that images of the living, absent and unaware, have been seen in the same way by these people pay no attention to this whatsoever. There was a certain man named Curma from the township of Tullium, which is near Hippo Regius. He was a senator modest in means, a simple man of the country who had achieved the position of magistrate only with some difficulty. After he had become sick, he was deprived of his senses and for many days he lay prone as though he was almost dead. There was the faintest breath in his nostrils, which you could barely feel when you brought your hand close, and this was the only indication that he was alive; otherwise he would have been buried like a corpse. He made no movement, took no nourishment, and neither his eyes nor any other sense of his body responded to any stimulus whatsoever. Yet he saw many visions as though in his dreams, which at length he finally reported when he woke up a few days later. And as soon as he opened his eyes, he said, "Someone should go to the house of Curma the smith and see what has happened there." When someone went there, they found that Curma the smith had died at that very moment when Curma the magistrate had returned to his senses and come back, as it were, from the dead. And to those who were present, Curma the magistrate indicated that Curma the smith had been ordered to be delivered up at the very moment when he himself had been dismissed. In fact, as his spirit returned to his body, he said that he had overheard that it was not Curma the magistrate, but Curma the smith, who had been ordered to be brought to the dwelling places of the dead.

Therefore, in these visions, just like in his dreams, among the dead whom he saw treated according to the diversity of their merits he also recognized some people he knew were still alive. Indeed, I might have perhaps actually believed him, if during those so-called dreams of his he had not seen certain individuals who are still very much alive, some of whom are priests from his own district, one of whom he heard say in the vision that he should be baptized by me at Hippo Regius, which, he replied, he had already done. Thus in that vision he had seen a priest, some clerics, and me myself, not yet dead, of course, in which afterward he did in fact see dead people. Now why do we not believe that he saw the dead in the same way he saw us, both absent and unknowing, and by extension he did not actually see them, but rather likenesses of them? The same principle applies to the places he saw. For he saw the place where the priest was in the company of the clerics and he saw Hippo Regius, where he thought he had been baptized by me. He was certainly not in these places at the time when it seemed to him that he was there. For he did not know what was going on in these places at that time, which he would have undoubtedly known if he had truly been there. Therefore, these visions have no basis in reality, but rather they have been sketched in shadow on certain images of things that are real.

POPE GREGORY THE GREAT: HOW CAN THE LIVING HELP THE DEAD?[1]

Augustine was unique among late ancient thinkers in his doubt that the dead communicated to the living in visions and dreams. Despite his immense authority on almost every aspect of Christian doctrine, his teachings on this matter were politely ignored by later thinkers. In the sixth century, Pope Gregory the Great (c. 540–604) told stories about the fate of the souls of ordinary Christians to a young disciple named Peter in the final book of his four-volume Dialogues, *which appeared in 594. In this treatise, Gregory warned his readers that torment "in fire" awaited the souls of the sinful dead. In a series of memorable stories, he showed that intercessory prayer and the celebration of the Eucharist gave the living the power to relieve Christian souls of their suffering in the afterlife. Moreover, in contrast to Augustine, the pope affirmed that the souls of the faithful departed communicated their need for help to the living through visions and dreams. These souls clearly had some kind of material existence; not only were they recognizable to their friends and loved ones, but they also felt the acute pain of the torments earned by their sins. Gregory's vindication of the reality of ghosts and the power of the living to intercede on their behalf made his* Dialogues *one of the most influential and widely read texts in the Middle Ages.*

When I was still a young man and not yet a monk, I heard a story from those who were older and more knowledgeable than me about a deacon of this apostlic see named Paschasius, whose most correct and splendid books concerning the Holy Spirit we still read. He was a man of wonderous sanctity, especially generous in giving alms, a supporter of the poor, while at the same time despising his own needs. But in the contest that took place between Symmachus and Laurentius over who should become bishop of Rome, during which the tempers of the faithful flared, Paschasius supported Laurentius. And even after Laurentius was defeated unanimously, the deacon nonetheless persisted in his support until the day he died, by loving and holding in high esteem a man whom the church had rejected as its leader by the judgment of the bishops. A short time later, during the papacy of Symmachus [498–514] shortly after Paschasius died, a man possessed by a demon touched the dalmatic draped over his coffin and immediately he was healed.[2] Then after a long time had passed, doctors advised Germanus, the bishop of Capua, whom I mentioned earlier, to soak in the baths of Angulus for the sake of his health. When he entered the baths, he discovered the deacon Paschasius standing and serving as an attendant in the hot steam. When he saw this, Germanus was very frightened and asked what such a great man was doing there. Paschasius answered him, "I have been assigned to this place of punishment for no other reason than the fact that I endorsed the candidacy of Laurentius against Symmachus. But I beseech you to pray to the Lord on my behalf. And you will know that your prayers have been heard, when you return to this place and find me gone." On behalf of Paschasius, the man of God Germanus bound himself in prayer. He returned after a few days, but he could not find Paschasius in that place. Indeed, because he had sinned not out of malice, but due to an error resulting from ignorance, Paschasius was able to be cleansed of his sin after his death. What we should believe is that he obtained this favor due to the generosity of his almsgiving, with the result that he could earn forgiveness after his death when he was no longer able to do good works.

At the same time, another monk of this monastery named John was a very promising young man, who surpassed his age with respect to his intellect, humility, kindness, and seriousness. During a sickness that nearly led to his death, an old man appeared to John in a nocturnal vision and touched him with his staff and said to him, "Rise, for you will not die at this time due to this sickness, but be prepared because you do not have a long time to live." Even though his doctors had lost hope in his recovery, John was immediately healed and recovered completely. He told everyone the vision he had seen and for two years he served God, as I said before, in a manner beyond his years. Three years ago, however, one of the brethren died and was buried by us in the cemetery of this monastery. While we were all departing after the burial, John lingered behind. When we went back for him, pale and trembling he told us afterward that he had heard the brother who had just died calling to him from the grave. Indeed, the aftermath soon taught us why, for ten days later John became feverish and died.

Our venerable brother Venantius, currently bishop of Luni, and the eminent Liberius, a very noble and trustworthy man, bore witness what they learned from their servants, who were present when the following event took place in the city of Genoa. For, as they told it, a man named Valentinus, the defender of the church of Milan, died. This man was very untrustworthy and distracted by all sorts of frivolities. He was buried in the church of the blessed martyr Syrus. Then, in the middle of the night, voices could be heard in the same church and it sounded as though someone was being violently thrown out of the church and dragged around outside. The sacristans ran to the sound of the voices and saw two extremely foul spirits who had tied up the feet of the corpse of Valentinus with some binding and were hauling him out of the church while he screamed and cried out loud. Terrified by the sight, the sacristans retreated to their beds. On the next day, however, they opened the tomb in which they had buried Valentinus and his body was no longer there. When they looked outside of the church where they had seen it thrown, they found it placed in another grave, its limbs bound, as though it had been dragged from the church. From this story, Peter, take away the lesson that people weighed down by grave sins who try nonetheless to be buried in a holy place will be judged for their presumption, for holy places do not free them from their sins, but rather compound them with the sin of rashness.

If sins can be forgiven after death, then the holy offering of the saving host is the best way to provide help for departed souls. It is for this reason that the souls of the dead sometimes beg for the Mass. For Bishop Felix, whom I mentioned before, heard the following story from a certain venerable priest, who was still alive two years ago, dwelling in the diocese of the city of Centum Cellae and serving at the church of St. John in a place called Tauriana. Felix claimed that, when the needs of the body demanded it, this priest was in the habit of washing in that place where hot waters produced a great deal of steam. One day when he arrived there, he encountered a stranger ready to help him by pulling his shoes from his feet, taking his clothes, offering a linen cloth to him as he came out of the hot water, and attending to his every need with great care. After this had happened a few times, on a certain day the same priest was about to go to the baths and thought to himself, "It is not appropriate to appear to be ungrateful to this man who has been so attentive to looking after me while I bathe, so it seems right for me to bring him something as a gift." So he brought two crown-shaped loaves of bread with him. As soon as he arrived at the baths, he found the man and as before he benefited from his attention in every way. He bathed and after he dressed and made ready to leave, he offered the gift that he had brought with him as a blessing to the man who had been so helpful to him, hoping that he would receive with kindness that which the grace of charity offered to him. But the man was mournful and upset and responded, "Why do you give these things to me, father? This bread is holy, so I cannot eat it. For indeed I was once the lord of this place, but for my sins I was sent back here after my death. If you wish to make an offering for me, give this bread to almighty God on my behalf, so that you may intervene for my sins. And you will know that your prayers have been heard when you come back here to wash and find me gone." With these words, he disappeared. Even though he seemed to be a man, by vanishing he revealed that he was a ghost. Then the same priest prayed for him in tears all week long and offered the saving Mass for him every day. And thereafter when he returned to the baths, he found that the ghost was no longer there. From this we learn how much the sacrifice of the sacred offering benefits souls, when the very spirits of the dead ask for it from the living and show us through signs how it absolved them from their sins.

But I should not remain silent about an event that I recall took place in my monastery three years ago. For there was a certain monk named Justus who was learned in the art of medicine. He was accustomed to devoting himself to my needs with care while I was in the monastery and to keep watch during my frequent bouts of illness. Then he was overtaken by some sickness and his end approached. During his illness, he was cared for by his brother and fellow monk Copiosus, who still practices medicine in the city of Rome. But when Justus knew that he had come to the end of his life, he divulged to his brother Copiosus that he had hidden three gold coins. Copiosus was not able to conceal this from the brethren. Searching carefully and looking through all of his medical supplies, they found the three gold coins hidden among his medicines.

As soon as I found out that a brother who lived in our community had committed such an evil deed, I was unable to bear it without anger because the rule of our monastery always demanded that all of the brethren hold everything in common and no individual was permitted to have anything that they called their own. With great sadness, I began to consider what I could do to purge the dying man of his crime and likewise provide an example to his living brethren. Therefore, I summoned Pretiosus, the prior of the monastery, and said, "Go and let none of the brethren visit Justus while he dies and let no word of consolation depart from their mouths. But when he is about to die and calls out for his brethren, let his own brother Copiosus tell him that he has been shunned by the entire community because of the gold coins that he kept secret. At the very least, may the bitterness of this moment scrape the guilt from his mind as he dies and thus may he be cleansed of the sin that he committed. Indeed, when he dies, his corpse should not be buried among the bodies of the brethren. Instead, make a grave in the dung heap and cast his body in there, and toss in as well the three gold coins he left behind, while all the brethren say in unison, 'May your money perish with you!' and thus cover him with earth."[3]

My intention was to teach two lessons: one to Justus as he died and the other to the brethren who yet lived, so that his bitterness at the hour of death might free this man from his guilt and such a great judgment brought on by his greed might prevent the remaining brethren from commiting the same fault. And so it was. For when Justus neared death and anxiously sought to commit his soul to the care of his brethren and not one of them deigned to heed his words or to speak to him, his brother Copiosus explained to him why everyone shunned him. Immediately he wept bitterly about the charge against him and departed from his body in a state of contrition. He was then buried as I had instructed. But all of the brethren were disturbed by this judgment and began one by one to bring forward to me all sorts of small and common items, even those things that the rule had always permitted them to have, for they greatly feared that they had something in their possession for which they could be punished.

When thirty days had passed since the death of Justus, my soul started to feel compassion for our deceased brother and I began to consider his faults with deep sadness and tried to come up with a way to save him from his plight. Then I summoned to me Pretiosus, the prior of our monastery, and said to him with sadness, "It has been a long time now that our brother Justus, who died, has been suffering in fire; we should show him our love and offer him help in any way that we can, so that he might be released. Thus, go and from this day forward for thirty days, have the brethren offer the Mass for him, so that no day may pass by when the life-giving offering is not made for the release of this man's soul." Pretiosus departed immediately and was obedient to my words.

Meanwhile I was occupied with other business and lost count of the days as they passed by. The same brother Justus who had died appeared at night in a vision to his own brother Copiosus. When he saw his dead brother, Copiosus asked him, "What is the matter, brother? How are you?" To which Justus responded, "Up to this moment, my situation was dire, but just now I am well, for today I was brought back into communion." Copiosus hurried off immediately to share this news with the brethren in the monastery. Indeed, the brethren carefully reckoned the days and realized that this was the thirtieth day on which the Mass had been offered on Justus's behalf. For Copiosus did not know what the brethren had been doing for his brother nor did the brethren know that Copiosus had seen Justus in a vision. Then at the very same moment when Copiosus realized what the brethren had been doing and they realized what he had just seen, it became abundantly clear that the vision and the thirtieth offering of the Mass were simultaneous, the reason being that the brother who had died escaped punishment through the saving power of the Mass.

THE ECOLOGY OF
THE OTHERWORLD
IN DARK AGE
EUROPE

In Pope Gregory's Dialogues, we see the formation of an authoritative tradition that death did not end the relationship between the living and the deceased. With the exception of the saints or especially wicked individuals, ordinary Christians would not proceed directly to heaven or descend irrevocably to hell when their souls departed from their bodies at the moment of death. Rather, weighed down by the accumulation of countless minor sins, almost everyone could expect to spend time in an otherworldly place where their souls awaited God's final judgment at the end of time. Some would suffer in cleansing fire to purify their souls; others would rest in peaceful repose, their only anguish caused by the absence of the direct presence of God. In the seventh century, a generation of Christian thinkers influenced by the writings of Gregory the Great set down in writing some of the earliest descriptions of the otherworld where the souls of the sinful dead resided. Long before the notion of purgatory became an official doctrine of the Christian church in the thirteenth century, early medieval monks imagined the ecology of a realm of souls with a vividness intended to inspire their readers to cultivate virtue in this life before death sealed their fate in the world to come.

THE VISION OF BARONTUS[1]

Written in the late seventh century, The Vision of Barontus *is one of the earliest examples of Christian visionary literature, which reached its full expression in the fourteenth century in Dante's towering* Divine Comedy. *In this story, a nobleman named Barontus, who had recently become a monk at the abbey of St. Peter at Lonrey near Bourges, fell ill and appeared as though dead. The brethren of Lonrey gathered around his body to pray for him. When Barontus revived the next morning, he related the story of his soul's voyage to the otherworld, his battle with the demons who sought to ensnare him, the aid he received from angels and the souls of dead monks, many of whom he had known in life, his meeting with Saint Peter, and his eventual return to the abbey. Written as a warning to his fellow brethren to lead lives of humility and virtue,* The Vision of Barontus *promoted the forgiveness of sins through private penance and especially through the giving of alms to the poor. In a rare stroke of luck, the monk who wrote the story down recorded the date of his composition: March 25, 678 or 679.*

Here begins the revelation of the blessed monk Barontus. I wish to remind you in turn, dearest brothers, of what happened recently in the abbey of St. Peter the Apostle, which is known by the name Longoretus.[2] A certain brother of noble birth, Barontus by name, having recently experienced a change of heart, entered the monastic life. After he had offered praises devoutly to God at matins in the church with his brothers, as soon as he returned to his bed he was immediately seized by a fever and brought to Death's door.[3] He began to fret with great tears and told his son, Aglioaldus by name, that he should seek out the deacon Eudo with all speed in the hope that the deacon would come to visit him out of brotherly love. Then and there, the boy dashed off with great lamenting and brought back the brother whom Barontus had summoned. But when this brother entered the house in which Barontus lay sick, he began to call his name over and over again, but Barontus was not able to respond to him. Instead he indicated his throat to his friend with his finger and waved his hands vigorously before his eyes as though defending himself. Then the fearful Eudo, relying on the weapons he had at hand, began to make the sign of the cross and with deep groans, he asked for holy water to be sprinkled in that house, so that the crowd of evil spirits might flee from there. But Barontus dropped his arms to his sides and closed his eyes and lay there half dead, unable to perceive anyone around him at all.

It was by that time almost the third hour [around nine in the morning] and the brethren came together to offer God their prayers in support of Barontus's life. When they saw that he could not move at all, they were overcome with tears in their sadness. In support of his soul they organized themselves into groups and took turns reciting the Psalms one after the other so that the heavenly doctor might return his soul to his body. So it happened that the brothers' recitation of the Psalter went on all day without interruption, until the time for the evening service arrived, when they habitually sang praises to God in the church. Barontus was in such rough shape, however, that no one who saw him had any hope that he would live much longer. But the servants of God, when they saw this, began to recite the Psalter with renewed vigor and on behalf of his soul to ask the heavenly Creator so that he who raised it up as though from Egypt would remove it to his eternal realm.[4] So staying up all night singing the Psalms, they arrived at the hour of cockcrow, when the power of Christ caused a miracle to occur there. It is not proper to remain silent about this throughout the entire Catholic church, for those who hear about it should be fearful of their sins and turn with their whole hearts to the service of

Christ, so that those who wish to emend themselves by sincere penance here and now do not in the end lament in perpetual punishment. As the brethren were singing the Psalms, Barontus woke up. He opened his mouth and blinked and uttered praises to God. The first words that came out of his mouth were "Glory to you, God! Glory to you, God! Glory to you, God!" When the brethren witnessed this, with a great trembling of excitement they began to give thanks to God, who had returned to life his servant Barontus, for no one believed that they would hear him speak again.

Then everyone gathered around him in a group and asked him to tell them in detail where he had been and what he had seen. As though waking from a long sleep, Barontus said, "When you saw me last night as we finished singing praises to Christ at matins, I was alive and well, but as soon as I returned to my own bed, I was suddenly overcome with drowsiness and fell asleep. But immediately in my sleep two loathsome demons arrived, whose terrifying appearance I found it hard to endure. They began to strangle me with violence with the intention of swallowing me down with the help of their bared fangs and thus carrying me off to hell. And confident that they would subdue me, they continued their attack until the third hour, when the archangel Raphael, radiant in the splendor of his brightness, arrived to help me. He ordered them not to treat me harshly anymore. But those proud demons resisted him, saying, 'If the brightness of God has not taken him from us, then there is no way that you can do so.' Then holy Raphael replied to them, 'If it is as you say, then let us go together to God's judgment and there let your sin be reckoned.' They argued back and forth all day until the time of vespers arrived. And the most blessed Raphael said to them, 'I am taking this soul with me from here to the seat of the eternal judge, but I am leaving the hope of his recovery here in his body.' For their part, the demons objected that they would never release my soul, unless God's judgment deprived them of it.

"Having heard this, Raphael extended his finger and touched my throat and poor me, I suddenly felt my soul being yanked out of my body. Let me now relate how small my soul seemed to me. It seemed to me to be as small as the chick of a hen, when it hatches from an egg. This little soul carried with it a head and eyes and other body parts, as well as sight, hearing, taste, a sense of smell, and touch, but it could barely speak until it came to the examination and received a body of air similar to the one it left behind." Barontus went on, "But their fight over my little soul was by no means easily settled. Holy Raphael was struggling to lift my soul back to heaven and the demons wanted always to cast my soul downward. But holy Raphael summoned his strength and began to lift me from the earth and to support me powerfully from the right-hand side. The demons fought against him, one seizing me roughly from the left-hand side and another kicking me hard from behind with his heels while uttering in the fullness of his wrath, 'I have already held you in my power once and did great harm to you, but now you will suffer forever in hell!'

"As the demon said these words, we rose above the forest surrounding the monastery and the bell over the church suddenly sounded for vespers. Then holy Raphael commanded the demons, saying, 'Retreat, you cruel beasts, retreat! You can harm this little soul no longer, for the church bell has sounded and the brethren have assembled to pray for him.' Nevertheless, the demons did not relent, but continued to bruise my side with savage kicks. And thus our course took us quickly over the monastery called Millebeccus.⁵ Here holy Raphael prayed in my favor and this verse came from his mouth, 'In every place of your dominion, bless my soul, Lord.'⁶ And as I heard this, I listened and looked and saw that very monastery and I recognized the entire community as they celebrated vespers and I even spied one of the brethren carrying green herbs for use in the kitchen. Dearest brothers, we ought to marvel with great trembling at the fact that my soul was taken far above the dwellings of the most holy men and had traveled a distance of twelve miles between the two monasteries in a moment's time. But when he had finished his prayer, blessed Raphael said, 'Let us visit this true servant of God [Abbot Leodoaldus], who lies sick in this monastery, for in his humility and good deeds he is distinct from others in the city of Bourges.' His grave illness had nearly led him to Death's door and he was no longer able to eat. Losing hope in his recovery, all of the brethren were busying themselves with nothing else but the arrangements for his funeral."

But after he found strength from a visit from the archangel, Abbot Leodoaldus related a great miracle that may terrify the hearts of unbelievers, who are not prodded to do penance for their sins and ask holy Raphael, whose name means "God's remedy," to come and cure them of their sins so that the Devil does not lead them away as captives to eternal punishment, from which they cannot escape back to the earthly joy in which they place their faith. Then the same abbot related that at the very time when brother Barontus said that he was with holy Raphael, a wondrous brightness was seen over the monastery in which he lay sick due to his illness and suffering with a severe pain in his chest. Then holy Raphael suddenly appeared, his shining face illuminating the entire monastery. He made the sign of the cross on the abbot's chest as he passed by and that very hour Leodoaldus was healed of the illness that had afflicted his chest so severely.

After all of these things took place, Barontus said, "As we traveled past this monastery, there rushed toward us four other exceedingly dark demons, who wished to rend me cruelly with their teeth and claws. And sinner that I am, I began to fear in earnest that they might snatch me away from holy Raphael and plunge me into the depths of hell, for there were now six of them and surely he alone could not hold them all back. But with his great strength holy Raphael did in fact hold them all back and as he was contending with them, two angels in white clothing and bearing a wonderful scent rushed to us and with speed they grasped hold of the feet of holy Raphael from behind and began to intone the antiphon, 'Have mercy on me, God, according to your great mercy.'⁷ Those demons immediately lost their strength. Two of them fell toward the ground and vanished and another two did the same. But the first two demons, who had been present when my soul was yanked from its body, never withdrew, but always stayed close by. And we carried on our voyage to the outskirts of hell and glimpsed the guardians of the infernal depths.

"And so after this second battle had taken place, we arrived at the first gate of paradise, where we saw many of the brethren from our monastery, who had gathered to await the day of judgment, when they were due to receive the fullness of God's presence with everlasting joy. Here are their names: Corbolenus, a priest, on whom God bestowed good things in life; Fraudolenus, a priest who conducted his life well; Austrulfus, a deacon, who departed from life suddenly by God's command; Leodoaldus, a reader, whom God blessed in a special way; and Ebbo, a reader, who was God's chosen servant. When they saw us in the company of the demons following intently on my left side, they were amazed and wished to speak with us. But for their part those malevolent demons did not want this to happen, but a great servant of God, Leodoaldus by name, petitioned holy Raphael by the maker of heaven and earth to permit me to rest for a little while. Then with humility he asked holy Raphael and me, unhappy as I was, which monastery I had come from and how I had erred so gravely that demons had such power over me. And I said to them, 'I am from the monastery of St. Peter at Longoretus and I do not deny that everything I suffer happened due to my own sins and wicked deeds.' Then those men, touched inside by a deep sadness because they recognized me as a brother from their monastery, began to groan, saying that the Devil had never before dared to seize any soul from our community. But in soothing tones holy Raphael began to offer them consolation concerning me, saying, 'I left some hope in his little body. If the heavenly Father so desires, he may return from here to there.' In response, these brothers asked holy Raphael with a humble prayer to lie [prostrate] on the earth at the same time with them and pray to the Lord for me, so that the ancient enemy might be prevented from devouring me, and for this purpose they all prayed.

"After they had finished their prayer, we came to the second gate of paradise, where we saw untold thousands of children adorned in white raiment singing praises to God in harmony as though with a single voice. And as soon as we came inside this gate through the midst of these saints, we saw a narrow path prepared along which we made our way to the next gate. But so great was the throng of virgins on each side to the right and to the left that no one other than God could see them all. And when they saw us, they began to call out in one voice, 'A soul is going to judgment.' And then they spoke again, 'You conquer like a warrior, Christ! You conquer! And may the Devil not take this soul to hell!'

"And then we came to the third gate of paradise, which had the appearance of glass. And inside there was a host of crowned saints with shining faces, sitting in their little dwellings and upon their seats, always giving thanks to God. And there was a multitude of priests, outstanding in their merits, whose dwellings had been built with gold bricks, as holy Gregory reminds us in his *Dialogues*.[8] And dwellings for many others were being built in great splendor and honor, but their inhabitants had not yet arrived. The person who does not hesitate to give bread to those who hunger builds these dwellings in heaven. And while I was carefully surveying this scene, one of our brothers who had already died, Corbolenus by name, approached me and pointed out to me in the same vicinity a dwelling built with great honor and said, 'This dwelling is intended for our abbot Francardus and the Lord has not prepared it for him undeservedly.' I will relate a little of what I know concerning his deeds because he raised me from the time I was a child. He was a devout man, fearful of God and learned in sacred reading. Because he was conscientious and charming, advantageous properties were given to this monastery, which provide the servants of God and pilgrims with consolation. He nurtured and taught the sons of noblemen. After a long illness, he has been cleansed to the point of purity. For all of the good things that he has done, God has prepared for him eternal joys. At last, we entered the third gate and began to make our way with all due haste. When the holy martyrs saw us, they immediately began to pray. As we noted earlier, they did not cease to call out in the same voice, 'You conquer, warrior Christ, who redeemed us by shedding your blood! May the Devil not take this soul to hell!' I say this without any word of a lie. I decided to relate this story to allow the sound of saintly voices to resound throughout the entire world.

"And then, finally, we reached the fourth gate of paradise and there I recognized one of our brothers, Betolenus by name, who lay for some time at the gate of our monastery, contorted in dire distress. But here he was in great comfort and he said to me that by the command of Saint Peter he had been put in charge of the lighting of churches throughout the whole world. He began to reprimand me because our church, which was built in honor of Saint Peter, was not lit throughout the night and the candles did not burn at every hour of the day and rest assured that Saint Peter, though far away, knew this to be the case. We were not allowed to go any farther, but I witnessed a miraculous brightness and clarity all around me that I could almost see even when I briefly closed my eyes.

"Then holy Raphael summoned one of his angels, whom he sent forth to call the apostle Peter in all haste to our side. The angel went with great speed and called Saint Peter. And he arrived without delay, saying, 'Why have you summoned me, brother Raphael?' Holy Raphael said, 'These demons are speaking against one of your little monks and they cannot be dissuaded from releasing him.' In response, blessed Peter turned his beautiful face to the demons and said, 'What manner of crime do you hold against this monk?' And the demons said, 'The worst possible sins!' And Peter said, 'Recount them.' And they said, 'He had three wives, which is not permitted. Moreover, he committed other adulteries and so many other sins, which we persuaded him to do.' And they recounted in detail those sins that I had committed from childhood onward and even those that I had forgotten about completely. And Peter said to me, 'Is all of this true, brother?' And I said, 'Yes, Lord, it is true.' And the most blessed Peter said to the demons, 'Even if this monk is guilty of some faults, he has also given alms'—truly, alms free you from death—'and has confessed his sins to the priests and done penance for these sins and furthermore he has received a tonsure in my monastery and gave up all of his worldly possessions for God and bound himself to the service of Christ. These good deeds offset all of the bad things that you have recounted. You cannot take him away from me now. Make no mistake that he is not your companion, but ours.' But those demons fought back with force against him and said, 'Unless the very brightness of God takes him from us, you cannot take him from us.' Then Saint Peter became incensed and repeated two or three times, 'Go back, foul spirit! Go back, enemies of God, ever opposed to him! Leave him alone!' But they did not want to release me, so the most blessed Peter suddenly brandished three keys, which looked like this, and moved to hit the demons on the head with them.[9] But spreading their wings, the demons sought to flee from him in rapid flight by the way that they had entered, but the most blessed apostle Peter forbade them from doing so, saying with authority, 'You do not have permission to depart in that direction, foul spirits!' Restricted in this way, those demons flew over the top of the gate and fled through the air.

"After the demons had fled, Saint Peter turned to me and said, 'Ransom yourself, brother!' And with great fear I said to him, 'What could I possibly give, good shepherd, for I have nothing here at hand?' And he said, 'When you return to your own pilgrimage in the world, reveal to everyone the twelve coins that you kept hidden without permission when you entered the monastic life and make haste to give them away. Begin on the first day of April and on the first day of each and every month throughout the cycle of the year place in the hand of a poor person one of those coins, each properly weighted and marked by the hands of a priest, so that you have authentic witnesses to the fact that you gave up all of the coins. And, as I said, place coins into the hands of pilgrims as well and thus send your ransom to the heavenly homeland. Beware lest you fall back into those sins, which you are liable to perpetrate due to human frailty, and take good care that at the end of the year not a single penny remains in your possession because, if you neglect to emend your ways from this point onward, you will sorely regret it when you die and your ruin will be much worse for you than it was before.' A certain old man, beautiful to behold and distinguished in his aspect, was standing next to the blessed apostle Peter and asked him, 'Lord, if he gives all of these coins away, will his sins be forgiven?' And the blessed apostle Peter replied to him, 'If he does as I have instructed him, then his sins will be forgiven immediately. And if he believes most firmly, let him receive my judgment.' And so I accepted his judgment. And Peter said to the old man, 'This is the price of the rich man and the poor man, a mere twelve coins.' After he had given me this warning, Saint Peter ordered two little boys, dressed in white garments, brightness shining from their faces and so lovely to behold, to take me back to the first gate, where the brothers of our monastery resided in peace. From there they led me back through hell so that I might see all of the torments suffered by the sinners and so that I might know what I should say to our other brothers who still lived. And finally they brought me unharmed to our monastery. Once they had received their order, those boys promptly obeyed and miraculously brought me all the way back to the place that I mentioned before.

"When the brethren saw me once more, they offered great praises and thanks to the heavenly doctor, who had freed me from the jaws of the Devil. After they had completed their prayer, they received the command from the most blessed men to lead me back to that homeland that I would one day leave again. They began to debate among themselves, which of them would take me back to my own earthly pilgrimage. They initiated a plan, approaching one of the brothers, Framnoaldus by name, who died in our monastery as a boy, by the will of God. His little body lies buried in the threshold of the church of Saint Peter. They asked him nicely to take me back to the monastery and in addition they made a promise to him, saying, 'If you take this brother back to the monastery, every Sunday he will clean your tomb and recite over it "Have mercy on me, God" all the way through to the end.'[10] Then they turned to me and said, 'Pledge this to us, your brothers, that you will fulfill what you have promised.' And I immediately made my promise and gave my word. And then they said, 'See that you do not do anything other than this and that you are not condemned as a liar.' Then brother Framnoaldus himself responded to them, 'I will obey your decision so that this man will fulfill what he has promised.' And the brethren gave thanks to God for his obedience.

"They gave him a candle to hold so that he might carry it to

Ebbo, the servant of God in the church. Ebbo should then make the sign of Christ upon the candle to prevent evil spirits from extinguishing it and disturbing our journey back, for they always strive in word and deed to call us back to the darkness. And those brothers said that brother Ebbo was celebrating the mysteries of the apostles in the church. So, leaving together, we came to him and the brothers asked him, 'Man of God, please make the sign of Christ upon this candle, for Saint Peter has commanded us to lead this pilgrim from here back to his monastery so that he might not suffer from the schemes of the demons on his way home.' Then brother Ebbo said to them, 'Most beloved brothers, let us make the sign together.' And as this man began to raise his hands to make the sign, a wondrous brightness began to radiate from his arms and fingers. And when I saw this, I began to consider carefully the nature of this great brightness that adorned his arms and fingers in this way. As I watched, they looked as though they were aglow with gold and gems. It was not without cause that his arms and fingers appeared this way. In as much as my inadequate mind perceives it, I will say a little about it. He was a person of high birth but he abandoned all of his worldly possessions, according to the teaching of the Lord, 'Go and sell all that you have and give it to the poor and come, follow me.'[11] Once he had fulfilled this command, thus beginning a new life of complete devotion, he handed himself over into the service of Christ. He acquired a tonsure, excised his sins, and renewed in this way he became a minister of Christ. His hands were always generous in giving alms. He traded earthly payments for eternal ones. His fingers and arms shone with light from doing these and other good deeds. For this reason, most beloved brothers, no one should hesitate to give alms, for in return the holy Lord allows the faithful to live as beings of light in eternal life."

The story goes on. After the servant of God Ebbo had finished making the sign upon the candle, he said to brother Barontus, "Listen, brother! If the demons try to ensnare you on your journey, say, 'Glory to you, God' and they will never be able to turn you from your path." "After these things had been accomplished, the most blessed Ebbo requested that the brothers should see me on my way and that I should visit hell in order to see and know the guardians of that place, so that I can tell our brethren all about it. And he said to them, 'We now know, brothers, that the demons cannot hinder him, for Saint Peter ordered him to return to his home so that he could improve his life.' Then the brothers fulfilled their orders by walking with me. When we arrived at a place between heaven and hell, I saw there an old man who was very beautiful to behold. He had a long beard and sat in peace on a tall chair. And when I saw him, I turned my head to my companions and asked them discreetly who this powerful and very eminent man was. Turning to me, they said, 'This is our father, Abraham, and you brother should always beseech the Lord, so that when he commands your soul to leave your body, he allows you to dwell in peace in the bosom of Abraham.'[12]

"Then, going on our way, we arrived at hell, but we could not see what was going on inside because of the gloom of the shadows and the great amounts of smoke. But I can tell you as much as God allowed me to see through the watchtowers manned by demons. I saw there countless thousands of people being held tied up and bound very tightly by demons, whose groans of sorrow sounded like the droning of bees returning to their hives. The demons dragged souls bound in sins to the torments of hell and commanded them to sit in a circle upon seats made of lead. I will explain in detail the ranks of the evildoers and the groups that they belonged to. The proud were being held there with the haughty, the indulgent with their kind, the perjurers alongside other liars, the murderers in the company of killers, the envious among the coveters, the detractors with the disparagers, the deceitful mingled with the deceivers. They were all groaning, for the reason that holy Gregory explained in his *Dialogues*, 'They bound them in bundles for burning,' etc.[13] There was an untold number of clerics there, who had violated their calling and stained themselves by being caught with women. Weighed down in their torments, they cried out with great lament. But this did them no good, for the reason that holy Gregory said, 'The one who has lost the opportunity for proper penance comes to the Lord with prayers in vain.'[14] Here I saw weary Vulfoleodus, a bishop damned for his deception, sitting in a filthy cloak like a beggar; there I saw Bishop Dido and we recognized other members of our family as well. Over here were those foolish virgins who applauded themselves for their virginity in the world and carried with them nothing related to good works. Demons held them under guard and they were groaning most bitterly. And there was one more thing I saw there that should provoke intense fear in sinners. All of those souls, who were held in the custody of demons and bound in chains and yet had done some good in the world, were offered manna taken from paradise, which is similar to dew, around the sixth hour of the day [that is, at noon]. It was placed before their nose and mouth and they received refreshment from it. And those who brought it had the look of deacons clothed in white raiment. But all of the others, who contributed nothing good in the world, were offered nothing in return, but with groans they closed their eyes and struck their chests and said in a loud voice, 'Woe to us, the wretched ones who did nothing good when we had the chance!'

"But after we had seen so much evil taking place, we carried on in the company of our brothers, whose names have been mentioned earlier, and with other travelers as well, who said that they were on their way to the city of Poitiers to visit the shrine of Saint Hilary. After a while, we landed in a pleasant meadow. Then, giving thanks to God, they returned to the heavenly homeland, leaving me and brother Framnoaldus, who had accepted the request to lead me back. Together we made our way to our monastery. And there appeared there a wondrous mystery of God, because the doors of the church were open in anticipation of our arrival. And Framnoaldus entered and prayed for a long time. And when he was finished, we went to his tomb, upon which he kneeled and prayed, 'Have mercy on me and raise me, Lord, when your kingdom comes.'[15] And he said to me, 'Behold, brother, where my little body lies! If you wish to fulfill what you have promised, you will have your whole reward.' After he said these words, he took from me the body of air that I had been given and the light and he departed.

"All help now lost to me, I, a sinner, was abandoned before the arch of the church of Saint Peter, placed in tribulation that I had not experienced so acutely since I left the presence of blessed Peter. I began to drag myself along the ground and to hasten back to my little body. But the great mercy of God sent a wind, which lifted me on high and in the blink of an eye carried me to the room where my body lay dead. But the moment that I looked inside, I saw the brethren keeping watch and my son, whose name is Aglioaldus, sitting across from my bed, holding his hand to his chin and nodding off to sleep from sadness and exhaustion. And the wind blew one last time and I entered into my body through my mouth. I uttered my first word in praise of God—'Glory to you, God!'—as Ebbo the servant of God taught me. And so after this I recounted in detail the entire story recorded above for our brothers, as I was instructed."

All of these events took place on the eighth Kalends of April in the sixth year of the reign of Theoderic, king of the Franks [March 25, 678 or 679].

DRYHTHELM RETURNS FROM THE DEAD[1]

The Venerable Bede, monk of the abbey of Wearmouth-Jarrow in Northumbria, provided an account of the other-worldly journey of a monk named Dryhthelm in his Ecclesiastical History of the English People (completed 731). Like Barontus before him, Dryhthelm's soul journeyed far from his body to visit the realm of sinful souls and to witness the variety of sufferings that they endured to prepare them for God's final judgment. In the newly converted territories of the Anglo-Saxons, the experience of Dryhthelm was a warning. Superficial conversion to Christianity was not enough to merit entrance into heaven. Only those believers who embraced the Christian faith with a true change of heart and a contempt for this world would experience God's abiding presence in heaven.

Around that time, a remarkable miracle occurred in Britain similar to those that happened long ago. For in order to arouse the living from the death of the soul, a certain man who was already dead returned to life and he recounted many things worthy of remembering that he had seen. I think that it is worth gathering some of them together briefly in this work. There was a man, the father of a family in the region of Northumbria called Cunningham, who was leading a religious life with the rest of his household. Laid low by a bodily illness and brought to Death's door as it grew worse day by day, he died in the early hours of the evening. When the sun rose, however, he returned to life and immediately sat up. Everyone who had been sitting around his body in mourning was struck with a great fear and turned in flight. Only his wife remained, for she loved him very much, though she trembled with fright. He consoled her by saying, "Do not fear, for truly I have now risen from the death by which I was held and I have been permitted to live among humankind once more. Nevertheless, from this time forward I must conduct my life very differently than I had before." He immediately got up and went to the oratory in the village, where he prayed well into the day. Soon thereafter he divided everything that he possessed into three separate portions. He gave one portion to his wife and another to his sons, but the third he retained for his own good by giving it directly to the poor. Not long thereafter he abandoned the cares of this world by entering the monastery at Melrose, which is enclosed almost entirely by a bend in the river Tweed. Once he had received his tonsure, he entered his own secluded cell, which the abbot had provided for him. There until the day of his death he lived a life of great repentance of mind and body, so that even if his tongue was silent, his life would have revealed that this man had seen many things either dreadful or desired that have been concealed from other men.

He told us what he had seen with the following words: "A man with a luminous appearance and bright clothing was my guide. We went forth without speaking in what seemed to me to be the direction of the rising of the sun at the solstice. As we walked, we arrived at a valley that was very broad and deep and seemed to stretch on forever to our left. One side of the valley was very terrifying with raging flames; the other was equally intolerable owing to fierce hail and cold blasts of snow gusting and blowing away everything in sight. Both sides were teeming with the souls of men, which seemed to be thrown back and forth, as though by the onslaught of a storm. When those poor souls could no longer endure the intensity of the immense heat, they leapt into the midst of the deadly cold. And when they could find no respite there, they leapt back to the other side to burn in the midst of those unquenchable flames. Since a countless number of misshapen souls was subject to the torture of this alternating misery far and wide as far as I could see without any hope of respite, I began to think that perhaps this was hell, for I had often heard stories about the agonizing torments there. My guide, who walked ahead of me, answered my thought: 'Do not believe this, for this is not the hell you are thinking of.'

"But when he led me a little way farther on, completely shaken by this terrifying scene, suddenly I noticed that the places before us began to grow gloomier and covered in darkness. As we entered this place, the shadows became so thick that I could see nothing else except for the outline and garment of my guide. As we progressed through the shadows in the lonely night, behold, suddenly there appeared before us thick masses of noisome flames spouting up into the air as though from a great pit before falling back into it again. When we arrived in this place, my guide suddenly disappeared and abandoned me alone in the midst of the shadows and this terrifying scene. As the masses of flames spouted to the heights and plunged to the depths of the pit over and over again, I saw that the tips of the rising flames were full of human souls, which like sparks ascending with smoke shot up to the heights and then, when the flames withdrew, fell back into the depths once again. Moreover, an incomparable stench poured forth with these flames and filled this entire realm of shadows. And after I had stood there for a long time, unsure what I should do or which way to turn or what fate awaited me, suddenly I heard behind me the sound of a great and most wretched wailing and at the same time raucous laughter as though some illiterate rabble was hurling insults at enemies they had captured. And as the noise became louder and finally reached me, I saw a crowd of evil spirits cheering and laughing as they dragged the souls of five people crying and wailing into the midst of the shadows. I could discern among these people one tonsured like a priest, a layman, and a woman. Dragging the souls with them, the evil spirits descended into the midst of the burning pit, and it happened that, as they went farther down into the pit, I could not clearly distinguish the wailing of the people and the laughter of the demons, for the sound was confused in my ears. In the meantime, insubstantial spirits rose up out of that flame-spitting abyss and rushing forward, they surrounded me. With flaming eyes and blowing a putrid flame from their mouths and nostrils, they tormented me. They also threatened to grab me with the fiery tongs that they held in their hands, but although they terrified me, they never dared to touch me. Surrounded on every side by enemies and blinded by the shadows, I cast my eyes this way and that way to see if by chance the help that I needed might arrive from somewhere. Back on the road along which we had come there appeared something like the brightness of a star shining among the shadows, which grew little by little as it hastened quickly toward me. When the light approached, all of the vile spirits who were trying to seize me with their tongs scattered and fled.

"It was in fact my guide whose arrival put the spirits to flight. Presently he turned to the right and began to lead me in the direction of the rising sun in wintertime. Without delay he led me out of the shadows and into gentle breezes of serene light. As I followed him in the open light, I saw before us an enormous wall, the height and length of which seemed to have no end. I began to wonder why we were approaching the wall, for I could discern no door or window or stairway anywhere along it. But once we had reached the wall, we immediately found ourselves on top of it, I know not how. And behold there was an expansive and pleasant meadow, filled with such a fragrance of blooming flowers that the sweetness of this wondrous smell quickly banished every trace of the stench of that dark furnace that still clung to me. Moreover, such a great light filled the entire place that the meadow seemed to be brighter than the day could ever be or even the rays of the sun at noontime. There were in this meadow countless groups of white-robed people and many parties of rejoicing companions. As my guide led me among these companies of the glad inhabitants of that place, I began to think that this was perhaps the kingdom of heaven, concerning which I had often heard people speak about. He replied to my thought, saying, 'No, this is not the kingdom of heaven as you imagine it.'

"When we had moved on and left behind these dwellings of

the blessed spirits, I saw before us a much greater grace of light than before, in which I could even hear the sweetest sound of people singing, but the fragrance of such a marvelous smell poured forth from that place that the smell I thought was incomparable a short time before paled in comparison to it, and the light of the flowering meadow seemed very thin and weak. Just as I was hoping that we would enter the sweetness of this place, suddenly my guide stopped. Without delay, he turned around and led me back by the way that we had just come.

"When we returned once more to those happy dwellings of the white-robed spirits, he asked me, 'Do you know what all of these things are that you have seen?' And I responded, 'No.' And he said, 'That valley, which you saw, so frightful with its fierce flames and harsh cold, that is the place where souls are required to be tried and punished because they failed to confess and make amends for the evil deeds that they committed for they waited to confess until the very moment of death, and so they died. But even though they delayed confession and penance until their death, all of them will enter heaven on the day of judgment. Moreover, the benefits of repeated prayers by the living and alms and fasting and especially the celebration of masses may even release them from this place before the day of judgment. Furthermore, that foul pit that vomited flames, which you saw, is the very mouth of hell. Whoever falls into it will not be freed for all eternity. That blooming meadow, in which you saw those very beautiful youths rejoicing and bright, that place receives the souls of those who died having done good works, but they are not so perfect that they merit arriving immediately in the kingdom of heaven. Nevertheless, on the day of judgment all of them will enter into the sight of Christ and the joys of the heavenly kingdom. For whoever is perfect in every word and deed and thought, as soon as they die, they will enter the heavenly kingdom, which is near to that place where you heard the sound of sweet singing accompanied by the pleasing fragrance and the brilliance of light. It is now time for you to return to your body and to dwell among the living once more. But if you apply yourself to paying attention to your actions with greater care and strive to behave and speak in the spirit of righteousness and honesty, then you will receive upon your death a place of dwelling among those rejoicing companies of blessed spirits you saw before. For when I abandoned you for a time, I did so in order to learn what would become of you when you die.' After he had told me these things, I returned to my body most displeased for I had delighted so much in the sweetness and beauty of the place I had seen and equally in the company of those whom I saw dwelling there. I did not dare to ask my guide any other questions, but meanwhile—I do not know how—I suddenly found myself back among the living."

The man of God did not speak about these and other things that he had seen to those who were inactive or careless with respect to their fates, but only to those who, terrified by the fear of torments or delighted by the hope of eternal joys, wanted to draw inspiration from his words for the fulfillment of their piety. For example, near his cell there lived a certain monk by the name of Haemgisl, a priest equal in his good work to his outstanding rank, who still lives as a hermit in Ireland and sustains the last age of his life with a diet of bread and cold water. Often coming to visit this man, Haemgisl learned from him through repeated questioning what kinds of things he experienced when he had departed from his body. Indeed, it was through Haemgisl's report that the few details that we composed above came to our attention. Moreover, he also related his visions to King Aldfrith, a very learned man in every way, who was well disposed to listen to him. At the king's insistence, he entered the monastery mentioned above and was crowned with a monastic tonsure. Whenever the king came to those parts, he went to the monastery very often to hear him speak about his visions. At the time, the community was governed by Æthelwold, an abbot and priest renowned for his simple and devout life, who now holds the seat of the bishop of the church of Lindisfarne with deeds worthy of that rank.

In that monastic community, the man received a more isolated dwelling place, where he could devote himself more freely to ceaseless prayers in the service of his Creator. And since his retreat was located on a river bank, he used to enter the water because of his great desire to punish his body and he frequently immersed himself under the waves. In this way, he kept himself in the water for as long as he was able, reciting psalms or prayers, remaining still while the water of the river rose up to his loins and even to his neck. And when he left the water, he never bothered to take off his cold and wet garments until they had been warmed and dried by the heat of his own body. When in the winter months, while broken bits of ice floated around him, which he himself sometimes had to break in order to make a place for him to stand or immerse himself in the river, those who saw him would say, "Brother Dryhthelm"—for that was his name—"it is amazing that you have the strength to bear such bitter cold for any reason!" And he responded simply— befitting a man with a plain disposition and a humble nature—"I have seen colder." And when they said, "It is amazing that you wish to endure such a harsh way of life," he responded, "I have seen harsher." Thus, until the day he died, with a tireless desire for heavenly joys he subdued his old body with daily fasting and he had a saving influence on many people both with his words and with his way of life.

SPECTRAL SERVANTS
OF THE CHURCH

From the eighth century onward, monastic communities played an increasingly important role in the relief of sinful souls suffering in the cleansing fires of the otherworld. During the reigns of Charlemagne (r. 768–814) and his successors, the abbeys of the Frankish heartland benefited from royal patronage, but they also bore the burden of imperial scrutiny. For the prayers of the monks to be efficacious, Charlemagne believed that all of the abbeys in his realm should embrace a uniform set of ritual practices and adopt a single authoritative code of conduct: the sixth-century Rule of Benedict. Benedict had taught his brethren to cultivate the virtues of obedience, humility, and silence and to avoid all sexual contact in emulation of the angels, whose heavenly ranks they aspired to join in the afterlife. These religious specialists spent their days engaged in lengthy liturgical services, the primary purpose of which was to sing praises to God to beseech his aid for the health of the king and his family, the well-being of the kingdom, and the salvation of all Christians.

The monks' mastery of their own wills gave their prayers an awesome efficacy, making them important intercessors for the souls of deceased Christians. Over the course of the Middle Ages, untold numbers of people made donations of revenue-producing land and other forms of wealth to cloistered communities in the hope that the prayers of the brethren would ease their suffering in the afterlife. For their part, monastic authors were quick to endorse their own communities as especially proficient in the virtues that gave their prayers the wings

to reach the ears of God. Many of them composed ghost sto-
ries as a way to promote the power of monastic prayer. Draw-
ing their inspiration from Gregory the Great's Dialogues,
these stories featured spectral visitations of recently dead
Christians who described their torments in the otherworld
and beseeched the monks to pray on their behalf. A second
visit confirmed their release from suffering, providing a valu-
able endorsement for the monks whose prayers helped to nav-
igate the passage of their souls to heaven.

IMPERIAL TORMENTS[1]

Throughout the ninth century, from the reign of Emperor Louis the Pious (r. 814–840) to the accession of King Louis the Child in 901, the monks of the abbey of Fulda maintained a chronicle known as the Annals of Fulda, *in which they set down the most significant events that happened year by year in the East Frankish kingdom. Along with the contemporary West Frankish chronicle, known as the* Annals of St. Bertin, *the* Annals of Fulda *are the most important primary source for the political history of the ninth century. During the year 874, the brethren of Fulda reported a dream of Louis the German, king of Bavaria (817–843) and Eastern Francia (843–876), in which the ghost of his father, Louis the Pious, entreated him to find relief for the suffering of his soul in the afterlife. Louis the German turned to the monks of the realm, in the hope that their prayers would free the soul of his dead father from torment. The story leaves the reader to ponder the outcome of their intercession.*

During the season of Lent in 874, when Louis the German had put aside the business of worldly affairs and was devoting his time to prayer, one night he saw in a dream his own father, Emperor Louis the Pious, in a state of suffering. The emperor said this to him in Latin, "I beseech you by our Lord Jesus Christ and by the majesty of the Trinity to free me from the torments, in which I am trapped, so that I can at last at some point obtain eternal life." Terrified by this vision, Louis the German sent letters to all of the monasteries in his realm so that the monks might intercede with their prayers before God for a soul trapped in torment. From this dream, it is clear that, although the emperor had done many things that were praiseworthy and pleasing to God, nevertheless he also permitted many things to happen in his kingdom that were contrary to God's law.

CLUNY AND THE FEAST
OF ALL SOULS[1]

No monastic community in the Middle Ages was as aggressive
or successful in promoting the efficacy of the prayers of its
brethren than the abbey of Cluny. Founded in 910 in Burgundy, Cluny upheld a rigorous standard of monastic conduct, a heavenly way of life that lent the prayers of its monks
a powerful influence with God. Beginning in the second half
of the tenth century, thousands of laypeople donated revenue-
producing land to the abbey in exchange for prayers on behalf
of the well-being of their souls (pro remedia animae). Around
the year 1030, Abbot Odilo of Cluny (r. 994–1049) established a new observance on November 2, the Feast of All
Souls, dedicated specifically to intercession on behalf of all departed Christians. On this solemn day, the brethren of Cluny
celebrated masses, sung psalms, and gave alms to the poor in
honor of the faithful departed.

The foundation of the Feast of All Souls was a bold and ulti-
mately successful claim on the part of the Cluniacs that their
prayers were more efficacious than those of other monastic
communities for releasing the souls of the sinful dead from
torment. To promote their community, the brethren of Cluny
circulated a legend about the inspiration for establishing the
Feast of All Souls. In the 1050s, a monk of Cluny named Iotsald composed an account of the virtuous life of Abbot Odilo,
which included the story of a hermit, who witnessed the beneficial effect of Cluniac prayers on souls suffering at the hands
of demons. According to Iotsald, the abbot allegedly founded

the Feast of All Souls when news of the hermit's story reached
him at Cluny.

Concerning the vision of a hermit.

Lord Bishop Richard related to me the story of a certain vision, which I had heard once before but I could not remember the details. "At that time," he said, "a certain devout man from the district of Rouergue [in southwestern France] was returning from Jerusalem. But when he had sailed halfway across the sea that stretches from Sicily to Thessaloniki, very strong winds struck his boat and drove it to an island, or rather a rocky outcropping, where a certain servant of God lived as a hermit. As he waited for a while for the sea to calm, the pilgrim tarried long enough to have a conversation with this servant of God about many different topics. Asked by the man of God where he was from, he responded that he was from the Aquitaine. Then the man of God asked if he had heard of a monastery called Cluny and if he knew Odilo, the abbot of that place. And the pilgrim responded, "I know the place and I know the abbot well, but I would like to know why you ask." "I will tell you," he said, "and I ask that you remember what you hear. There are places nearby from which, by the manifest judgment of God, a scorching inferno spouts with tremendous heat. In those flames the souls of sinners are purged by a variety of torments. A host of demons bear the task of perpetually renewing their torture; day in and day out, they heap more punishments upon the sinners, whose suffering grows more and more intolerable as a result. I have often heard them lamenting and making no small complaint, for the souls of the damned may be freed from their torments through the manifold mercy of God by the prayers of devout people and by the giving of alms to the poor, which occurs frequently in holy places. As you can imagine, they direct their strongest pleas not to be forgotten above all to the monks of Cluny and their abbot. For this reason, by God I beseech you, if you manage to return home safely, that you make known to the monks of Cluny everything you heard from me and you tell them on my behalf that they should apply themselves more and more to prayers, vigils, and the giving of alms for the relief of those souls trapped in punishment, so that through their good works joy may be multiplied in heaven to the detriment of the Devil." When the traveler returned to his own country, he dutifully reported this story to the holy father Odilo and devout brethren of Cluny. Hearing this, they were in no small way amazed with a great joy in their hearts. Giving thanks to God, they augmented their prayers with yet more prayers, heaped alms upon alms, and immediately applied themselves to work so that the dead might find rest. It was on this occasion that the holy father Odilo established a new tradition throughout all of his monasteries. Just as the monks celebrated the Feast of All Saints on the first day of November, on the following day [November 2], they held a commemoration for the respite of all the souls of the faithful during which they celebrated masses privately and publicly with the singing of psalms and offered alms generously to all of the poor who came to the abbey. Through these good deeds, the Devil would lament greatly to lose what he thought he had and Christian souls in their suffering would rejoice at the hope of mercy.

A LESBIAN GHOST[1]

Cardinal bishop Peter Damian (c.1007–1073) was a strong advocate for the prayers of the monks of Cluny, but he believed that the souls of the sinful dead could also be freed from torment by the intercession of the saints. The following ghost story is unusual in two respects. First, the ghost in question was a lesbian in life, who admitted that she had disgraced herself in her youth "by succumbing to wanton lust with girls my own age" and suffered in the afterlife because she forgot to confess these sins to her priest. Second, the intercessory prayer of the monks plays no role in the release of her soul. Rather, it is the arbitrary mercy of the Virgin Mary, the queen of the world, that has freed a veritable city of departed Christians from torment. The shades of the souls she has redeemed lingered in Rome for one last night on earth to pay their respects to the Virgin in churches dedicated to her throughout the city before embracing the eternal rest that her mercy has won for them.

A very devout priest named John related to me an event that happened in Rome a few years ago, which I will tell you in turn. On the feast of the Assumption of Mary, the blessed mother of God [August 15], the Roman people according to their custom devote themselves to prayers and litanies throughout the night and with lanterns lit visit churches in many parts of the city. In the basilica on the Capitoline Hill dedicated to the honor of the same blessed Virgin, a certain woman caught sight of her godmother, who had died almost a year before. Because she was unable to get close enough to speak with her due to the vast number of people crowding together in the church, she resolved to wait for her godmother on the corner of a narrow lane, where there was no doubt that the old woman could not escape her notice as she left the basilica. As her godmother walked past, the woman spoke to her in haste, "Are you not my godmother Marozia, who recently died?" she asked (for that was the name of her godmother while she lived). The old woman responded, "Yes, I am." "So how are you doing now?" the young woman asked. Her godmother said, "Until today a heavy punishment oppressed me because I had disgraced myself in my youth by succumbing to the enticement of wanton lust with girls my own age. And I am sad to say that for some reason I forgot about this and even though I went to the priest for confession, I did not receive his judgment on this sin. But today the queen of the world answered our prayers and freed me with many others from those places of punishment, and such a great multitude of souls has on this day been rescued from torment by her intervention that their number exceeds the entire population of the city of Rome. For this reason, we are visiting the holy places dedicated to our glorious lady all over the city to show our thanks most joyfully for the great benefits of her mercy." Since the godmother could not tell if the young woman believed her story, she added, "So that you believe without a doubt that my story is true, know that a year from today, on this very same feast day, you will most certainly die. But if you live any longer, which is not possible, you will prove that I was clearly a liar." And once she spoke these words, the godmother vanished before the young woman's eyes. Soon thereafter the young woman donned sackcloth and mindful of what she had heard concerning her impending death, she began to live her life more prudently. What more is there to say? After nearly a year had passed, on the vigil of the Assumption she became sick and on the day of the feast itself she died, just as her godmother had told her. Here we should note and consider with fear that this woman suffered punishment for a sin which she had forgotten until the virgin Mother of God intervened on her behalf.

THE HAUNTING OF THE
CLOISTER[1]

Abbot Peter the Venerable of Cluny (r. 1122–1156) was one of the most formidable monastic leaders of the twelfth century. He defended the interests of European Christendom by composing treatises against the truth claims of Jews, Muslims, and heretical Christians. An authoritative power broker active at the highest levels of secular and religious society, Peter wrote hundreds of letters to kings and nobles, popes and bishops. As abbot, his influence extended to the dozens of monastic foundations across Europe that looked to the abbey of Cluny for inspiration and oversight. In the 1140s, Peter composed a treatise entitled Two Books Concerning Miracles, *in which he recorded many instances in his time when God intervened in the affairs of humankind by working wonders for people to behold. Among these miracles, Peter related numerous ghost stories, in which tormented souls haunted the abbey of Cluny to beseech the brethren for the relief that only monastic prayer could provide.*

These tales of the restless dead served several purposes for Peter the Venerable. Monastic ghost stories demonstrated clearly that his Cluniac brethren were powerful intercessors for the souls of departed Christians, even those of wicked individuals who had grown rich by preying on the resources of the abbey. But the abbot of Cluny was also writing against the teachings of a heretical Christian group known as the Petrobrusians. Among other false beliefs, these heretics had denied that monastic prayer for the dead had any efficacy to relieve the suffering of sinful souls. Peter's ghost stories, verified by

the most trustworthy witnesses, proved wrong the rival claims
of the Petrobrusians, while at the same time promoting the
abbey of Cluny as the most important center of intercessory
prayer in all of Christendom.

Concerning those events which happened in and around Cluny.

With the help of the Lord, let us now turn from those topics
we have already discussed, which pertain to the reverence of
the divine sacraments and to the sincerity of confession and to
other topics no less useful in so much as they apply to the edification of morals. First, I will explain, as best I can, about visions or revelations of the dead, which I have been able to learn
about from different sources. In fact, these visions are said to
happen frequently, especially in our day and age. For many men
who are worthy in faith affirm that apparitions of the dead appear to the living and often tell them many things that have
proven to be true. I believe that the telling of such events would
be worthwhile to my readers, especially to those who despise
the present life out of their love for the life to come and struggle
to attain to it through correct faith and pious works. For it is a
huge relief for them, and in these wretched times to which they
submit with groans day by day it is a great consolation when
they hear a story about the fatherland, from which they are
banished on this pilgrimage and to which with sighs they long
to return, that arouses their faith and hope more and more.

I have heard many stories concerning such events from many
people. I have not retained any order of time in telling their
stories because I was not able to remember it clearly from the
words of those who told me or I did not care to retain it, even
if I could. For what use is there to know such a thing, whether
it happened before or after, so long as it corresponds truly
with what took place? It is much more important to inquire
into the events of the times, rather than the times of events. Indeed it seems to me fitting that we begin with local stories before proceeding to those from farther away, and for this reason
let us start right away with events that we have heard to have
taken place in and around the abbey of Cluny.

Cluny is the most renowned abbey in almost the entire
world with respect to Christian worship, the severity of discipline, the number of monks, and the observance of every aspect of the monastic way of life; it is a unique and open refuge
for sinners, through which many penalties have been lifted
from the dead and a great many riches have been stored up in
the heavenly kingdoms. There innumerable multitudes of men,
casting from their shoulders the heavy burdens of the world,
have submitted their necks to the sweet yoke of Christ. There
people of every profession, authority, and rank have trans-
formed a haughty and excessive life in the world into the humble and poor life of monks. There the venerable fathers of
those churches, fleeing the hardships of ecclesiastical adminis-
tration, have chosen to live a safer and more serene life, prefer-
ring to be on the bottom rather than on the top. There the
tireless and unyielding struggle against spiritual wickedness
earns palms of victory on a daily basis for the soldiers of
Christ. As the inhabitants of this place cast down their flesh
continuously in spiritual combat, it is true according to the
apostle: "to live is Christ, and to die is gain."[2]

From here the balsam of spiritual virtues has poured forth,
the entire house of the world has been filled with the scent of
the ointment, while the ardor of monastic life, which had
barely cooled in this time, grew hot by the example and zeal of
these men. Gaul, Germany, even Britain across the sea bears
witness to this; Spain, Italy, and all of Europe acknowledge
this as well: they are teeming with monasteries, among which
some have been newly founded and others rebuilt from an ancient state of disrepair. There the community of monks, arrayed by God in their ranks like heavenly troops, along with
other training exercises in holy virtues, apply themselves in
this manner to divine praises day and night, so that it is possible to understand that this utterance by the prophet also applies to them: "Blessed are those who dwell in the house of
God; Lord, they will praise you forever and ever."[3] But why do
I recount some parts of the world, when their reputation
reaches from our place in the utmost west all the way to the
east and it does not escape notice in any corner of the

Christian world? For this is the vineyard, these are the branches, which are truly the vines belonging to Christ, and pruned by the farmer, their father, they bear a great deal of fruit, according to the message of the Gospel. Concerning this vine, it is written in the Psalms: "It stretched forth its branches all the way to the sea and its shoots to the river."[4] It is understood that although this was written concerning the synagogue of the Jews taken out of Egypt and especially concerning our church in the present day, even so nothing prevents us from understanding that it concerns this Cluniac church as well, which is by no means a lowly limb in the vineyard as a whole.

Concerning the wondrous apparition of Stephen, who was called "the White."

It has been freeing to digress here for a little while, but since this subject does not pertain directly to our purpose, and it is not possible to explain in writing so much material briefly and while hastening on to other topics, it is necessary to put this subject on hold at present so that we may proceed as we promised to the benefits gained from the revelations of the dead.

In the first place, what I am about to say was told to me by certain individuals whose testimony I am compelled to believe as readily as my own. For their way of life and conduct demands that I place faith without a shadow of a doubt no less in what I see with my own eyes than what I hear from them. These men told me the following story. There was at Cluny a monk called Bernard Savinelle, concerning whom they say that sometimes in certain circumstances he behaved in a frivolous manner, but once he was corrected he learned the habit of regular discipline. After he had suffered the disgrace of words as well as the disgrace of blows, he bore his correction with the utmost patience and after his chastisement he displayed a mild demeanor as he hastened to whatever task was at hand.

One night while the brethren were celebrating the night vigils with praises to God, Bernard left the choir where he was singing with the others and headed to the dormitory. While he was climbing the stairs, suddenly Stephen, who is commonly

called "the White," formerly abbot of the monastery of Saint
Egidius, who had died a few days before, blocked his way. Bernard did not recognize him at first sight; believing him to be
someone else, he hastened toward the dormitory. But the ghost
of the dead man that had appeared broke the silence with
words, saying, "Where are you going? Stay and hear what I
am about to say to you." Bernard was truly stunned but also
angry that this monk was breaking the rule by speaking at
night and in an improper place and he expressed these words
using sign language.[5] But when that dead abbot, who had returned with the intention of speaking rather than remaining
silent, kept on talking, Bernard was compelled by his rebel-
lious actions to stop making signs and asked him who he was
and what he wanted. The abbot said, "I am called Stephen,
abbot of Saint Egidius, a sinner in many ways both before my
abbacy and thereafter. For these sins I now suffer harsh penalties, from which I can be freed more quickly through the inexpressible mercy of God if someone assists me. Therefore, I
pray to you that moved by my plea you might beseech the lord
abbot and all of the brethren to pour forth prayers before almighty God for my freedom and to do everything that they
can to release me from such great evils." When Bernard responded that he would indeed do what the ghost asked, but
feared that no one would believe his story, the dead man who
was speaking added, "So that no one can have any doubt concerning the things that you will tell them, know that eight days
from now you will depart from this life. After you have foretold the time of your death to them, once it has taken place
your demise will prove that you spoke the truth." Once he said
this, he immediately vanished before the monk's eyes.

And then Bernard returned from the dormitory to the
church. Understandably he was greatly troubled by the news
of his impending death and passed the night in contemplation
of it. At dawn, he revealed what had happened to him first to
the prior, then to the venerable and holy father Hugh, and finally to the great and revered community of the brethren. Afterward the story reached the ears of everyone, but as it is
human nature almost always to discern different things from

the same event, indeed a few believed him, but many more maintained that he was making it all up. Even so, everyone waited upon the death of this man, which the brother had announced as the judgment by which they would be free from every doubt. And behold on the very next day the one who reported this vision was struck by illness; deteriorating slowly, he neared the end of his life. Even to his last breath, he affirmed resolutely everything he had said. Within the predicted eight days, he came to a good end and thus by his death he proved that he had been a messenger of truth.

Concerning a similar apparition of Bernard, who was called "le Gros."

Similar to the miracle of Stephen the White, in fact almost exactly the same, was a miracle concerning Bernard le Gros, which I heard from those witnesses we mentioned above. Bernard was a man famous for his noble background and his power in this world. He owned fortifications near to the monastery of Cluny and he inflicted many evils upon this place and other neighboring churches. Then he changed his heart and decided to put an end to his evil deeds. He approached the venerable father Hugh [abbot of Cluny from 1049 to 1109] and made it known that he wished to make a pilgrimage to Rome to pray for his sins. If it was permitted for him to return, he promised that he would renounce the world and become a monk of Cluny. He reached the city of Rome, where in the presence of the glorious bodies of the highest apostles and martyrs he atoned for the crimes of his previous life with prayers and, when he had run out of alms, by whatever satisfaction he could. After he had spent forty days in this manner in the city, which is the customary amount of time given to a sinner to perform penance, he departed from Rome. On his way home, he went as far as Sutri. While he was tarrying in that city, which is quite close to Rome, a sickness that he had contracted earlier grew worse and he died. There he was cared for respectfully and buried by his traveling companions, as is permitted only while one is on pilgrimage.

A few years later, the steward of a certain villa under the

jurisdiction of Cluny was making his way in the middle of the day through a forest near to the castle of Uxelles. Bernard himself had recently built this castle, from which his plunderers would ride out to seize everything they could far and wide. As I was saying, while he was making his way, the steward suddenly encountered the very same Bernard. When he saw this man sitting on a mule and dressed in new fox fur and remembered that he was dead, the steward was terrified. Then, when he calmed down, he asked if the ghost was the person he seemed to be and why he had returned. He received the following response, "You should know that I am Bernard, once the lord of this region. Everyone who resides nearby knows that I committed many evil deeds during my time, for which I am now suffering most terribly in turn. But what tortures me above all else is the construction of that castle over there, which, as you are well aware, was recently built at my command. Even though I seem to have escaped eternal damnation because near the end of my life I did penance for my evil deeds, I still need a great deal of help to free my soul. For this reason, I have been permitted to return to implore the mercy of the abbot of Cluny. I have followed his entourage for quite some time and yesterday when he spent the night at Anse I was there among his followers. I ask that you go to him now and pray earnestly that he might have mercy upon me." And when the steward to whom the ghost was speaking asked him why he was wearing a fox-fur cloak, Bernard responded, "I bought this cloak when it was new and on the very same day that I wore it for the first time, I gave it away to a beggar. Just as it was new when I gave it, thus it always remains new and it provides an inexpressible comfort to me in my torment."

With these words, the apparition of Bernard disappeared and the steward hastened to fulfill what he had agreed to do. He went to the blessed abbot, to whom he had been sent, and told him everything that had happened down to the last detail. Full of the spirit of charity, the abbot listened to the dead man's request with a kind disposition and devoted many offerings and many masses as help for the soul of one struggling under the eternal judgment. It is worthwhile to believe that through these works Bernard would be freed from his hardships and find the rest of the faithful according to divine direction. For there would be no reason that this ghost, concealed in the hidden folds of the judgments of God, would be permitted to appear among the living to seek its freedom if nothing useful might result from its return. Indeed, it seems as though it would have been sent forth for no purpose unless some result followed from its journey. Moreover, the ghost would not have sought aid from the sacraments nor from the performance of holy works if he had known that these things would have been no use to him. Since he asked to be assisted by these means and these works were efficacious in providing relief for him, Bernard demonstrated that he was worthy of their help.

As for the steward to whom the apparition had first appeared, the holy abbot predicted that his death was near. For often when manifestations of the dead appear in our day in this manner, the story goes that whoever spoke to the deceased finds themselves dead not long thereafter. Motivated by his fear of the ghost and by the warning of the holy abbot, the steward immediately renounced the world and became a monk. A few days later, his life came to an end.

WARNINGS TO THE LIVING[1]

*By the thirteenth century, monastic authors were writing
ghost stories as warnings to the living to promote virtuous behavior not only among the wealthy and powerful, but also
among men, women, and children of all stations. The prolific
Cistercian author Caesarius of Heisterbach (c. 1180–1240)
compiled many such stories in his* Dialogue on Miracles.
*Couched in the form of a conversation between a monastic
teacher and his disciple in emulation of Pope Gregory the
Great's* Dialogues, *this massive compendium of over seven
hundred exemplary tales provided raw material for preachers'
sermons and thereby reached a wide audience of monks and
laypeople alike. The democratization of the monastic ghost
story reflects the concern of the thirteenth-century church to
hold all Christians responsible for their moral conduct, especially in the wake of the Fourth Lateran Council, which convened in Rome in 1215 by the order of Pope Innocent III. The
statutes of the Fourth Lateran Council insisted upon the active involvement of laymen and laywomen in their own salvation. Among its many innovations was the call for every
Christian to participate in the ceremony of the Mass at least
once every year. Unlike earlier tales in the monastic tradition,
the ghost stories told by Caesarius sometimes ended with the
eternal damnation of the soul in question. The warning to his
audience was clear. Every detail of the Christian's life was
subject to an intense scrutiny and even the most virtuous activities, like the giving of alms to the poor, contributed nothing to your eternal reward if they were not performed with
pious intent.*

Concerning the dead knight who at night hung serpents and toads at the door of his son in place of fish.

When he died, a certain knight bequeathed to his son goods he had obtained by usury.[2] One night he came knocking forcefully at the door. When a boy came running and asked why he was knocking there, he answered, "Let me in. I am the lord of this property" and gave his name. Looking through the opening and recognizing him, the boy responded, "My lord is most assuredly dead; I will not let you in." When the dead man went on knocking and received no answer, at length he said, "Take these fish, which I eat, for my son. Look, I am hanging them on the door." When they went out in the morning, they found a multitude of toads and snakes in a tangled mass. Truly this is the food served in hell, which is cooked in a sulfurous fire. NOVICE: What is your opinion about those people who live a bad life and nevertheless give many alms to the poor? MONK: It does not benefit them for eternal life.

Concerning a Bavarian, who appeared to his wife after death and said that almsgiving had not helped him.

Not many years have elapsed since the death of a very wealthy official of the duke of Bavaria. One night the castle in which his wife was sleeping trembled so much that it seemed as though there was an earthquake. And behold, the door of the chamber in which she was lying opened and her husband entered, accompanied by a giant figure, blacker than black, who pushed him by the shoulders. When she saw and recognized her husband, she called him to her and made him sit upon a seat at her bedside. She felt no fear, but as she was only wearing a nightgown, she draped a part of the bed covering over her shoulders, for it was cold. She asked her husband about his condition and he responded with sadness, "I am consigned to eternal punishments." Hearing this, his wife grew very frightened and asked, "What are you saying? Did you not give alms in abundance? Your door was open to every pilgrim. Do these good deeds provide no benefit to you at all?" He responded, "They provide no advantage at all for eternal life, for I did them out of empty glory rather than out of love."

When she tried to ask him about other things, he answered abruptly, "I was allowed to appear to you, but I can linger here no longer. Behold my hellish handler stands waiting for me outside. Indeed, if the leaves of every tree turned into tongues, they still could not describe my torments." After this, he was summoned and driven away; the entire castle trembled as before at his departure and his lamenting cries echoed for a long time. This vision was and remains especially renowned in Bavaria, as our monk Gerard (formerly a canon of Ratison) was witness. He related this story to us. See how in all of these stories the scripture is fulfilled that says, "The mighty will be mightily tormented."[3] NOVICE: This example and others like it should be preached to the mighty. MONK: Because the lives of the priests themselves are for the most part bad and wayward, they flatter the mighty instead of pricking them.

Concerning the cleansing of a certain usurer of Liège.

In our time a certain usurer in Liège died and the bishop denied him burial in the cemetery. But his wife went to the apostolic see to beg for his burial and when the pope refused, she made the case for her husband in this way, "I have heard, lord, that man and wife are one, and that the apostle says that a man without faith can be saved by his faithful wife.[4] Hence whatever shortcoming my husband had, as a part of his body I will make it up most freely; indeed, I am prepared to be enclosed on his behalf and to make satisfaction to God for his sins." Having won over the cardinals to her side, her husband was restored to the cemetery by the order of the Lord Pope. Next to his tomb, she had a little dwelling made, in which she enclosed herself and devoted herself day and night to almsgiving, fasts, prayers, and vigils to please God for the sake of her husband's soul. After seven years had passed, this man appeared to her in somber garb and gave her thanks, saying, "May God reward you, for because of your labors I have been freed from the depths of hell and from the worst punishments. If starting today you devote yourself to similar benefits on my behalf for another seven years, I will be freed completely." When she had accomplished this, he appeared to her again, this time in white garb and with a smiling face and said, "Thanks to God and you, for today I have been freed." NOVICE: Why did he say that he had been freed from the depths of hell, when no redemption may be found there? MONK: The depths of hell means the bitterness of purgatory. It is the same when the church prays for the dead: "Lord Jesus Christ, king of glory, free the souls of all the faithful departed from the power of hell and from the depths of the lake, etc."[5] The church does not pray for the damned, but for those who can be saved. And the power of hell, the depths of the lake, or the mouth of the lion are all taken there to mean the bitterness of purgatory. By no means would the usurer have been freed from punishment, if he had not shown contrition in the end.

Concerning a scholar who after his death struck and broke a board in Preuilly.

In the kingdom of France there is a house of the Cistercian order called Preuilly. In this house a miraculous event recently took place, as our abbots told us when they returned last year from the General Chapter meeting.[6] For several of them testified that they had heard the story from the abbot of the house where the vision took place. A certain young man in the same house became a novice and his master soon followed him. Once he had become a monk, this young man behaved so strictly and was so solitary that the abbot feared for him and quite often scolded him because his zealousness set him apart. But this young man did not heed these salutary warnings and persisted in his willfulness and then after a few years he died. One night when the abbot was standing in his stall at Lauds and was looking toward the presbytery, he observed three people coming toward him glowing like three candles.[7] As they came closer, he recognized all of them. In the middle was the aforesaid scholar and at his side were two lay-brothers, all of whom had recently died. Then the abbot, remembering the willfulness of the scholar, asked him a question, saying, "How are you holding up?" When he responded, "Well," the abbot added, "Are you not suffering some punishment due to your willfulness?" "Yes," he said, "great and many torments, but because my intention was good, albeit indiscreet, the Lord had mercy upon me and I was not damned." And the abbot said, "Why is that lay-brother"—he pointed at him with his finger—"brighter than the other, when this one abandoned the monastic life at one point, and the other from the time he entered the order never strayed seriously from the path." The monk responded, "Because after his fall this man rose stronger still and was more zealous than the other." Meanwhile, as the choir sang the verse, "He will keep the feet of his saints, and the wicked will be silent in the darkness," the scholar, wishing to leave some sign of his presence there, struck the board under the feet of the singers so hard with his heel that it broke.[8] Then he disappeared. Truly, as a testimony to such an obvious miracle, the abbot did not allow the broken board to be repaired or replaced. NOVICE: These events should be learned by monks who become useless to themselves and others due to their indiscrete zeal. MONK: On their account, Saint Benedict says in his rule that the eighth grade of humility is when the monk does nothing except what the communal rule of the monastery or the example of his elders encourages him to do.[9] NOVICE: Just as certain monks in their stiffness are too willful, so, too, are others too flippant with words or signs. MONK: And those monks also earn their punishment.

Concerning the cleansing of Margaret, a nun from Mount St. Savior.

About three years ago there was a certain young girl—I believe that she was nine years old—in Mount St. Savior, which is a house of our order, who died on Advent Day.[10] Truly, on a bright day as the community was standing in the choir, this dead girl entered the church. Approaching the altar, she bowed very deeply, then walked to her place in the choir where she had been accustomed to stand. Another girl of about the same age saw her standing there next to her and knowing that she was dead, this girl was struck with great horror, so that everyone noticed. When this girl was asked by the gracious lady abbess, from whose mouth I heard the story I am about to relate, why she appeared so alarmed in the choir, she responded, "In such and such a way did Sister Gertrude come into the choir

and when during the vesper services mention was made of Our
Lady, at the collect standing next to me she prostrated herself
down to the ground. When the collect was finished, she
rose again and left. This was the cause of my horror." Fearing the Devil's deceptions, the abbess said to the girl, "Sister
Margaret"—this was her name—"if Sister Gertrude should
come to you again, say to her '*Benedicte*,' and if she responds
to you '*Dominus*,' ask her where she has come from and what
she is looking for."[11] On the following day, the ghost came
again and, after she had responded "*Dominus*" to Margaret's
greeting, the girl added, "Good sister Gertrude, from where
have you come at this hour and what do you seek among us?"
The ghost responded, "I come here to make amends. Because I
whispered with you gladly in the choir, uttering half-spoken
words, for this reason I have been ordered to atone in this
place, where I happened to commit my sin. And unless you beware of the same sin, when you die you will suffer the same
punishment." When she had made satisfaction four times in
this manner, she said to the girl, "I have now completed the
reparation for my sin; you will not see me again." And so it
was. For as the girl watched, the ghost proceeded toward the
cemetery, passing through its wall by some miraculous power.
Behold, such was the cleansing of this young girl. NOVICE:
Whoever said that a punishment of this kind is more acute
than any punishment of this world is not right in the head.
MONK: We will discuss this topic more fully in the following
chapter. But Margaret was so frightened by the warning of the
dead girl that she became sick and approached the end of her
life. Having fallen into a trance, she lay so still that everyone
thought that she was dead. After an hour she woke up and
swore that she had seen certain of the sisters in the presence of
Our Lady and some of them she did not see there. She also
said that the same glorious Virgin Mary held a crown in her
hand, which she said belonged to the priest named Steppo.
This same Steppo had been a priest. He was a very devout and
incredibly charitable man, who served God and the sisters on
the same Mount St. Savior. But so that you know that one
should not care by what manner of death a just man dies, the

same Steppo, when he was struggling with a painful illness last year, suffered a brain seizure and went completely mad, with the result that he uttered many blasphemies. After he had died and was buried, the Lord, wishing to show his merits, consented to work miracles at his tomb. Sick people, so I hear, sleep on the tomb and wake up healed.

Concerning the punishment of Rudinger and his drink.

In the diocese of Cologne not far from the city of Cologne, there was a certain knight by the name of Rudinger. He was so entirely given over to wine that he would attend celebrations at different country estates for the sole purpose of drinking good wine. When he became ill and was about to die, his daughter asked him to appear to her within thirty days. Responding "I will do this if I can," he died. Indeed, after his death he appeared to his daughter in a vision, "Behold I am here just as you asked." And in his hand he was carrying a small clay cup, which is commonly called a *cruselinum*, with which he used to drink in taverns.[12] His daughter asked him, "Father, what is in that cup?" He responded, "My drink is made from pitch and sulfur. I am always drinking from it and I cannot empty it." Then he disappeared. And immediately the girl understood, as much from his previous life as from this punishment, that there was little or no hope in his salvation. For in the here and now wine goes down easily, but in the end it will bite you like a snake.

NIGHT IS THE
DEAD'S DOMINION

Concern for the fate of Christian souls inspired the ghost stories told by medieval monks, but not all of the dead who returned to the world of the living did so to petition their friends and loved ones for prayers. Others returned solely out of spite, bent on wreaking havoc in their former communities. Malevolent ghosts and walking corpses first appeared in medieval narratives in the eleventh century and the popularity of stories about their ruinous rampages remained strong until the end of the Middle Ages. These tales of the walking dead have several features in common. The people in question were almost always men of unsavory character, whether the runaway peasants described by Abbot Geoffrey of Burton, the "evil Welshman" of Walter Map's tale, or William of Newburgh's aptly named "Houndpriest." Malice alone may have brought their bodies back to life, but some authors blamed the machinations of Satan for their unnatural behavior. The animated corpses of these villains were dangerous not only because of the violence they committed, but also because of the disease that their polluted presence spread through the air. Even more striking, however, is the common fund of folk wisdom from which these stories drew the practical knowledge for dealing with the restless dead. Learned prelates and uneducated villagers alike generally agreed that the only way to put a stop to rampaging corpses was decapitation, the removal of the heart, and the burning of the carcass. Bishop Hugh of Lincoln's high-minded remedy—placing a letter of absolution on the corpse in its grave—was an exception to what seems to have been a long-standing tradition about effective remedies for laying the malevolent dead to rest.

SPIRITS OF MALICE[1]

Thietmar, bishop of Merseburg (r. 1009–1018) was a well-informed churchman who moved in the upper circles of society in the Ottonian empire of northern Europe. A powerful man who owed his ecclesiastical office to the patronage of Emperor Henry II, Thietmar composed a sprawling history of the political elites of his time: kings and bishops and the family intrigues that bound them together. But he also had a keen interest in the supernatural. At the beginning of his Chronicle, *Thietmar related several anecdotes about the restless dead. Unlike the ghost stories told by contemporary monks at Cluny and elsewhere, the bishop's tales had more than a hint of malice. This should not surprise us, for the town of Walsleben, where one of these events allegedly took place, had been the scene of terrible violence a century before, when pagan Slavs slaughtered the Christian inhabitants of the place. The ghosts of these Christians lingered in a local church, where they observed the rites owed to God like their living counterparts. But pagans haunted this landscape as well. In the commercial center of Deventer, a priest who interrupted a ceremony performed by heathen ghosts was burned alive and reduced to ash upon the altar in a manner similar to the immolation rituals performed by the pagan Slavs who once lived there.*

I will relate certain events that were verified to have happened in Walsleben [in modern Brandenburg, Germany], a city that had been rebuilt after its destruction, so that no Christian may have any doubts concerning the future resurrection of the dead, but rather may proceed with all haste through their desire of holy things to the joys of blessed immortality. The priest of the church there was accustomed to sing matins in the darkness of the early morning.[2] But when he came to the cemetery, he saw therein a great multitude of people bearing offerings to a priest who was standing before the doors of the church. At first, he paused, and then, protecting himself with the sign of the cross, he fearfully walked among them, none of whom he recognized. When he entered the church, a woman who had recently died and was well known to him asked what he wanted. Once she had learned from him why he had come, the woman proclaimed that they had already looked after all of those things and that he did not have long to live. Afterward, he told this to his neighbors and it proved to be true.

During my time in Magdeburg—just as I have heard it from trustworthy witnesses, for I was a resident of the city at that time—the guards, who were keeping watch one night in the church of the merchants, saw and heard things similar to the episode I have just reported, and led the dignitaries of the city to that place. While these dignitaries were standing at a distance from the cemetery, they saw lights burning in candleholders and they heard two men singing the invitatory and all the morning prayers in order.[3] When they approached, however, they perceived nothing at all. On the next day, when I related this story to my niece Brigida, who directed the convent of St. Lawrence like a shepherd and was then suffering from an illness of the body, she was not surprised at all and straightaway told me this tale by way of a response, "In the time of Bishop Baldric, who had governed the holy see of Utrecht for more than eighty years, the prelate renewed and consecrated a church in a place called Deventer that had been destroyed by the passage of time and commended it to one of his priests. One day, in the early morning, as the priest made his way there, he saw the dead making offerings in the church and in the cemetery, and he heard them singing. As soon as he related this to the bishop, he was ordered to sleep in the church. But on the following night, he was thrown out by the dead along with the bed, on which he was resting. Alarmed by this treatment, he lamented the situation in the presence of the bishop, who ordered him to persist in guarding his church, once he had been marked by the relics of the saints and sprinkled with holy water. Obedient to his lord's command, he tried once more to sleep in the church, but fear's persistent sting kept him awake. And behold, arriving at the accustomed hour, the dead lifted him up, placed him in front of the altar, and burned his body until only fine ashes remained. When the bishop heard this, he was moved in the spirit of penance to order a three-day fast in the hope that he might help both himself and the souls of the dead. I could say much more concerning all of these matters, my son, if my infirmity did not hinder me. As the day is conceded to the living, so the night is the dominion of the dead." As Saint Paul warns, it is not fitting for a mortal to know more than is beneficial to moderation.[4]

THE BLACKENED HEARTS
OF STAPENHILL[1]

*Revenants appeared with alarming frequency in the literature
of Anglo-Norman and Angevin England. In his account of the
miracles attributed to Saint Modwenna, written between
1118–1150, Abbot Geoffrey of Burton (r. 1114–1150) recorded acts of vengeance undertaken by the saint against
those who had threatened the interests of the abbey in Stapenhill, Stratfordshire, where her bones lay buried. Among these
stories was the unusual tale of two peasants who fled their obligations to the abbot and sought the protection of a local
count, whom they roused to anger against their monastic
master by "speaking wickedly" against him. Saint Modwenna
protected her monks from the count's aggression, but the two
fugitive peasants suffered a terrible fate. They died suddenly
and received burial, but then, to the horror of their neighbors,
they proceeded to wander around at night, sometimes carrying their coffins on their backs, sometimes in the form of wild
animals. Even worse, they called out to their living neighbors
and brought disease in their wake. After most of the villagers
had died, the bishop allowed the locals to put a stop to the
revenants. Their bodies were dug up, their heads cut off and
placed between their legs, and their hearts were burned on a
fire, until they cracked open and released evil spirits in the
form of crows. Anglo-Saxon burial sites, including one at the
village of Stapenhill itself, sometimes contain corpses decapi-
tated in this way, which lends support to the argument that
Abbot Geoffrey of Burton was describing a traditional way of
dealing with the threat of the wandering dead.*

When an insult against the church occurred once again, the Lord inflicted punishment because of the merits of the virgin Modwenna with a terrifying judgment of the kind I am about to describe. For there were two villagers living in Stapenhill under the jurisdiction of the abbot of Burton, who fled to a nearby village called Drakelow. They wrongfully abandoned their lords, the monks, in their desire to live under the authority of Count Roger the Poitevin. The abbot of the monastery sent word and had their crops seized, for the villagers had not yet removed it from their barns, and then he had every last grain of it moved to the abbey's granaries in the hope that he could in this way summon them back once more to their proper dwellings. But those villagers, going off and spreading lies, brought a querulous complaint to the count, riling him up and saying the worst possible things to him, to such an extent that the count became furious with the abbot to the point that the count threatened to kill the abbot wherever he might find him. Then, in his wrath, the count gathered a multitude of peasants and knights with carts and weapons and sent them in haste to Stapenhill to the granaries of the monks in a great show of force and ordered them to seize with violence all of the crops therein, both the stores of the abbey, which provided for the monks, and also the crops belonging to those wicked fugitives, concerning whom we have already spoken. Then, not content with this, he again sent many men and knights to the fields of the abbey near a place called Blackpool with the command to destroy the church's crops with all of their might. The count encouraged them especially to draw out the ten knights, who were family members of the abbot and members of his entourage, if they could devise some way to provoke them to a pitched battle. When he understood what was happening, the abbot forbade his knights from going outside under any circumstances, while he and the monks, with bare feet and much groaning, entered the church and with many tears set down on the ground the shrine of the blessed virgin Modwenna, where her most sacred bones lay at rest. Together they all cried out to the Lord with the sum of their effort, beseeching and praying for his immense power from the bottoms of their hearts, so that he might deign to lend aid to his servants in his blessed goodness, if he so desired, and that he might reveal his willingness to help those struggling in such difficulty with a manifestation of his power.

Meanwhile, as all of the monks were inside offering prayers with unanimous intent, the ten knights disregarded the abbot's prohibition and without the knowledge of him or his monks, they took up arms with shared intent. Boldly mounting their horses, they galloped onto the field, ready for battle, a few against many. Spurring his horse to charge, one of the abbot's knights suddenly struck the count's steward and knocked him to the ground with such force that the violence of the blow broke one of his legs. This feat of strength terrified the entourage of their enemies as the battle commenced. Then another of the abbot's knights likewise spurred his horse quickly to charge in the same way. He struck a knight from the household of the count with a tremendous show of force and knocked him into a nearby stream, hurling him into the mud a long way from his horse. The rest of the monks' knights, each and every one of them, fought so valiantly in this battle that the ten of them put to flight more than sixty opponents and, to the great disgrace of the vanquished, these few men chased a great many more from the field of battle through the merit of Modwenna and the power of God.

The evening of the very next day, the two fugitive peasants, through whom and because of whom this whole evil affair had begun, were sitting down to eat when both were suddenly struck down dead. On the very next evening, both of them were laid in wooden coffins and buried in the churchyard at Stapenhill, the village from which they both had fled. What followed was exceedingly strange and especially astounding. On the same day on which they were buried, they appeared at dusk, while there was still a hint of light, at Drakelow, carrying upon their shoulders the wooden coffins in which they had been buried. Through the next night they wandered through the paths of the village and the nearby fields, sometimes in the form of men carrying wooden coffins on their shoulders, sometimes in the likeness of bears or dogs or other kinds of animals. Moreover, they spoke to the other peasants, banging on the walls of their homes and crying out to everyone who could hear, "Get moving, quickly, get moving! Get up! Get up and come!" When these uncanny events had repeated themselves every evening and every night for quite some time, a disease struck the village and all of the peasants living there suddenly found themselves in such a dire situation that within three days, with the exception of three individuals whom we will talk about later, every last one of them succumbed to sudden death in the strangest way.

The count was stunned and struck with a great fear when he realized that such strange events had begun to unfold. He immediately repented and came to the monastery with his knights. Seeking pardon with humility, he made a binding peace with the abbot and the monks, petitioning them with prayer to placate God and the virgin Modwenna, whom he had offended. In the presence of everyone, with faithful devotion, he ordered Drogo, the reeve of the village, to pay twice the amount for all of the damages that he had inflicted. And so he left the monastery with relief and departed without delay to his other lands. Then Drogo, returning quickly, restored double what was owed to the monastery and, begging pardon once more, departed to other regions with all haste for he wished to escape the destruction wrought by death. The two peasants who still remained in the village—Drogo had been the third—became sick and languished for a long time. Furthermore, they lived in fear of the dead men, those phantoms who carried their wooden coffins on their shoulders in the evening and at night, as we described above. With the permission of the bishop, they sought out the graves of these men, dug them up, and found their bodies intact, but the linen wrappings over their faces were stained with gore. The peasants cut off the heads of the corpses and placed them between their legs in the graves. Then they ripped the hearts out of the bodies, which they buried once more in the earth. They carried the hearts to a place called Dodefreseford, where they burned them from morning until the evening. Finally, once the hearts had been burned, they cracked open with a great sound as though due to immense pressure and suddenly everyone there clearly saw an evil spirit in the shape of a crow flying from the flames. Soon after these things occurred, the deathly sickness and the phantoms disappeared once and for all. The two peasants who were lying sick in their beds recovered their health as soon as they saw the smoke rising from the fire where the hearts had been burned. They got up immediately, gathered up their children and wives and everything they owned, and gave thanks to God that they had escaped. They made their way to a neighboring village called Gresley, where they remain to this day. Thus, the village known as Drakelow was abandoned and for a long time no one dared to live there, fearing the judgment of the Lord that had happened there so strangely and marveling at the wonders that the All-Mighty worked through the holy virgin Modwenna.

THE EVIL WELSHMAN[1]

Writing toward the end of the twelfth century, Walter Map (1140–c. 1208/1210) composed a treatise called On the Trifles of the Courtiers. *This work of satire was a patchwork of historical anecdotes drawn from personal experience and fantastic stories based on oral sources. The short tale of an evil Welshman who returned from the dead to plague a small village in Wales permitted Walter to praise the bravery of the English knight William Laudun, when the traditional remedy for laying a wandering corpse to rest had failed.*

I know about a strange portent that happened in Wales. An English knight named William Laudun, strong at arms and of proven bravery, came to Gilbert Foliot, at that time bishop of Hereford, but now bishop of London, and said, "Lord, I have come to you seeking counsel. Recently, a certain evil Welshman died faithlessly in my village. After four nights had passed, he returned to our village night after night. He will not stop summoning his neighbors, one by one by name. Those who he summons quickly become sick and within three days they die, so that now very few of them are left." Marveling, the bishop said, "Perhaps the Lord bestowed the power on an evil angel of that lost soul to animate his dead body. Let the body be dug up, cut the neck through with a shovel, sprinkle a great quantity of holy water on the body and in the grave, and bury it again." Even after this was accomplished, those residing nearby were nonetheless plagued by the old phantom. So one night, when very few people were still alive, the summoner called William's name three times. But because that man was brave and quick and prepared for this event, he leapt up with his sword drawn and followed the fleeing demon back to its tomb where he struck its head from its neck as it fell into its grave. Since then, the demolition caused by that wandering plague ceased, doing no more harm to William himself or to any of the others. We know for certain the outcome of this case, but we do not know the cause.

RAMPAGING REVENANTS[1]

William of Newburgh (c. 1130–c. 1200) collected stories about the living dead for inclusion in his History of English Affairs, *which surveyed the history of England from 1066 to 1198. It was not difficult for him to find information on the rampages of reanimated corpses in the north of England because, as he claimed, "numerous examples from our own time are at hand and testimonies of the fact are abundant." Animated by the spirit of malice or the Devil himself, these malevolent creatures threatened physical violence to those dearest to them in life and threatened to depopulate their former abodes by spreading airborne diseases through their restless wanderings. William was a skilled storyteller. He went to great lengths to set the scene by providing detailed information on the shortcomings of the evil men fated to return from the dead. He also relished recounting the bravery of his heroes—monks and villagers alike—who risked their lives to save their towns from walking corpses and fought down fear to keep watch in graveyards at night as they waited for the dead to rise.*

In those days an incredible event happened in the county of Buckingham, which I learned about first from friends in that district and afterward heard a fuller account from Stephen, the venerable archdeacon of that county. A certain man died and, according to custom, through the respectable duty of his wife and family he was buried on the evening of the Lord's Ascension.[2] On the following night, however, he entered the

room where his wife lay sleeping. Not only did he terrify her
when he woke her up, but he also nearly crushed her under the
immense weight of his body. The very next night, he afflicted
his terrified wife in the same way. Frightened of the danger, to
ward off the anxiety that he would come a third time, she remained awake in the company of watchful companions. Again
he came, but he was repelled by the shouts of the watchers
and, when it was clear that he could do no harm, he departed.
Once he had been driven away from his wife, he plagued his
own brothers in the same way, who lived in the same village.
Following the example of his cautious wife, they, too, stayed
up all night with their companions, prepared to face and drive
off the danger. Nonetheless he appeared once more, hoping
that his brothers might be overcome by sleep, but once he was
driven off again by the watchfulness and bravery of the sentinels, he ran riot among the livestock, both indoors and outside
the house, as the wildness of these animals and their unusual
behavior made plain.

Once he had established himself as a serious threat to his
friends and neighbors alike, he made it necessary for everyone
to keep watch by night. In that village, there was a general
watch in effect in every dwelling, while individuals remained
wary of his unexpected approach. After he had run riot in this
way for some time at night alone, he began to wander about
during the hours of daylight, formidable to all, but seen by
only a few. Indeed, it often happened that when he encountered a group of people, he was only visible to one or two of
them, even though his presence was not concealed to the others. Alarmed beyond measure, these men finally decided to
seek the counsel of the church. With a tearful lament, they
told the whole story to the archdeacon I mentioned earlier,
while he was presiding solemnly over a meeting of the clergy.
The archdeacon immediately set the affair down in writing for
the venerable bishop of Lincoln, who was residing in London
at that time, and decided that it was best to wait for his authoritative opinion regarding this strange circumstance. For
his part, the bishop was amazed by this story and conducted a
careful inquiry with his advisors, who told him that such

prodigies have happened in England quite often and explained with many examples of previous incidents that the people would find no peace unless the body of this most wretched man was dug up and burned. The venerable bishop found this idea most unseemly and unworthy. So, shortly thereafter, he sent a letter of absolution, written in his own hand, to the archdeacon, with the command that the tomb be opened so that it might be made clear with faithful inspection what state the body was in. The bishop also ordered that the letter be placed on his chest, and the tomb sealed up again. Once the tomb was opened, the corpse was found exactly as it had been laid there. The bishop's letter of absolution was placed on his chest, and the tomb was sealed once more. He was never seen to wander again nor permitted to inflict harm or terror upon anyone thereafter.

In the northern parts of England as well, we know of another prodigy, not unlike this one and equally strange, that happened around the same time. At the mouth of the river Tweed and under the jurisdiction of the king of Scotland, there is a noble town called Berwick. In this town there lived a man of wealth, but a scoundrel, as became clear afterward. After his death he was buried, but at night he went forth from his grave through the workings—as some believe—of Satan. And followed by a pack of loudly barking dogs, he wandered about hither and thither. Thus he struck all of his neighbors with terror before returning to his tomb at daybreak. After this had happened for several days in a row, and no one now dared to be found out of doors after sunset (for everyone dreaded an encounter with the deadly monster), the townspeople of upper and middling backgrounds met to discuss what should be done, the more simple among them fearing that by chance due to negligence they might be beaten black-and-blue by this undead monster, the more thoughtful believing with good reason that, if a solution was not found quickly, the very air would become infected and corrupted by the repeated wandering of this foul corpse, causing disease and the deaths of many people. The need to avoid these perils was made abundantly clear by many comparable examples. Therefore, they enlisted ten young men, renowned for their boldness, to dig up the abominable corpse. Once they had chopped it limb from limb, they set it alight and made it food for the fire. When this was done, the affliction ceased. For this monster, while it was being animated—as it is said—by Satan, it is said to have told certain people who it encountered by chance that they would not have any peace so long as he was unburned. Therefore, once he was burned, tranquility seemed to be restored to them, but then a disease, which originated as a result of the monster, killed a large number of the villagers. Nor did this sickness rage so terribly elsewhere, even though it was prevalent in every part of England at that time, as will be explained more fully in its proper place.

It would not be easy to believe reasonably that the bodies of the dead should rise from their graves—by what agency I do not know—and should wander around to cause terror or calamity for the living only to return to the same tomb that opens of its own accord to receive them, except that numerous examples from our own time are at hand and testimonies of the fact are abundant. It would clearly be strange if such things happened long ago, since no such account can be found in the books of ancient authors, who applied their formidable energy committing to writing everything worth remembering. For if they neglected by no means to write down even events of moderate significance, how could they have suppressed an event at the same time so amazing and so horrifying, if by chance it had occurred in their age? In contrast, if I wanted to record every event of this kind that was revealed to have taken place in our time, the undertaking would be at once too difficult and too tiresome. Let me add only two more recent accounts beyond those already recorded and insert them into our story, since the occasion permits, as a warning to posterity.

A few years ago, the chaplain of a certain noble lady died and received burial at that noble monastery called Melrose. This man had very little respect for the sacred order to which he belonged and acted very much like a layman. What especially blackened his reputation as a minister of the holy sacraments was his dedication to the vanity of hunting with the result that he was known to many by the notorious nickname

Hundeprest, that is, "Houndpriest." And indeed while he was alive, this preoccupation of his was alternately ridiculed by people or thought to be a refined pastime, but it was only after his death that the guilt deriving from it became clear, for he rose from his grave at night. He was unable to sow terror or cause harm in the monastery itself due to the merits of the holy monks who lived there. After that, he wandered around outside the abbey and carried on with great groans and a hideous murmuring, particularly around the bedchamber of his former mistress. After this had happened a few times, she became very anxious and shared the enormity of her fear and sense of danger with one of the monks who visited her concerning an affair related to the abbey. She demanded with tears that prayers more earnest than usual be poured forth on her behalf as though for one suffering in agony. The monk sympathized graciously and with good reason with her anxiety, for she seemed most deserving of numerous prayers from the holy community of that place, and he promised a prompt remedy through the mercy of the Highest Provider.

The monk returned to the abbey and joined forces with another monk of the same age and temperament and two strong young men, with whom he kept watch over the cemetery where that wretched priest lay buried. These four men, furnished with weapons and bravery, spent the night in that place, safe in the support that they provided for one another. Midnight had just passed and no sign of the monster had appeared. Then it happened that three of them, leaving alone in that place the one who had brought them all together, went into a nearby house, as they explained, to ward off the chill of the night with a fire. Then, when this monk found himself alone in that place, the Devil, believing that he had found the right moment to break the monk's courage, roused his vessel, which had seemed to have lain quiet longer than usual. Seeing the monster from a distance, at first the monk grew stiff with fear, for he was alone, but he soon recovered his courage. When it was clear that there was no place to run, he valiantly intercepted the onslaught of the horror, which rushed toward him with a terrible roar, and buried the battle-ax he was wielding deep into its body. When it received this wound, the monster let out a cry and, turning its back, fled away, though not quite as quickly as it had advanced. The amazing monk harried his fleeing foe from behind and forced it back into its own tomb, which gaped open for the monster on its own accord. Once it had snatched its guest from the sight of its pursuer, the tomb appeared to close right away with the same ease. When these events were taking place, the companions who had sought relief from the night's chill near the fire left the house and ran late to the scene. When they heard what had happened, at dawn they assisted in digging up that cursed corpse and dragging it away from the tomb. Once they had cleansed the monster of the dirt that came out with it, they found on its body the great wound that it had received and in the tomb a large amount of gore, which had flowed from it. And so they carried the corpse beyond the walls of the abbey for burning and scattered the ashes. I have told this story in plain language, exactly as I heard it myself from devout men.

Another haunting, not unlike this one but more destructive, happened at the castle called Anantis, as I learned from an old priest, a well-known and influential man who had lived in those parts and remembered this event taking place in his own presence. A certain man who had committed evil deeds, fleeing from the province of York in fear of the law or his enemies, came to the lord of the aforementioned castle, to whom he was known, and settled there. Having found by chance a line of service suitable for a man of his character, he worked hard to increase rather than correct his own depravities. He took a wife, to his own detriment, as became clear thereafter. For, hearing certain rumors concerning her, he was stricken by the spirit of jealousy. Eager to learn if these rumors were true, he made as though he was about to go on a long journey and would not return for several days. He returned that evening, however, and secretly entered his bedroom with the help of a servant. There he lay on a beam overhanging his wife's chamber so that he might prove with his own eyes if anything threatened the honor of his bed. Seeing his wife having sex with a young neighbor, forgetful of his purpose due to his wrath, he fell and landed heavily on the ground next to where they were lying. The adulterer made his escape, but his wife, concealing the fact with her cunning, took care to lift her fallen husband gently from the floor. When he had recovered somewhat, he reproached his wife for her adultery and threatened punishment. But she said, "Make the sign of the cross on yourself, my lord, for you are saying strange things, which should not be attributed to you, but to the sickness that has a hold on you." Then, shaken by the fall and struck numb throughout his entire body, as you can imagine, he was laid low by a disease. The old priest I mentioned, who told this story to me, visited him as a duty owed to piety and advised him to make confession for his sins and to receive the eucharist according to custom like a Christian. But this man was caught up in recalling what had happened to him and what his wife had said and decided to postpone until tomorrow—a tomorrow he would not see in the body—what he was advised to do today. For on the following night, destitute of Christian grace, in the grips of the misfortunes he merited, he shared in the sleep of death. And although he was unworthy, he received a Christian burial, which was no benefit to him at all. During the night, by the machination of Satan, he came forth from his tomb. With a pack of dogs following after him emitting terrifying barks, he wandered through the courtyards and around the houses. Everyone locked their doors and no one presumed to leave on any business from nightfall until sunrise for they feared to be beaten black-and-blue should they perhaps encounter this rampaging monster. But in fact these precautions were of no use, for the air had become infected by the rambling of that grim cadaver, filling every house with disease and death by its pestilent breath. Already the town, which a short time before was populous, now seemed nearly empty of people, as the survivors of the destruction fled to other regions, so that they would not die as well. Saddened by the ruin of his parish, the old priest, from whose mouth I heard this story, endeavored to summon together wise and devout men on the sacred day of the Lord called Palm Sunday, who would in this great predicament provide useful counsel and revive with whatever consolation they could muster those miserable villagers

who remained.[3] Therefore, after he had delivered a sermon to
the people and performed with solemnity the rituals appropriate to that venerable day, he summoned to his table his religious guests in the company of other honorable people who
were present. While they were eating, two young men who had
lost their father to the destruction caused by the plague, mutu-
ally encouraging one another, said, "This monster has cost us
our father and it will quickly destroy us as well, if we do nothing about it. Therefore, let us do something bold that will not
only ensure our safety but also avenge our father's death. There
is no one to stand in our way, for a feast is underway in the
house of the priest and the whole village is silent, as though
completely deserted. Let us dig up the cause of this pestilence
and burn it with fire." Thus, they found a shovel with a blunt
edge and proceeding to the cemetery they began to dig. And
just when they thought that they would have to dig even deeper,
suddenly before they had removed very much earth, they un-
covered the corpse, swollen to an enormous size, its face blood-
ied and bloated beyond measure. It seemed as though the burial
cloth, in which it had been wound, was nearly torn to pieces.
Spurred on past fear by their wrath, the young men inflicted a
wound on the unmoving carcass, from which flowed a continuous torrent of blood as though it was filled with the blood of
many people, like a leech. Then they dragged it outside the village and hastily constructed a pyre. But one of them said that
the pestilent corpse would not catch fire until its heart had been
removed, so the other cut open its side with blows from the
blunt shovel and thrusting his hand inside, he pulled out that
cursed heart. After the corpse had been torn apart and given to
the flames, the guests dining with the priest learned what had
taken place and ran to the spot in order to be able to testify to
this event. When that infernal monster was thus completely destroyed, the pestilence that had prowled among the people
ceased, as though the air, which had been corrupted by his
loathsome activity, was cleansed by the fire that had consumed
that wretched cadaver. Now that I have explained these events,
let us return to the course of history.

THE GHOSTS
OF WAR

The restless spirits of slain soldiers were among the most common ghosts in Greek and Roman antiquity. Killed by violence before their time, the phantoms of "the great armies of battle dead," as Homer called them, hovered near their tombs or played out their final conflicts on the fields where their corpses lay unburied. The ghosts of the dead lingered on for centuries after ancient conflicts. In the Middle Ages, reports of phantom armies or roving hordes of dead warriors increased in the eleventh century and were especially common in the period of the Christian Crusades to win back the Holy Land from the Muslims (1095–1291). The appearance of the dead in battle dress often foretold a slaughter, but warrior souls also marshaled to come to the aid of pious Christian lords who had fought against the enemies of God or who had been diligent in giving alms for the relief of souls in purgatory. By the twelfth century, a tormented troop of dead soldiers and their grim entourage known as Hellequin's Horde roamed across northern Europe, their "mad course of endless wanderings" a penalty for the sins they had accrued in life.

TERROR IN TONNERRE[1]

*In the 1030s, a monk of Cluny named Rodulphus Glaber col-
lected stories for a chronicle of his time entitled* The Five
Books of Histories. *By his own account a wayward individual
ill-suited to life as a monk, Glaber painted a vivid portrait of
Christian society in northern Europe in the generation before
the First Crusade. Among stories of warring kings, holy abbots, and vile heretics, Glaber penned several accounts of
contemporary omens that portended terrible events, like the
appearance of a dragon in the sky before the outbreak of a
devastating civil war. One of these tales was the report of a
ghostly army seen by a priest on the outskirts of the town of
Tonnerre in Burgundy, the appearance of which foretold a
terrible battle that took place there the following year.*

In truth, we should remember very carefully that whenever
prodigies are clearly revealed to people who are still alive
whether by good or by evil spirits, it often happens that those
who see them do not live for very long thereafter. We have
learned many examples of this from which we will commend a
few to memory, so that whenever it happens, people might
show caution rather than be deceived. When Bruno was the
bishop of Langres, there was a certain priest with a devout
reputation named Frottier, who lived in the town of Tonnerre.
One Sunday evening, as it grew dark and he was about to sit
down to dinner, he went over to the windows of his house to
relax for a bit. Looking out, he saw approaching from the
north a host of horsemen, vast in number, marching westward

arrayed as though for battle. After he watched them for some time, he grew anxious and summoned one of his servants to bear witness to this incredible sight. While he was calling out for the servant to come, the horsemen faded from view and suddenly vanished. The priest was overcome with such a great fright that he could hardly keep himself from crying. Thereafter he fell sick and in the same year, just as he had lived well, he died. Those who saw this were witnesses to the fact that he had been taken away from this life by the portent he had seen. For the very next year, Henry, the son of King Robert who ruled after his father, was moved by wrath and came to Tonnerre with a vast army, which resulted in an immense slaughter of men on both sides of the fight.

HELLEQUIN'S HORDE

Scholars have discovered the roots of stories about the wandering army of the dead known as "Hellequin's Horde" in pagan antiquity and Germanic traditions, but the most detailed descriptions of this unearthly manifestation emerged in Latin texts from the twelfth and thirteenth centuries. Walter Map described their origin in his satirical book On the Trifles of the Courtiers. *According to Map, a pygmy king doomed an ancient monarch of the Britons named Herla and his entourage to an endless, fruitless march. While Map's use of this story served his satirical purpose—Herla's court prefigured the vain and hectic court of his employer King Henry II—other authors invested this ancient story with a message about the Christian afterlife. The most vivid rendering of the horde's activity came from the Anglo-Norman monk and historian Orderic Vitalis (c. 1075–c. 1142), who told how a priest named Walchelin had a nocturnal encounter with a vast column of dead soldiers and their entourage. He identified them as "Hellequin's Horde" and described them as a purgatorial procession of suffering sinners, doomed to trudge ever onward until they earned relief from their punishment. Among them, Walchelin recognized many people he knew in life, including his beloved brother, who begged his sibling for the respite brought by prayers and alms given to the poor on his behalf.*

(A) THE PYGMY'S CURSE[1]

Legends tell of one court and one alone that is similar to this court of ours [of King Henry II]. This, they say, was the court of Herla, a king of the most ancient Britons, who was put in contrast by another king, a veritable pygmy, for the smallness of his stature was no greater than that of a monkey. According to the story, this little man rode on a large goat and could be described as a kind of Pan, for he had a fervent expression, a large head, a red beard so long that it reached his chest, which was covered in spotted fawn skin, and his legs ended in the hooves of a goat.[2] Herla spoke with him one on one. The pygmy said, "I am the king of many kings and princes, a people without number; I come willingly, having been sent by them to you. And although I am unknown to you, I rejoice in the fame that has elevated you above all other kings. For you are indeed the best of your kind and related to me in place and blood, and you deserve to adorn your wedding ceremony gloriously with me as your guest, when the king of the Franks gives to you his daughter in marriage. This is in the works without your knowledge and behold his ambassadors arrive today. Let there be a binding agreement between us: first I will attend your wedding and then you will attend mine on the same day next year." Once he had said these words, quicker than a tiger, he turned around and vanished before our eyes.

The king returned home in a state of amazement, received the Frankish ambassadors, and accepted the proposal. When he was sitting ceremoniously at his wedding, behold the pygmy appeared before the first course with a great multitude of creatures like him. They sat down to dine, filling the tables, more of them sitting outside rather than inside in tents belonging to the pygmy, which were pitched in an instant. From these tents rushed servants with vessels made entirely of precious stones constructed with a skill beyond imitation. They filled the palace and the tents with dishes of gold and precious stone; they served nothing on platters of silver or wood. Wherever they were needed, there they were. They took nothing from the palace or anywhere else, pouring forth everything from their own supplies; and everything that they brought with them fulfilled the wishes and desires of everyone present. Everything that Herla had prepared sat untouched; his own servants sat still for their services were neither sought nor needed. The pygmies circled around, earning the gratitude of everyone, shining like lights among the crowds with the richness of their raiment and gems, troubling no one with word or deed, either by their presence or their absence. Then, while his servants were in the midst of their work, their king addressed King Herla thus, "Best of kings, with God as my witness I am here at your wedding according to our agreement. If I can fulfill any part of your contract more so than what you now see, I will see to it gladly down to the last detail. If not, then do not defer the return of such great honor when I seek it from you." After he said these words, without waiting for a response, he retreated to his tent and around dawn he departed with his entourage.

The very next year, the pygmy appeared suddenly in the court of Herla to request the fulfillment of their pact. The king agreed and once he had prepared enough supplies for the repayment of the debt, he followed where he was led. Soon they entered a cavern in the face of a very tall cliff. After passing through darkness into a light which did not seem to come from the sun or the moon, but from many lanterns, they arrived at the homes of the pygmies, a dwelling place every bit as handsome as the palace of the Sun described by Ovid.[3] There they celebrated the wedding, and the pact with the pygmy king was fulfilled appropriately. When he received permission to leave, Herla departed laden with gifts and presents of horses, dogs, hawks, and every accoutrement that allowed one to excel at hunting or fowling. The pygmy king escorted them as far as the darkness, where he presented Herla with a bloodhound that was small enough to carry. He warned the king in no uncertain terms, however, that no one in his whole entourage should ever dismount from their horses until the dog leapt down from his arms. With these words, he bid the king farewell and returned to his own country.

A short time thereafter, Herla returned to the light of the sun and to his kingdom. There he spoke to an old shepherd, seeking news concerning his queen, whom he mentioned by name. Looking at the king with wonder, the shepherd said, "Lord, I can hardly understand a word you say, for I am a Saxon, while you are a Briton. But I have not heard the name of that queen, except that people say that there was once a queen of the most ancient Britons who went by the same name. She was the wife of King Herla, who, the story goes, disappeared with a pygmy at this very cliff and was never seen in the world again. It has been two hundred years now since the Saxons took over this kingdom and drove out Herla's people." The king was stunned for he thought that he had tarried only three days; it was all he could do not to fall off his horse. Then some members of his entourage, forgetful of the pygmy's warning, dismounted from their horses before the dog did, and immediately turned to dust. The king, understanding the reason for their distintegration, forbade under a penalty akin to death that no one should dismount their horse until the dog came down. But the dog has never come down.

And the story goes that King Herla forever follows a mad course of endless wanderings with his entourage who know neither rest nor respite. Many people have often claimed to have seen Herla's army, so they believe. But in recent times, some maintain that in the first year of the coronation of our King Henry [1154–1155], Herla's horde stopped coming to our country in its great numbers, as before.[4] At that time, many Welshmen claimed to have seen it plunge into the Wye, Hereford's river. Since then, this phantom patrol has ceased; it is as though they passed their wanderings on to us when they traded theirs for rest.

(B) A DARK HOST OF THE DEAD[5]

I do not believe that I should pass over or commit to silence an event that happened on the first of January to a priest in the diocese of Lisieux. In a village called Bonneval, there was a priest named Walchelin who served at the church of Saint Aubin, a former monk who became bishop of Angers and a confessor. On the first of January in the year of our Lord 1091, this man was summoned, as duty dictated, to visit a sick person by night on the far reaches of his parish. As he was returning home all alone and making his way far removed from any settlements, he began to hear a loud noise like that of a great army and he believed that it was the household guard of Robert of Bellême marching in haste to lay siege to Courcy. The moon in its eighth phase, in the sign of ram, was then shining brightly and showed the way for travelers. The priest was young, bold, and strong, large of body and nimble. When he heard the sound of men approaching in disorder, he became afraid and began to weigh many options in his mind, whether he should flee so that he would not be assaulted by lowly minions and shamefully robbed, or whether he should raise a defiant hand in his own defense if someone confronted him. At length he spied four medlar trees in a field some way off from the road. He decided to run to them quickly and hide until the horsemen had passed by. Then a man of enormous size carrying a giant mace blocked his way as he ran, and with his weapon poised over his head, the man said, "Stand still and go no farther!" The priest immediately did as he was told and, leaning on the staff that he was carrying, he stood very still. The stern warrior stood beside him and, doing the priest no harm, watched as the army passed by. Behold, a huge horde of people on foot went past and they were carrying on their necks and shoulders animals and clothing and all manner of furniture and household goods just like pillagers do. They were all lamenting excessively and urging one another to hurry. The priest recognized among them many of his neighbors who had recently died and he heard them bemoaning the great torments by which they were being tortured because of their sins. Then a horde of coffin bearers followed and the giant quickly joined their march. Nearly five hundred biers were being carried and each one was shouldered by two carriers.[6] Furthermore, upon the biers sat men as small as dwarves, but they had huge heads like barrels. Indeed, two Ethiopians were carrying a giant tree trunk and upon the trunk a wretched man, cruelly bound, was being tortured and he was crying out, emitting screams amid his dire torments. Then a terrifying demon, which was sitting upon the trunk, goaded the bleeding man mercilessly on his legs and back with fiery spurs. Walchelin actually recognized this man as the murderer of a priest named Stephen and realized that he was suffering unbearably for the blood of the innocent man that he had spilled two years previously, for he had died before he could complete his penance for such a terrible crime.

Next followed a cohort of women, whose multitude seemed without number to the priest. They were riding in the manner of women, sitting on sidesaddles in which burning nails had been affixed. The wind was frequently lifting them up the length of a cubit from the saddle and then dropping them back upon the spikes.[7] Wounded by the hot nails in their buttocks and tormented frightfully by the stabs and the burning, these women cried out, "Woe, woe!" and openly bemoaned the sins for which they were suffering such punishments. Indeed, it was for the enticements and obscene delights that they had indulged in while they were alive that they now endured dreadful fires and stenches and many more torments than they could ever tell, and they bemoaned their punishments, crying out with wretched voices. In this troop, the priest recognized certain noblewomen and he saw horses and mules with empty litters belonging to women who were not yet dead.

Terrified by these sights, Walchelin began to contemplate their many possible meanings. Not much farther along he saw a crowded column of clergymen and monks and also noticed their leaders—bishops and abbots—with their pastoral staffs. The clergymen and bishops wore their black caps; the monks and abbots were dressed likewise in their black cowls. They were groaning and lamenting and a few of them called out to Walchelin and asked for the sake of their past friendship that he pray for them. The priest related that he had seen many prelates of sterling reputation there, who men now believed to have joined the saints in heaven. Indeed, he saw Bishop Hugh of Lisieux and the famous abbots Mainer of Saint-Évroul and Gerbert of Saint-Wandrille and many others who I cannot recall by name. I will not try to commit their names to writing. Human perception often fails, but the eye of God pierces to the marrow. A human being sees what is on the surface, but God looks upon the heart. In the kingdom of eternal blessedness an everlasting brightness shines upon all things and there perfect sanctity, having obtained every delight, exults in the sons of the kingdom. Nothing without order happens there; nothing polluted enters there; nothing sordid and contrary to honesty is found there. Whatever sin the filth of the flesh has committed is burned away by a cleansing fire and is made clean by many kinds of purgation according to the decision of the eternal judge. And just as a vessel, scrubbed clean of rust and carefully polished all over, is placed in a treasury, so too the soul, cleansed from the contagion of every sin, enters paradise, and there, fortified with every happiness, it rejoices without fear or concern.

After he had seen these terrible things, the priest trembled uncontrollably and, supported by his staff, he waited for worse things to come. Behold, a teeming army of soldiers followed next. They sported no color except for black and a flickering fire. All of them were mounted upon huge horses and girded with every conceivable weapon as though they were hastening to war, and they flew pitch-black standards. Richard and Baldwin, the sons of Count Gilbert, who had recently died, could be seen there, as well as many others who I cannot hope to number. Among the rest, Landry of Orbec, who had died that same year, began to speak to the priest, and relayed his messages to him with terrifying shouts, beseeching him emphatically to convey his instructions to his wife. But the hordes behind and up ahead interrupted his words and said to the priest, "Do not believe Landry, for he is a liar." He had been viscount and advocate of Orbec and had risen far beyond his humble origins through his innate intelligence and honesty. But in lawsuits and pleas, he judged according to his will and perverted his judgments in return for money, a servant more to greed and fraud than to any moral standard. For this reason, he deserved to be shamed in his suffering and openly called a liar by his companions. In this judgment, no one flattered him and no one beseeched him for his clever pleading. Truly, because he was accustomed to closing his ears to the cries of the poor, now in his torments he was judged to be contemptible and unworthy of a hearing.

After the great cohort of many thousands had marched on, Walchelin began to think to himself, "Without a doubt, this is Hellequin's horde. I have heard from many people that they had once seen it, but incredulous I mocked their stories because I never saw any firm proof concerning such things. Now I truly do see the spirits of the dead, but no one will believe me when I tell them what I have seen unless I can show some sure proof to the living. Therefore, I will catch one of the riderless horses that follows the horde. I will mount it swiftly, ride it home, and show it to my neighbors to earn their belief." Soon he grabbed the reins of a pitch-black horse, but this animal shook itself from his grasping hand and, running as though winged, it galloped after the dark host. The priest was disheartened by his failed attempt, but he was young in age, bold and agile, indeed swift of body and strong. Prepared, he stood in the middle of the road and held out his hand to an approaching horse that appeared most ready to be taken. The horse stopped to allow the priest to mount and, exhaling from its nostrils, it produced a great cloud in the shape of the tallest oak tree. Then the priest put his left foot in the stirrup and, once he had seized the reins, placed his hand on the saddle. Suddenly he felt an intense heat, like a burning fire, under his foot and an indescribable chill penetrated his heart through the very hand that held the reins.

While this was happening, four horrific horsemen arrived and asked with booming voices, "Why are you stealing our horses? You will come with us. None of us harmed you, yet you have tried to take what is ours." The priest was very frightened and let go of the horse, and as three of the horsemen were about to seize him, the fourth one said, "Let him be, and allow me to speak to him, because I want to send my instructions to my wife and my sons through him." Then he addressed the fearful priest directly, "Listen to me, I beg you, and relay to my wife what I command." The priest responded, "I do not know who you are and I would not recognize your wife." The soldier said, "I am William of Glos, the son of Barnon, who was once the well-known steward of William of Breteuil and his father Count William of Hereford. Among mortals I made unfair judgments and seized plunder, and I am guilty of more crimes than anyone can relate. Usury torments me more than all other sins. I lent my money to a certain man in need, and I received a mill that he owned as security. When he was unable to repay the loan, I retained the mill for the rest of my life, disinheriting the rightful heir when I left it to my own heirs. Behold, I carry the burning iron of a mill-shaft in my mouth, which seems to me heavier to carry than the castle at Rouen. Therefore, tell my wife Beatrice and my son Roger to help me by restoring with all haste to the rightful heir the surety from which they have received much more than I ever gave." The priest responded, "William of Glos died long ago and a message of this kind would find no acceptance by any of the faithful. I have no idea who you are, nor who your heirs might be. If I should presume to tell this story to Roger of Glos or to his brothers or to their mother, they would ridicule me as a madman." Persisting further, William beseeched him resolutely and put forward with urgency many recognizable signs of his identity. But the priest, though he understood all that he heard, nonetheless pretended that he did not understand at all. Finally, overcome by William's insistent prayers, Walchelin agreed and promised that he would fulfill what he was asked to do. Then William repeated the details of his story once more and in a long tale he related many things to the priest. Meanwhile, the priest thought to himself that he would not dare to relay the commands of this wretched undead to anyone. "It is not right," he said, "to proclaim such things. There is no way that I will share what you have imparted to me with anyone." The enraged knight thrust out his hand, seized the priest by the throat, and uttered threats as he dragged him along the ground. The captive man could feel the hand that held him burning like fire, and in great distress he cried out, "Holy Mary, glorious mother of Christ, help me!" As soon as he called upon the most pious mother of the son of God, help ordained by the All-Mighty appeared at once. For a knight approached carrying only a sword in his right hand and brandishing the naked blade as though about to thrust, he said, "Why are you cursed men murdering my brother? Leave him alone and go!" Off they galloped at once in pursuit of the dark host.

When they had gone, the knight tarried on the road with Walchelin and asked him, "Do you not recognize me?" The priest responded, "No." The knight said, "I am Robert, the son of Ralph the Fair, and I am your brother." As the priest marveled at this unexpected turn of events and was tormented greatly on account of everything that he had seen and felt (as I have described), the knight began to recount for him many details of their shared childhood and to relate well-known proofs to him. The priest remembered well everything that he heard, but not daring to confess with his mouth, he denied everything. At last the knight said, "I marvel at your hardness and stubbornness. I took care of you after the death of our parents and I loved you more than any other person. I sent you to schools in France, I supplied you with clothing and cash in abundance, and I strived hard to help you in many other ways. Now you seem to have forgotten these things and disdain to recognize me at all." Once these truthful stories had been offered in abundance, the priest was then convinced by the knight's assertion and openly acknowledged his brother's account with tears. Then the knight said to him, "By all rights you deserve to die and to come with us now as a participant in our suffering because you took what was ours with a wicked rashness. No one else has ever dared to do this, but the mass that you sang today saved you from death. Also I have now been allowed to appear to you and to show you how wretched I am. After I last spoke with you in Normandy, blessed by you I traveled to England. There I met the end of my life by the Creator's command, and I have endured immense punishments for the sins by which I was so greatly burdened. The weapons that we carry burn like fire and they taint us with a terrifying stench and they oppress us greatly with their massive weight and they burn with a fire that does not go out. Up to now I have suffered unspeakable torment from punishments of this kind. But when you were ordained in England and you sang your first mass for the faithful departed, your father Ralph was released from punishment and my shield, which caused me such pain, fell off. I still carry this sword, as you can see, but this very year I await in faith for my release from this burden."

When the knight was relating these things and others like them and the priest was listening to him carefully, he saw at the knight's heels around his spurs a mass of blood in the shape of a human head. Marveling, the priest asked, "Why do you have such a great clot of blood on your feet?" And the knight responded, "It is not blood, but fire, and it weighs more than if I was carrying Mont Saint-Michel.[8] Because it was my custom to wear spurs that were bright and sharp so that I could gallop quickly to spill blood, I rightfully bear this enormous load upon my heels, by which I am weighed down so intolerably that I cannot evoke the extent of my pain to anyone. The living should constantly consider these things and tremble, indeed beware, lest they suffer such dire penalties for their own sins. I cannot speak with you any longer, brother, because I am compelled to follow in haste this wretched host. I beg you, remember me and assist me with your pious prayers and alms. For I hope to be saved one year from Palm Sunday and to be freed from all of these torments by the mercy of the Creator. Be mindful of your own fate and lead your life wisely, for it is already stained with many sins, and know that it will not last long. For the time being, keep silent. The things which you have inadvertently seen and heard, do not speak of them for now and do not try to tell anyone about them for three days."

Once he had said these things, the knight departed in haste and the priest was seriously ill for a week. Then, at last, he began to recover and went to Lisieux, where he told the entire story to Bishop Gilbert and received from him the remedies that he required. He lived in good health for another fifteen years. I heard from him personally all the things that I have written and many other things that have been lost to oblivion and I saw on his face the wound caused by the touch of the terrible knight. I have recorded these things for the edification of my readers, so that the just may be strengthened in their goodness and the wicked may be recovered from evil. Now I will return to the matter at hand.

AN ARMY WHITE AS SNOW[1]

In the middle of the twelfth century, a story attributed to Abbot Maiolus of Cluny (d. 994) concerning the appearance of an army of dead souls during a war between two dukes illustrated vividly the benefits for elite laymen of offering suffrages for the dead. Eusebius of Sardinia was a pious nobleman who had given over the revenues of an entire city to offer continuous alms for the poor and masses for the faithful departed. When his rival, Ostorgius of Sicily, took control of this city by force, God sent a vanguard of souls, "an army white as snow," who had been liberated from purgatorial suffering to win it back for Eusebius's holy purpose. Around 1150, a Cluniac monk told the story of the two dukes in the form of a long poem suitable for monastic rumination, amplifying its themes to create a dramatized lesson on the duties and rewards of knightly piety, but the story circulated most widely in the decades around 1200 as an exemplum, *a pithy moral tale intended for religious instruction that may have been redacted for use in sermons to laypeople.*

Concerning two dukes who warred against each other and were brought to terms of peace through a wondrous vision of souls.

I will tell you, my brothers, of an event involving two men that occurred in recent times, one that I heard about through a trustworthy and reliable report. It is a story to teach us the virtue of giving alms and inspire us never to tire of doing so. For alms not only benefit those who are still physically alive by securing forgiveness for their sins; rather, because they obtain salvation and redemption for souls, alms also give comfort to the dead, who no longer have opportunity to repent.

There were two dukes, one of Sardinia, the other of Sicily, who opposed each other in an enduring conflict that went on now in one's favor, now the other's. The duke of Sardinia was called Eusebius, the duke of Sicily Ostorgius. Eusebius had the greatest zeal possible concerning the dead, doing all that he could for them by celebrating masses, bestowing alms, and paying a tithe of all his goods. Moreover, he set apart for God and for the liberation of faithful souls one of the more prosperous cities in his possession; from that city he received nothing for his own use, but instead he caused tithes from all his realm and holdings to be brought there. In that place he assembled a very great multitude of the poor and continually fed and clothed them, and there throughout the churches celebrations of the Mass took place.

Now the other man, Ostorgius, was richer and mightier than Eusebius with respect to his kingdom and army, but in virtue he was much his rival's inferior. In all his earthly treasure, Ostorgius could not compare with him who so stored up for himself treasure in heaven; nor with his army could Ostorgius compare with him who, without knowing it, was readying for himself a greater host of reinforcements from the captives he was redeeming, as the event to be told hereafter makes plain.

And so Ostorgius advanced on the city that I just mentioned, the one set in service both to God and to the care of souls; he attacked it by ambush and captured it. When Eusebius, who was away at the time, heard this news through a messenger, he bore it with the deepest sadness and distress, so much so that he said he would rather have lost half his kingdom than this City of God (as he called it). Exhorting both himself and his men, he said, "O good soldiers, what shall we do? Shall we let pass unavenged this injury both to God and to ourselves? Rather let us, who are few, bravely and in God's name confront the many. May that man win whom the just and almighty King of heaven has ordained to win. For even if victory should go to the enemy, it would be a glorious thing for us to fall for the sake of divine justice."

His troops concurred and gave assent to his speech. Summoning his army around him, the duke went in pursuit of the enemy; laying an ambush in a very well-fortified place, he waited for the foe to show himself. The sentries appointed for Eusebius's camp, taking up position in a higher place, sought a vantage far and wide over the territory and were scanning it all around with their keen eyes, when, suddenly, there appeared a white vanguard that they could discern from far away. From what they saw, they immediately suspected that it belonged to the enemy, and so they stood attentive, waiting anxiously. As the persons they spied drew ever nearer, Eusebius's men at last perceived the great battle line of an army white as snow, riding on snow-white horses, with snow-white banners and arms of dazzling brightness. Immediately astonished at something so unheard of, they rushed to tell their anxious commander the news. Eusebius, now poised between hope and fear, roused his spirit in hope that the strangers were on the side of good, since he had heard they were white in color; at the same time, because he perceived them drawn up for battle, he feared they might pose some hostile threat.

And so, after seeking the counsel of his chiefs, he dispatched to the place four apt men to ask the strangers where they came from, where they were heading, and whether they came in peace or as enemies. As those emissaries approached, horsemen were likewise sent from the white host to give suitable answers to the questions of Eusebius's men. The duke's messengers offered peaceful greetings to the others as they met. They returned the greeting with the utmost courtesy. When Eusebius's men asked them the reason for their coming or for their arms being of such a kind, the others, perceiving them to be taken aback by the strange sight, first encouraged them with this friendly reply, "Stand firm; do not fear and do not hesitate. We come to you in peace, but armed against your enemies. We belong to the retinue of God, the highest King, and now we have come, as most faithful helpers to your lord, to overcome his enemy in battle." They added these words as well, saying, "Go and explain to your commander about us, that he should neither delay to come converse with us nor have fears about anything else." Returning with great joy, the messengers related to Eusebius the whole encounter in due order.

At once revived to hope as if emerging from a tomb of fear and sorrow, Eusebius rejoiced, felt triumphant, and now hastened to the place, relieved as if the victory were already obtained. As he approached the spot, he, too, met four snow-white riders coming toward him; he questioned them and heard the same reply that his own men had related. When the white riders in turn asked him whether he felt sorrow at the injury of having the city taken from him, he replied that, indeed, he felt extreme sorrow, and especially because he had dedicated this city to God and to the salvation of faithful souls. To this, the riders said, "Now sorrow no more, for whatever you have given or intended to give to God, who is himself the giver of all good things, will not perish for you even if some misfortune should snatch it away; rather it will remain a hundredfold for you in heaven. But, lest we draw out your state of worry any longer, we will now demand twice over from your enemy all that is yours by right, and, what is more, he will either surrender himself to you or we will bind and hand him over to your authority. Only take heed and, after readying your army, hasten to follow us." Then the duke journeyed back, commending himself to the will of God and to the trustworthiness of those strangers; he formed what troops he had into just a single legion and, confident in divine aid, advanced to battle against a force of sixty thousand. The army of white riders that went ahead of him formed a battle line forty thousand strong, it seemed, against Ostorgius.

Now Ostorgius, when he saw them approaching in such arms, was dumbstruck by something so unprecedented, and he, too, sent with all haste to inquire who they were and what they wanted. To his messengers the riders gave the same replies as they had to Eusebius's, namely that they were of God's own retinue; that they came, moreover, in order to seize the messengers' leader, Ostorgius, in retribution for his injury to God, and would do so if he did not immediately present himself to them and make satisfaction to God and to God's ally, Eusebius, for having invaded the city. After the messengers conveyed to their lord these tidings (so far as they understood them), he grew exceedingly frightened and sought the counsel of his men. And when he had listened to them, he set out together with all his troops for the place to which he had been commanded to go; and, questioning those men from the snow-white army who came forth to meet him, he heard for himself what one group of messengers after another had heard concerning the retinue of God. This time, in addition, the riders made dire threats against him, saying that divine wrath was drawing near him who had dared to steal, through deceit and treachery, a city donated to God. Goaded by fear, Ostorgius sued for peace, promising to make whatever amends they wished for his rash behavior. They all then rode back to the army of white horsemen, and as they were conversing, behold, Eusebius came upon them with his own troops. Immediately Ostorgius restored to him in double measure all that he had ever taken, and, beyond that, he surrendered himself along with all his men to Eusebius, as he had been ordered to do.

With affairs thus peacefully resolved, the army to which I have so often referred addressed Eusebius most amiably and asked him whether things had turned out well enough for his liking. When he, with many expressions of thanks, responded that he was indeed pleased, he also attempted subtly to find out who they were. Without delay, they replied, "We are those souls of the departed that the Lord's generous indulgence has released for your acts of kindness and your alms, and to whom, now freed from captivity to the Devil and to sin, he has given radiant dwellings in everlasting peace. Therefore, have no misgivings about what you have done on our behalf, because in return for such great kindness you have especially received God's favor, as well as the favor of all the saints and all the faithful dead. Know now that you have rescued all of us whom you see, and through the Lord's kind and gracious providence you will rescue many more still, so long as you do not abandon your present designs. Carry on, then, and, now that you have been admonished by our words and faithful service, strive to accomplish ever more perfectly the good that you hitherto performed out of kindness alone, so that the captives whom you set free before the just Judge may in turn intercede for you in his presence. For those who have been redeemed through you are praying that you would have a long life and health, so that many others who are yet to be redeemed through you may also rest in peace and, together with us, implore for you the forgiveness and grace of the eternal Judge and Lord." Having said these words, they asked for the duke's leave and appeared to travel back by the same route they had come. It can only be surmised, not expressed, how great an almsgiver for the dead he thereafter became, since he had previously done so many good deeds while not even aware of their great profit, which now he knew firsthand.

We have learned of these things through the telling of the master and abbot Maiolus from the monastery of Cluny, a man of highest authority, who, during the conflict between the two rulers, was detained as a prisoner while he was busy overseeing the abbeys that were under his care in those lands. But even if, at this point, someone is willing to trust Maiolus as an authority for the story, it is possible that the same person may not so easily give credence to the event itself, a thing strange and previously unheard of. Perhaps someone will also raise the objection that the spirits of souls are described in the story as having appeared in bodily form, and absurdly so, since spirits, being incorporeal, can avail themselves of nothing that is corporeal. Against this objection one should respond that, for incorporeal spirits, which are invisible to our bodily eyes, it is necessary to appear acting as bodies do, by which means they are able to be seen and understood. But you will say, "Where do their horses and weapons come from?" Well, when in dreams you perceive yourself to be sailing or riding, where do those horses or ships come from? Just as your spirit, by using a corporeal form, creates an image of the activities you perform with your body, so, too, the events in this story were able to happen, and there is nothing absurd about them.

But, lest I appear to have rashly advanced this argument on my own, did not Elisha see a vision of this kind, as we read in the Book of Kings (that is, when the king of Syria sent the might of his army to capture him)?[2] And did not Elisha, by praying to God, cause his servant [Gehazi] to share in the vision with him, so that he would have that man as a trustworthy witness? For he saw how the entire mountain there, where the two men stood together, shone all around them with the brilliance of a heavenly army; and he saw how great a force of horses and fiery chariots fortified the place. No one can justifiably doubt that those were angelic spirits; and so, since this sort of vision was revealed through heavenly spirits, it should not seem incredible that something similar happened involving human souls that have now cast off their flesh. The fact that souls, after shedding their bodies, imitate the habits of their bodily activities is no greater a cause for wonder than the fact that angelic spirits, when assuming human form, produce the appearance of these same activities in themselves. But all questioning can be more quickly resolved if one calls to mind that anything the divine Majesty wills it can also accomplish. Whatever the present story may amount to, let us with whole and unquestioning faith regard one thing as certain and persuade ourselves of it with trust: namely that whatever good we do for the departed faithful both benefits them by conferring eternal rest and salvation, and benefits us, who do such works, by meriting God's grace and fellowship with those who are faithful to him. Therefore, we should not neglect the care for the dead, especially our loved ones and our brothers [in monastic life]. On the contrary, the more uncertain we are concerning their fates, the more attentively should we come to their aid, so far as our means allow, and commend them to our most kind Redeemer by our daily prayers, and mourn less for the death of their bodies than for their having sinned against God, the just Judge.

NORTHERN HORRORS

The cultures of medieval Scandinavia encountered Christian missionaries as early as the eighth century, but the process of conversion took many hundreds of years. With Christianity came literary culture; in the thirteenth century, Scandinavian Christians from Iceland and Denmark preserved the heroic traditions of their people in sagas written in Latin and Old Norse. These historical tales featured mighty heroes embarking on perilous voyages to unknown lands (including North America) as well as legendary feuds between the ancestors of prominent families. Many of these stories were set in the distant past of the tenth and eleventh centuries. Their purpose was primarily to entertain, but they also preserved with evident pride tales of the pre-Christian past that informed the identity of medieval Scandinavians. While the people of the north embraced their new Christian faith, they refused to abandon the heroes of their own antiquity.

The restless dead play a prominent role in the Scandinavian sagas. Unlike the ghosts of the Christian tradition, which appear to the living to appeal for suffrages to relieve their torment in purgatory, the dead in the sagas were usually a nuisance to their family and friends. Sometimes they lingered in their old homes as an unsettling presence. More often, however, they killed livestock, destroyed property, and terrorized individuals as much with their violence as with their ghastly appearance. Left unchecked, they could turn a settlement into a wilderness. Laying the malevolent dead to rest was a heroic feat of strength. In Scandinavian lore, the decapitation of a corpse could stop its wandering, as could the impaling or burning of its body. But only the bravest of warriors were willing to "struggle under great pressure and in considerable peril" against the unearthly strength of walking corpses.

THE RAVENOUS DEAD

In the early thirteenth century, a cleric named Saxo Grammaticus (c. 1150–1220) in the entourage of Absalon, archbishop of Lund, wrote a history of his people in Latin called The Deeds of the Danes. In sixteen books, he told the story of the Danish people from the time of King Dan, the putative founder of the royal dynasty, until 1187. Decades in the making, Saxo's massive work braided information drawn from ancient and medieval historical traditions and legendary material from oral sources into a sweeping narrative of the Danish past. While supernatural elements were few and far between in The Deeds of the Danes, the story of the burial of Asvith and the voluntary entombment of his oath-bound friend Asmund provides unsettling testimony that friendship in life was no protection from the insatiable hunger of the restless dead.

Another version of this story appeared in the Old Norse saga known as The Story of Egil One-Hand and Asmund Berserkers-Slayer, written in the fourteenth century. In this tale, two exceptionally strong lads competed against each other in every test of strength they could devise. Agreeing that they were equal in prowess, they decided to join forces, becoming blood brothers and promising to share the plunder from their battles with berserkers and giants. Their pact included the promise of one final struggle between them: the one who lived longer had to endure three nights buried alive in the same chamber as the corpse of his friend.

(A) A RENDING GHOUL[1]

In the meantime, Asvith was consumed by an illness and entrusted with his dog and his horse to a cave in the ground. Because of their oath of friendship, Asmund allowed himself to be buried alive with him and food was furnished for him to eat. And then Erik happened upon the tomb of Asvith by chance as he traversed the highlands with his army. Believing that there were treasures therein, the Swedes broke through the hill with their mattocks. Only then did they realize that they had opened a cave of much greater depth than they had first imagined. To explore the cave, it was necessary for someone to be lowered into it while tied to a dangling rope. One among the most eager young men was chosen by lot for the task. When Asmund saw the young man being lowered in a basket attached to a cord, he immediately threw him out of the basket and climbed into it himself. He then gave a signal to those who were standing on the surface and holding on to the rope to raise the basket. They pulled the basket up in the hope of great wealth and they beheld instead the unexpected sight of the man they had hauled up. Terrified by his sudden appearance and believing that a dead man had returned to life, they cast aside the rope and fled in all directions. Indeed, Asmund's face was terrifying to behold for it was covered in gore like that of a mangled corpse. He tried to call them back as they ran away, shouting that they were falsely afraid of a living man. Looking at him, Erik marveled at the sight of Asmund's bloody countenance, for his entire face was stained red. Indeed, Asvith had returned to life at night, and had torn off Asmund's left ear in their repeated struggles, leaving the horrible spectacle of a raw and unhealed scar. When asked by the onlookers to relate how he had received the wound, this is what he said:

"Why are you so amazed to look upon me, emptied of all color?
Truly, any living man becomes diminished among the dead!

Every dwelling in this world is unfortunate and difficult for those
    on their own;

wretched are those who luck has deprived of other people's aid.
This cave and empty night and darkness and this ancient hollow
have snatched away all pleasure from my eyes and from my soul.
The dreadful earth, this rotten tomb, and a heavy tide of foulness
have diminished the fairness of my once youthful face,
and have sapped the great vigor that I used to have.
Beyond all of this, I have retained my strength against the undead
while struggling under great pressure and in considerable peril.
Asvith returned from the dead and rushed upon me with tearing claws,
returning with Stygian strength to renew fierce battles after his death.

Why are you so amazed to look upon me, emptied of all color?
Truly, any living man becomes diminished among the dead!

I do not know by what daring of the god of darkness
the spirit of Asvith was sent forth from hell
to devour the horse with his ferocious teeth
and to offer the dog to his unspeakable jaws.
Not content with eating the horse or the dog
he turned his grasping claws on me
and, having slashed my cheek, he ripped off my ear.
Hence the semblance of my torn face inspires horror,
stained with blood from this cruel wound.
But that monster did not escape unpunished,
for I quickly lopped off his head with my sword
and stabbed his body with a piercing stake.

Why are you so amazed to look upon me, emptied of all color?
Truly, any living man becomes diminished among the dead!"

(B) CONTESTING WITH A CORPSE[2]

Aran said to Asmund, "We must never test each other's skill
with weapons, since we'd both end up dead. I'd like us to enter
a sworn brotherhood, each of us pledging himself to avenge
the other, and sharing equally each other's money, now and in
the future." It was also a part of their pact that the one who

lived the longer should raise a burial mound over the one who was dead, and place in it as much money as he thought fit; and the survivor was to sit in the mound over the dead for three nights, but after that he would be free to go away . . .

Less than a month after their arrival [in Tartary], Aran died suddenly one day as he was going into his palace. The corpse was dressed for burial according to custom. Asmund had a burial mound raised over Aran and beside the corpse he put in the mound Aran's horse with a saddle and bridle, his banners and armor, his hawk and hound. Aran was seated on a chair in full armor.

Asmund had another chair brought into the mound and sat himself down there, after which the mound was covered up. During the first night Aran got up from his chair, killed the hawk and hound, and ate them. On the second night he got up again from his chair, killed the horse and tore it to pieces; then he took great bites of horseflesh with his teeth, the blood streaming down from his mouth all the while he was eating. He offered to let Asmund share his meal, but Asmund said nothing. The third night Asmund became very drowsy, and the first thing he knew, Aran had got him by the ears and tore them off. Asmund drew his short-sword and sliced off Aran's head, then he got some fire and burned Aran to ashes. Asmund went to the rope and was hauled out of the mound, which was then covered up again. Asmund took all of the treasures in the mound with him.

OLD GHOSTS, NEW LAWS[1]

The thirteenth-century Eyrbyggja Saga *was the story of several generations of Norse settlers in Iceland from their arrival in the late ninth century to the early eleventh century, when Christianity had finally taken a firm hold on Icelandic society. The ghosts in this saga are inconsistent in their behavior, as are the responses of the story's protagonists. The specter of Thorolf was a malevolent presence until brave individuals built a wall around his grave to prevent his wandering and finally laid him to rest by burning his blackened corpse and spreading his ashes in the sea. By contrast, the ghosts of Thorodd and his drowned companions were much more civil. They attended their own funerary feasts (a good omen, according to Icelandic lore!), but when they lingered too long in their old abodes, their families compelled them to leave by charging them with trespassing and then banishing them completely through Christian rituals of purification. This story illustrated how the new laws of Icelandic society, both civil and religious, now held sway over the unruly ways of the pagan past.*

After Thorolf died, a good many people found it more and more unpleasant to stay out of doors once the sun had begun to go down. As the summer wore on, it became clear that Thorolf was not lying quiet, for after sunset no one out of doors was left in peace. There was another thing, too; the oxen that had been used to haul Thorolf's body were ridden to death by demons, and every beast that came near his grave went out of its mind and howled itself to death. The shepherd at Hvamm often came running home with Thorolf after him. One day that autumn neither sheep nor shepherd came back to the farm, and next morning, when a search was made for him, the shepherd was found dead not far from Thorolf's grave, his corpse coal-black, and every bone in his body broken. They buried him near to Thorolf. All the sheep in the valley were found dead, and the rest that had strayed into the mountains were never seen again. Any bird that happened to land on Thorolf's cairn dropped dead on the spot. All this grew so troublesome that no one would risk using the valley for grazing any longer.

At night the people at Hvamm would hear loud noises from outside, and it often sounded as if there was somebody sitting astride the roof. That winter, Thorolf often appeared on the farm, haunting his widow most of all. A lot of people suffered badly from it, but she was almost driven out of her wits, and eventually the strain of it killed her. Her body was taken up to Thorsardale to be buried beside Thorolf's cairn, and after that the people of Hvamm abandoned the farm.

Thorolf now began haunting the whole valley, and most of the farms were abandoned because of it. His ghost was so malignant that it killed people and others had to run for their lives. All those who died were later seen in his company.

Everyone complained about this reign of terror and thought it was Arnkel's business to put a stop to it. Those who thought themselves safer with Arnkel than anywhere else were invited to stay at his farm, as Thorolf and his retinue caused no harm when Arnkel was around. As the winter wore on, people grew so scared of Thorolf's ghost that they were too frightened to travel, no matter how urgent their business.

So the winter passed. Spring brought fine weather; and when all the frost in the ground had thawed, Arnkel sent a messenger over to Karsstad asking the Thorbrandssons to come and help him carry Thorolf away from Thorsardale and find him another resting place. It was the law in those days, just as it is now, that everybody must help bury the dead if asked to give assistance. All the same, when word reached the Thorbrandssons they said they had no reason to help Arnkel and his men out of their troubles. But their father Thorbran said, "You ought to do whatever the law requires. You must not refuse to do what you've been asked." So Thorodd said to the messenger, "Go and tell Arnkel that I will stand in for my brothers. I'll go up to Ulfar's Fell and meet him there."

The messenger went back and told Arnkel. He got ready at once and set out with eleven men, a few oxen, and some tools for digging. First they went up to Ulfar's Fell, where Thorodd Thorbrandsson joined them with two more men, then they all traveled together across the ridge into Thorsardale and up to Thorolf's cairn. When they broke into the cairn they saw his body was uncorrupted and very ugly to look at. They pulled him out of the grave, laid him on the sled, hitched up a powerful pair of oxen, and hauled him up as far as Ulfarsfell Ridge. By then the oxen were so exhausted they had to get another yoke of them to haul the corpse west along the ridge. Arnkel wanted to take Thorolf all the way to Vadilshofdi and bury him there, but when they came to the end of the ridge, the oxen panicked and broke loose. They ran down the ridge, then north by the hillside, past the farmstead at Ulfar's Fell, and so down to the sea, where they both collapsed. By now Thorolf had grown so heavy that the men could hardly shift him, but they managed to drag him up to a small knoll nearby, and there they buried him. This place has been known as Twist-Foot's Knoll ever since. After that Arnkel had a wall built right across the knoll just behind the grave, so high that only a bird in flight could get over it, and here Thorolf rested quietly enough as long as Arnkel lived. You can still see traces of the wall.

———

In the summer that Christianity was adopted by law in Iceland [c. 1000], a ship from Dublin put in at Snæfell Ness. Most of the crew came from Ireland and the Hebrides, but there were some Norwegians, too. They lay at Rif for a good part of the summer, then with a fair wind sailed up the fjord to Dogurdar Ness, where a number of people from the neighborhood came to trade with them.

There was a Hebridean woman on board called Thorgunna, and the crew said she had some valuable things with her, difficult to get in Iceland. When Thurid of Frodriver heard about it, she was very keen to see all this finery, for she was a vain woman and extremely fond of elegant clothes and rich adornment. She traveled to the ship to see Thorgunna and asked if she had something very special in ladies' clothing. Thorgunna said she had nothing for sale, but added that she had plenty of fine things to wear herself, so that she had no need to feel ashamed to go to feasts and other gatherings. Thurid asked her to show her her things. Thorgunna did so, and Thurid thought them attractive and tastefully made, but not particularly expensive. Thurid made an offer for them, but Thorgunna refused to sell. Then Thurid invited her to come and stay with her, for she kept thinking about all the fine things she had seen and hoping she could get them from her later on.

"Yes, I'd like to stay with you," said Thorgunna. "But there's something you should know. I'm not all that keen to pay cash for my board and lodging. I'm still a strong woman, and I don't mind working as long as I do not have to do heavy work. But I will make up my own mind about how much of my money I pay out."

Thorgunna spoke very stiffly, but that did not prevent Thurid from urging her to come and stay with her, so Thorgunna had her baggage put ashore, a heavy trunk, which she kept locked, and a lighter one, and both were taken to Frodriver. As soon as she arrived, she asked to be shown to her bed, and was given a place in the inner part of the main room. She opened the big chest and took from it a set of bedclothes, beautifully made. She spread English sheets on her bed, laid a silk-covered quilt on top, then took bed curtains from the chest and a canopy as well. It was all so marvelous, no one could remember having ever seen anything like it.

"How much would you take for the whole set?" asked Thurid.

"I don't care how refined and ladylike you are," said Thorgunna, "I am not going to sleep on bare straw just to satisfy you."

Thurid was far from pleased about this, and it was the last time she offered to buy Thorgunna's things from her.

Thorgunna spent every day weaving, unless there was hay-making to do, and when the weather was good, she used to work at drying the hay in the home meadow. She had a special

rake made for her, which she let no one else touch. Thorgunna
was a massive woman, tall, broad built, and getting very stout.
She had dark eyebrows and narrow eyes, and beautiful chestnut
hair. Her manner was always very proper, and she used to go to
Mass every morning before starting work, but she was hard to
get on with and wasted little time on conversation. People
thought she must be in her fifties, though she was a woman who
still had a lot of life left in her.

By this time Thorir Wood-Leg and his wife Thorgrima
Witch-Face had come to live at Frodriver, and soon there was
trouble between them and Thorgunna. Kjartan the farmer's
son was the only one there Thorgunna took to, and she liked
him a lot, but he kept his distance, which she found extremely
irritating. Kjartan was thirteen or fourteen at the time, a big
lad and very manly.

The summer was wet, but there were good drying spells in the
autumn once the home meadow at Frodriver had been mowed,
and nearly half of that hay was fully dry. One day was ideal for
drying, calm and clear, with not a cloud in sight. Thorodd was
up early that morning and arranged the work for the day. Some
of the farmhands were to cart the hay home and others to stack
it. He told the women to help with the drying of the hay, and
shared out the work between them. Thorgunna was given as
much hay to dry as would have been winter fodder for an ox.

Everything went smoothly to begin with, but in the early afternoon a black cloud began to form in the north, just above
Skor, and soon it swept across the sky, making straight for the
farmstead. It looked as if the cloud would bring rain, and
Thorodd told them to start stacking the hay, but Thorgunna
kept turning hers as hard as she could, and refused to begin
stacking it even though she had been told to. The dark cloud
raced across the sky, and when it was just over the farmstead
at Frodriver, things were so overcast they could see nothing
beyond the meadow, and hardly an arm's length inside it.
After that there was such a heavy cloudburst that all the hay
on the ground was drenched. The cloud vanished suddenly,
and when the weather cleared up again, they saw that the
shower had been one of blood.

In the evening there was a fine drying spell, and the blood dried quickly, except on the hay that Thorgunna had spread. Neither this nor the rake she had used would dry.

Thorodd asked Thorgunna what this omen could mean, but she said she couldn't tell. "Most likely it forebodes the death of someone here," she said.

Thorgunna went home in the evening and straight to bed. She took off the blood-soaked clothes she was wearing, lay down on the bed, and gave a heavy sigh. People could see that she had been taken ill. The shower had fallen nowhere else, only on Frodriver. Thorgunna refused food that evening. The next morning Thorodd went to see her about her illness and to find out when she thought she might be feeling better. She said she believed this illness would be her last.

"I've found you to be the most sensible person here," she said, "and that's why I'm telling you what to do with the things I leave behind. You may not think much of me, but everything I tell you will turn out exactly as I say, and nothing good will come of it if you don't follow my wishes. This first omen is a clear indication that something serious is bound to happen unless every step is taken to prevent it."

"You're probably not far from the truth," said Thorodd. "I promise to follow all your instructions."

"Here's what I want," said Thorgunna. "Should I die of this illness I want my body taken to Skalholt, because something tells me it will soon be the most venerated place in the land. I know there are priests there to sing Mass for me as well, and that's why I want you to take me there. In return you can have sufficient of my belongings to repay you handsomely for all your trouble, but before you start dividing up my property, Thurid is to have the scarlet cloak. I'm doing this to make her less unhappy about the disposal of the rest of my things. Next, out of all the things I'm leaving with you, take whatever you and your wife want most, to cover your expenses. There's a gold ring of mine that must be given to the church, but my bed and all its furnishings I want burned to ashes, for they'll never do anyone much good. I'm not saying this because I begrudge these things to anyone who could use them, but I must be firm about it. I wouldn't like to be responsible for all the trouble people will bring on themselves if they don't respect my wishes."

Thorodd promised to do all that she asked of him. Soon after, her illness took a turn for the worse and she lingered on only a few days before she died.

The body was taken to the church and Thorodd had a coffin made for it. Next day he carried the bedclothes outside, gathered some firewood, and made a bonfire. When his wife, Thurid, came and asked what he was up to, he said he was going to burn them, just as Thorgunna had asked.

"If I have my way," she said, "I'm not having you burn valuable things like this."

"She meant every word when she said it wouldn't do to ignore her warning," said Thorodd.

"It only goes to show what an envious woman she was," said Thurid. "She was too mean to let anyone else enjoy them, and that's why she told you to do it. Whatever we decide to do, I can't see what harm can come of it."

"I don't think ignoring her wishes will do us much good," he said.

But Thurid put her arms round his neck and begged him not to burn the bed furnishings. She kept pleading with him until he agreed only to destroy the eiderdown and pillows, while Thurid took the quilt, the bed curtains, and the canopy. All the same, neither of them felt really happy about it. After that they got ready to send the corpse off for burial.

For the journey Thorodd chose men he could rely on and gave them his best horses. The corpse was wrapped in an unstitched linen shroud and laid in a coffin. They set off, taking the usual route south across the moor, and nothing much happened on their journey till they came south of Valbjarnarvellir. As they crossed the sodden moorland there, the packhorse kept throwing off the coffin. On they went, south to the Nordur River, and crossed it at Eyjar Ford through very deep water. The weather was squally with sleet and heavy rain. Eventually they came to a farm called Nether Ness in Stafholtstungur and asked to stay the night, but the farmer refused to give them hospitality. It was getting very late, and they thought they could

go no farther, as it seemed unwise to risk fording the Hvit River
at night, so they unloaded the horses, carried the coffin into a
storehouse near the door, walked into the living room, and took
off their clothes, intending to spend the night there, without
food if necessary.

The household went to bed before it grew dark. They hadn't
been long in their beds when they heard loud noises coming
from the larder, and some of them went to see if thieves had
broken into the house. When they came to the larder, there
was a tall woman, stark naked, not a stitch of clothing on her,
getting a meal ready. The people of the household were too
scared when they saw her to come anywhere near. As soon as
the corpse bearers heard about it, they went to see for themselves what was going on. The woman was Thorgunna, and
everyone thought it best to leave her in peace. When she had
finished doing what she wanted in the larder, she carried the
food into the living room, laid the table, and served the meal.

"Before we part, you may end up very sorry that you didn't
treat us more hospitably," said the corpse bearers to the
farmer.

"We'll gladly give you food and anything else you need,"
said the farmer and his wife.

And as soon as the farmer had made them welcome, Thorgunna walked out of the room and didn't reappear.

Now a lamp was lit in the living room, and the travelers
were helped out of their wet clothes and given dry things. They
sat down at the table and made the sign of the cross over the
food, and the farmer had every corner of the house sprinkled
with holy water. The travelers ate their food, and it did them
no harm at all, even though it had been prepared by Thorgunna. They spent a very comfortable night there.

In the morning they got ready to be on their way, and the rest
of the journey went without a hitch. Everyone who heard what
had happened at the first farm thought it best to give them all that
they asked for, and nothing else happened on the journey. They
came to Skalholt and handed over the precious gifts Thorgunna
had left for the church there, which the priests accepted with

pleasure. So Thorgunna was buried, and the corpse bearers set off for home. They had an easy journey and got back safely.

The farm at Frodriver had a large living room with a bed closet behind it, as was usual in those days. In front of the living room there were two storerooms on either side of the door, one for dried fish and the other for flour. They used to have a great fire burning in the living room every evening, and people would sit beside it for hours on end before they had their evening meal.

The evening the corpse bearers came back [from burying Thorgunna], the people at Frodriver were sitting by the fireside when they saw a half-moon appear on the paneled wall. Everyone could see it. The moon kept circling round the room, backing from left to right, and stayed in sight as long as people remained at the fire.

Thorodd asked Thorir Wood-Leg what it meant, and Thorir said it was a fatal moon. "There'll be deaths here," he added.

It went on like this for a whole week; every evening the same weird moon appeared in the living room.

The next thing to happen was that the shepherd came home one day, badly shaken. He had little to say, but when he did speak, he was very ill-tempered. He avoided other people and kept muttering to himself, so everyone thought he must have been bewitched. This went on for some time. When two weeks of winter had passed, he came home one evening and went straight to bed and lay down. Next morning, when people went to see him they found him dead. He was buried at the church there, and not long afterward massive hauntings began at the place.

One night Thorir Wood-Leg went out to the privy to relieve himself, and when he was on his way back to the house, he saw the shepherd standing in front of the door. Thorir tried to get inside, but the shepherd barred his way. Thorir began walking away, but the shepherd came after him, picked him up, and threw him hard against the door. This gave Thorir a nasty shock and a good many bruises, but he struggled back to bed. Later he became ill, then died, and was buried at the church there. After that, the pair of them, Thorir Wood-Leg and the shepherd, were often seen together. As you might expect, people were terrified.

After Thorir's death, one of Thorodd's farmhands fell ill. He lay in bed for three days, and then he died. Soon people started dying one after another, six of them in all. This was just about the beginning of Advent, but in those days, people in Iceland didn't observe the fast.

The storeroom was stacked so full with dried fish that the door would hardly open. The pile of fish went right up to the crossbeam, and people had to use a ladder to get at it from above. Then things started happening. Night after night, as people were sitting at the fire, they could hear something tearing at the dried fish, but when they went to look, not a living thing could they see there.

That winter, shortly before Christmas, Thorodd went out to Ness to get more dried fish for himself. There were six of them together in a ten-oared boat, and they spent the night at Ness. In the evening, after Thorodd had gone and the fire had been lit, people came into the living room and saw a seal's head coming up through the floor. One of the servants was the first to notice this as she came in. She grabbed a club in the doorway and hit the seal on the head, which only made it rise up out of the ground a little more. Then it turned its eyes toward the canopy from Thorgunna's bed. One of the farmhands came up and started hitting the seal, but it kept rising farther up with every blow, until its flippers emerged. At that the man fainted, and everyone was paralyzed with horror, except for young Kjartan, who rushed up with a sledge-hammer and struck the seal on the head. It was a powerful blow, but the seal only shook its head and gazed around. Kjartan went on hammering the head and driving it down like a nail into the floor until the seal disappeared, then he flattened out the floor above its head. Throughout the winter it was always the same story; Kjartan was the only one who could put fear into the ghosts.

The next morning Thorodd and his men put out from Ness with their dried fish, and they were all drowned off Enni. The boat and the fish were washed ashore there, but the bodies were never found.

When the news came to Frodriver, Kjartan and Thurid invited their neighbors to a funeral feast, at which they used the
Christmas ale. On the first evening of the feast, when all the
guests were seated, Thorodd and his companions came into
the room drenched to the skin. Everyone welcomed Thorodd
and his men, and thought this a happy omen because in those
days it was believed that drowned people had been well received by the sea goddess, Ran, if they came to their own funeral feast. At that time a good many heathen beliefs still
prevailed, though people were baptized and supposed to be
Christians. Thorodd and his men walked across the main
room, which had two doors, and into the living room. They
ignored the greetings people gave them and sat down at the
fire. The people ran out of the living room, but Thorodd and
his men stayed on until the fire began to burn very low, then
they went away. As long as the funeral feast lasted this continued: every evening the drowned men would come to the fire. It
gave people at the feast plenty to talk about, but some of them
thought it would stop once the feast was over.

After the feast all the guests went back home and the place
seemed rather dull without them. In the evening after the
guests had gone the fire in the living room was lit as usual, and
as soon as it was ablaze, Thorodd and his companions came
in, all of them soaking wet. They sat down at the fire and
began squeezing the water out of their clothes. No sooner had
they taken their seats than Thorir Wood-Leg and his six companions came into the room, all of them covered with earth.
They started shaking the dirt out of their clothes and throwing mud at Thorodd and his men. The people ran out of the
room, as you would expect, and that evening they had to do
without light, heating stones, and everything else the fire provided. The next evening they lit a fire in another room, hoping
the dead men would not come there, but things turned out otherwise. Everything happened just as before, and both parties
came to sit by the fire. On the third evening, Kjartan suggested
they should light a large fire in the living room, and another
fire in a separate room for the household, so they tried that. As
it turned out, Thorodd and the other dead men came and sat at

the large fire, while the living sat at the smaller one, and so it continued throughout the Christmas season.

By that time the noises in the fish pile had grown much louder, and day and night people could hear the fish being torn up. Soon the time came for the fish to be eaten, and they had a look at the pile. Someone got on top of it and saw a tail sticking out. It had the look of a singed oxtail, but was covered with short seal hair. The man on the stack took hold of it. First he tried to pull it out himself, then called for others to come and help him. Several people, men and women, joined him on the stack and kept pulling at the tail, but they couldn't budge it an inch. Everybody thought the tail was dead, but as they were struggling to get it out, the tail tore right through their hands, and the skin was ripped off the palms of those who had been pulling hardest. The tail was never seen again. They started clearing the fish out of the storeroom, and when they got down into the pile, they saw that all the meat had been torn off the fish and only the skins left behind, but no sign of a living creature in it anywhere.

Shortly thereafter Thorgrima Witch-Face, Thorir Wood-Leg's widow, fell ill, and after a short spell in bed she died. On the very evening of her burial she was seen in her husband's company. Then the sickness that had been raging when the hairy tail had made its first appearance broke out again, this time killing more women than men. Six people died one after another, and the hauntings and night walkings drove others away from the farm. There had been thirty servants there in the autumn, but eighteen of them had died, five more ran away, and by midwinter there were only seven of them left.

After these weird events had been going on for some time, Kjartan set off one day over to Helgafell to see his uncle Snorri and ask his advice about what should be done to put an end to them. At that time there was a priest staying at Helgafell, sent to Snorri by Gizur the White. Snorri asked the priest to go with Kjartan to Frodriver along with his son Thord the Cat and six other people. They must burn the canopy from Thorgunna's bed, said Snorri, and then summon all the dead to

a door-court.² After that the priest was to sing Mass, conse-
crate water, and hear people's confessions. They rode to Frodriver, and on the way there they asked the neighbors to come
with them.

It was Candlemas Eve when they came to Frodriver, and the
fire had just been lit. Thurid had been taken with the same illness
as those who had died. Kjartan went straight into the living room
and saw Thorodd and the other dead people sitting by the fire as
usual. He pulled down the canopy from Thorgunna's bed,
plucked a brand from the fire, then went out and burned to ashes
all the bed furnishings that had once belonged to Thorgunna.

Next Kjartan summonsed Thorir Wood-Leg, and Thord the
Cat summonsed Thorodd for trespassing on the home and
robbing people of life and health. All the dead ones at the fire
were summonsed in the same way. Then the door-court was
held and charges made, the proper procedure of ordinary law
courts being observed throughout. The jury was appointed,
testimony was taken, and the cases were summed up and referred for judgment. As sentence was being passed on Thorir
Wood-Leg, he rose to his feet, "I sat here as long as people
would let me," he said, then went out through the other door
where the court was not being held.

After that, sentence was passed on the shepherd, and he
stood up. "I'll go now," he said, "and it seems I should have
gone sooner."

When Thorgrima Witch-Face heard her sentence, she stood
up, too. "I stayed as long as you let me," she said.

So they all were sentenced one after another, and as they
were sentenced, they got up, made some such remark, and left
the room. It was clear that none of them wanted to go.

Thorodd was the last to be sentenced. When he heard the
judgment, he stood up. "There's no peace here," he said, "we'd
best all be on our way." And with that he walked out.

Then Kjartan and the others went back inside, and the priest
carried holy water and sacred relics to every corner of the
house. The next day he sang all the prayers and celebrated
Mass with great solemnity, and there were no more dead

people haunting Frodriver after that. Thurid began to improve
and got well again. In the spring after all these strange events,
Kjartan engaged new servants. He farmed at Frodriver for a
long time, and people thought him a very courageous man.

————————

Thorodd Thorbrandsson was still farming at Alftafjord and
owned the estates at Ulfarsfell and Orlygsstad as well. Thorolf
Twist-Foot's ghost haunted these farms in such a violent fash-
ion that no one would live there. Bolstad was now derelict, for
once Arnkel was dead, Thorolf had begun to haunt there, too,
killing men and beasts alike, so that no one has ever had the
courage to farm there since. After Bolstad was abandoned,
Thorolf Twist-Foot moved on to Ulfarsfell, where he did a
great deal of damage. Everyone on the farm was terrified
whenever Thorolf Twist-Foot appeared on the scene. The
farmer at Ulfarsfell was Thorodd's tenant, so he went to Karsstad to complain, saying everyone felt that unless something
was done, Thorolf would never stop until he had cleared the
neighborhood of men, beasts, and all. "I can't stay there any
longer unless something is done about it," he said.

Thorodd listened to his tenant, but was not sure how to deal
with the problem. In the morning he had his horse brought
along, told his servants to join him, and asked some of his
neighbors to come, too. Off they went to Twist-Foot's Knoll,
where Thorolf was buried, broke open the grave, and saw
Thorolf lying there, uncorrupted with an ugly look about him.
He was as black as death and swollen to the size of an ox.
They tried to move the dead man, but were unable to shift him
an inch. Then Thorodd put a lever under him, and that was
how they managed to lift him out of the grave. After that they
rolled him down to the foreshore, built a great pyre there, set
fire to it, pushed Thorolf in and burned him to ashes. Even so,
it took the fire a long time to have any effect on Thorolf. A
fierce gale had blown up, so as soon as the corpse began to
burn the ashes were scattered everywhere, but all that they
could get hold of they threw into the sea.

STRANGE TALES OF MYSTERY AND TERROR

By the later Middle Ages, tales about petitioning ghosts and unruly corpses had become commonplace throughout northern Europe. As we have seen, in the decades around 1200, Caesarius of Heisterbach composed stories of restless souls for a primarily monastic audience in the tradition of Gregory the Great, Peter Damian, and Peter the Venerable. But in the writings of Caesarius and his contemporaries, we can also discern the inflection of new developments in Christian doctrine. At the Fourth Lateran Council (1215), Pope Innocent III called upon all Christians to take greater responsibility for their own salvation by making confession to a priest at least once a year and by participating more frequently in the Mass. Moreover, it was during the thirteenth century that the doctrine of purgatory—the existence of an intermediate place in the afterlife where the souls of sinful Christians underwent a cleansing by fire in preparation for entry into heaven—received its official definition at the First Council of Lyon (1245).

Christian authors immediately recognized the utility of ghost stories in promulgating these new church doctrines and responded by including laymen and laywomen as actors in their tales with much greater frequency than before. For the first time, we see a much more pronounced concern for the otherworldly fate of everyday people in a literary tradition previously aimed almost exclusively at the religious and secular elite. Beginning in the thirteenth century, medieval Christians at all levels of society, from royal courts to rural villages, heard strange tales of mystery and terror about the returning dead *that prompted them to weigh with much greater care than before the moral decisions of their daily lives in light of the destiny of their very own souls. One of the recurrent features in these tales that the storytellers do not fully explain is the need for the ghosts to be "conjured" by the living in order for them to communicate their sins and the terms of absolution that will finally lay them to rest. The Latin verb conjurare is a legal term that dates back to the early Middle Ages. In the context of these ghost stories, it means to beseech someone to state their identity and purpose with the invocation of God's name.*

RECREATION FOR
AN EMPEROR[1]

*In the first decades of the thirteenth century, a successful
administrator and canon lawyer of English origin named
Gervase of Tilbury (c. 1150–c. 1228) compiled a massive
compendium of stories to provide recreational reading for his
friend and patron Emperor Otto IV (1175–1218). Born in
England, Gervase became an international traveler, who stud-
ied and taught in northern Italy before entering the service of
powerful secular and ecclesiastical leaders, including Henry II,
king of England (r. 1154–1189), William of the White Hands,
archbishop of Rheims (r. 1176–1202), King William II of Sicily
(r. 1166–1198), and Imbert, archbishop of Arles (r. 1191–1202).
During his travels, Gervase collected hundreds of stories about
history, geography, cosmology, and the marvels of the natural
world and assembled them into an encyclopedia called* Recreation for an Emperor (Otia Imperialia). *His goal was didactic;
many of the stories had morals about the benefits of being a
good king and a good Christian. But Gervase took an obvious
delight in crafting a compelling narrative, especially on the topic
of marvels. Unlike miracles, which were the result of divine
power, marvels were natural phenomena, the causes of which
human beings did not yet fully understand.*

*Among the "marvels of every province" recorded in his
work, Gervase related stories about animals with human
characteristics, enchanted places, and spirits both malevolent
and benign, like poltergeists and fairies. Ghosts haunt his
tales in great numbers. Some of these accounts resemble the
exempla told by his contemporary Caesarius of Heisterbach,*

in which the souls of the faithful departed return to ask for in-
tercessory prayers and the performance of the Mass to relieve
their suffering in purgatory. Others have a pronounced tone
of malice, like an anecdote about the ghost of a dead husband,
who returns to murder his wife for breaking a vow that she
had made to him in life. By far the longest ghost story in Ger-
vase's collection is his account of the revenant of Beaucaire.
This was the ghost of a boy who returned periodically to the
realm of the living, but was visible only to the eyes of his
young female cousin, the person he loved most in life. Once
rumor of his presence spread, crowds of churchmen and curi-
osity seekers interviewed this young woman, who directed
their questions to the ghost and reported his answers back to
them. The ghost's answers were impeccably orthodox, which
lent credibility to a girl who had the uncanny power to medi-
ate between the living and the dead.

From this, ever blessed Augustus, you understand the teaching
about the blessing that should be given before a meal by a
priest just as we remember what our Lord Jesus Christ did,
both the blessing at the table and the thanksgiving after the
meal along with a hymn.[2] You should not disregard the fact
that some priests rush through the blessing at the beginning
of a meal because of their eagerness to eat, while others skip
the thanksgiving at the end due to the lethargy induced by a
full stomach. Because of this, I have decided to relate an event
that took place recently within the borders of your empire. In
the abbey of Saint-Ruf, built by the most holy pope Adrian
in the city of Valence, the cellarer of that place could not find
the time for longer prayers because of the overwhelming concern and urgency of his business in the world.[3] When he gave
thanks after a meal, he changed the psalm "Have mercy upon
me, God" to the psalm "Praise the Lord, all nations," so that
he could finish up with the verses in short order and free himself more quickly to attend to the business of his abbey.[4] He
conducted himself in this way until he came to the end of his
life and died. And then one day when a devout monk was

walking alone in the abbey during a time of solitude and praying without pause, he unexpectedly saw before him the cellarer who had died not long ago. The monk said a blessing and
asked the cellarer where he had come from, where he was
going, what he was doing, and inquired with concern what he
was suffering among the dead. The cellarer responded that
after many accusations made against him by their ancient ad-
versary, the Devil, he still obtained hope of salvation. But he
asserted that among all of his sufferings he was tormented
most severely because, putting the world before God, he neglected the psalm of mercy in favor of the shortest psalm of
all, despite the fact that the mercy of God should always be
sought, especially by the righteous, who should concern themselves more with forgiveness than with the rewards that they
are owed. Asking if the brethren could do anything to offer
him relief, the monk learned that the cellarer could be freed
after a year if the community performed constant vigils, alms,
prayers, and especially sacrifices of the mass on his behalf.
Then the two of them agreed that if the cellarer had not been
freed in a year, he would appear once again to the monk when
the year had passed to explain what help he still needed concerning his condition. And so, when they had agreed upon
this, the cellarer disappeared. The monk explained the situation to his brethren in the chapter meeting. A year later he met
the soul of the cellarer again, now rejoicing in its freedom
from the distress of its torments due to the abundance of
prayers and masses. From this, we should consider the magni-
tude of the severity of justice and the reckoning of judgment,
and the greatness of the mercy of our compassionate Lord, so
that we should fear to cause the Lord offense and at the same
time we should be taught not to lose hope in the mercy of God.

———

There are volcanoes near the town of Pozzuoli [near Naples in
Italy]. The sand on their summit is hard on the feet and prevents the progress of those climbing up because of its great
heat. An old story relates that John, who was once bishop of
Pozzuoli, was a holy man and outstanding in every good
work.[5] Unremitting in prayer, he was walking along singing

the office of the dead when he heard the wailing of souls suffering in the hollow center of the fiery mountain. Then the bishop ordered a lamenting spirit in the name of our lord Jesus Christ to say whose soul it was and for what crime it had been condemned to be punished. With a human voice, the conjured soul responded in a familiar idiom inflected with tears that it was the spirit of a neighbor known to the bishop, which had been assigned to the harsh and punishing fires of Avernus.[6] The holy man asked if it had any hope at all of salvation. The spirit responded that it could still be saved by masses and prayers, if mass to the Lord was offered on its behalf every day for an entire year. At this, the bishop asked, "O Christian soul, by what signs and indications will I learn that you have been saved?" The soul responded, "If you return to this place after a year has passed and you summon me by the name of God, I will answer you if I am still in this place of torment. If I do not answer, you will know for certain that I have been set free by the mercy of God and your prayers."

What happened then? After a year had passed during which he had busied himself with masses and prayers, the bishop reported that the soul he had conjured was never heard again, from which the man of God presumed that it had been truly freed from its punishment. For they say that the souls of the dead appear frequently to their family and friends by divine dispensation, sometimes in the visions of sleepers, sometimes in plain sight in the likeness of their former bodies, so long as they are in places of punishment near and adjacent to our world, and they make known the misery and urgent need of their condition, but when their time in purgatory is over and they are carried up to joys on high, they do not present themselves to our sight any longer.

We know that a watchful eye on a pristine marriage bed is maintained not only by the living, but also by the dead. For in your kingdom of Arles and in the province and county of Aix, there was a nobleman outstanding in lineage, remarkable in morals, favored with respect to military rank: William de Moustiers. He married an equally illustrious wife, who was adorned with social grace, prudence, and virtue. After they had children, William met his end. When he was making his last request, he charged his wife on her marriage vow not to take as her second husband the man whom he considered to be his archenemy. He added that if she did marry him, he would murder her with the salt mortar that he had at hand. His wife readily agreed to a life of widowhood, for her soul was so troubled by the intensity of her sadness that she would have agreed willingly to any condition.

What happened then? William died and after several years had passed, his surviving wife, persuaded by the advice of her friends, married the knight who was the archenemy of her former husband—the man whom he had forbidden her to marry. Mindful of her promise of faith and the warning that went with it, she resisted for a short time, but was forced into the marriage even though her soul was unwilling. When she expressed her concern about the dead man's threats, her friends assured her that the dead had no power to harm the living. The lady was married and when she returned home from the church after the ceremony, just as she had sat down for a little while with her friends, with a sudden scream she spoke the following words, "Woe, poor me, who presumed to break the promised faith of my marriage bed! Behold my husband is here, ready to kill me with the mortar." Immediately, in full view of the festive gathering, the dead man lifted up the mortar and crushed his lady's skull. And although everyone saw the mortar being lifted up, no one saw who committed the deed. Even so, the testimony of the lady's scream and her subsequent death were more than enough to identify her attacker.

It is often the case that many people have ridiculed us when we try to describe the punishments of hell, for they maintain that what we say about the otherworld is worthless, adding that we have made it up. They do not believe what they have read in the Bible unless they have heard it directly from someone who has either risen from the dead or who has appeared to the living after death. Indeed, they ask how anyone can know this information if they have not seen it or experienced it themselves. To this I reply that the weakness of our present age does not allow anyone to return to life after four days in the grave and to announce what happens among the dead.[7] And, indeed, not all of the dead who are permitted to return to us as apparitions are allowed to make known what they have seen, like when Paul, caught up in the third heaven, saw secrets of God "which no one is allowed to utter."[8] But Lazarus is called "the betrayer of hell" because he wrote many things about the condition of the souls of the dead, although this book is either not accepted by the church or it is reckoned among the apocryphal works, whose authenticity is in doubt. He is called the betrayer of hell, not because he reported all the things that he saw in hell, but because he revealed some of the many things he saw there, in so far as the the power of God granted him dispensation to do so.[9] But now, for the incredulous and for those who defend, not their ignorance, but their stubbornness by asserting the impossibility of returning to this world after death, I will share an unprecedented experience that has recently been made known among us: let hearts marvel, let minds be amazed, and let limbs tremble at the novelty of it!

In the month of July in the year of our Lord 1211, being the thirteenth year of the pontificate of Lord Innocent III and the second year of your imperial rule, there was in the kingdom of Arles, in the diocese and province of Arles, in a town called Beaucaire, an eleven-year-old girl, whose parents were upstanding and prosperous citizens, faithful and hard-working. This girl had a cousin who was born in the city of Apt. This young man was in his early adolescence. He was a beardless, vigorous, and likeable person, but he was cast out from Apt for certain offenses typical of young men his age. While he was making his way to Beaucaire, he received a life-threatening wound through no fault of his own but rather due to a misfortune that he did not cause. Seeing the approach of death, he forgave the harm that he had suffered and sent off the man who killed him. Once he had made confession and received the viaticum with due contrition, the young man died and was buried.[10]

After three or five days, he appeared to the girl, whom he had loved so much in life, while she was keeping vigil by lamplight at night. She greeted him, but not without fear, partly because of the faintheardedness typical of her tender age, partly because nature has implanted deep in the hearts of mortals a fear of the dead and encounters with them cause a certain agitation of the mind. But, in the habit of those who return from the dead by divine consent, the young man eased the girl's fear and spoke soothing words to her. He said, "Cousin, do not fear. For I have come to you by divine permission, drawn by my old affection for you. Please do not think that I can harm you in any way. I am allowed to speak to you alone and to relay my replies to others through you."

Hearing this, the girl asked the speaker how and for what reason he could return to this place, since he was dead. But when he heard the word *dead* the young man was stunned. He groaned and, as though wounded and struck by the word, he pleaded, "O my sweetest girl, never let that word escape from your lips! For the harshness of death is so great and so beyond compare that once someone has tasted death, they cannot endure the very mention of the word without their spirit returning to torment."

While the ghost and the girl were talking, the mother and the father of the girl, who were still awake, could hear the words of their daughter, but they could not hear the voice of the ghost. They asked their daughter what she was saying and to whom she was talking. She replied, "Can you not see my cousin William, who recently died? He is standing right here and speaking with me." Stunned and amazed, her parents made the sign of the cross, for they saw no one else there and could only hear the girl speaking.

Without delay, the ghost disappeared. He did not return again until a week later, when the father and mother of the girl had gone with neighbors and friends to the abbey of Saint-Michel de Frigolet, about two miles away, to commemorate the dead.[11] About nine in the morning, the ghost appeared to the girl as she was standing in her father's chamber. When she saw him, the girl greeted him in a friendly manner and then asked where he had come from and in whose company he had returned to this world. He replied that he had a dwelling in the air among the spirits and that he had to endure the pains of the fire of purgatory. He added that at that very moment the prior and brethren of the abbey of Saint-Michel had sprinkled him with the sweetest and most refreshing water, and had conveyed such an enormous benefit to him through their masses and prayers.

The girl asked the ghost to show her his companion. So he presented on his left, as though from behind his back, a horned devil, terrifying to behold, a frightful thing that spouted fire and spit flames. As is the custom in Provence, the girl reached for the holy water that was kept in the chamber and sprinkled it on the devil, which immediately vanished. The ghost affirmed that the sprinkling of the holy water yielded the greatest benefit for him by providing relief from the fire.

Pope Gregory was clearly referring to this fire in his *Dialogues* when he said that spirits are tortured by a corporeal fire because, if an incorporeal spirit can be contained in the body that it vivifies, why can that spirit not also be held for punishment in the place where it is mortified?[12] And so it happens that a corporeal element can burn an incorporeal spirit. And just as one star shines more brightly than some and less brightly than others, so too the one fire of Gehenna torments some spirits more and some less; but it never ceases to burn those whom it burns.[13]

After a few days had passed, news spread throughout the region, and those living nearby, moved by a sense of wonder and novelty, began to visit the girl. To put to the test the rumors of what the girl had done, an intimate friend of ours, a knight from the town of Saint-Gilles, went to Beaucaire. After he had conveyed many other questions to the ghost through the mouth of the virgin, he asked, "Well, my girl, ask your cousin if anyone has done something helpful for him today." To this question, the ghost responded that this very knight had offered two silver coins on behalf of his soul to a poor man on the road leading out of Saint-Gilles. The knight confessed that he alone knew of this act of charity.

On another day, the prior of Tarascon arrived to probe the truth of the things he had heard. When the prior asked the girl

if she had seen her cousin recently, she responded that he arrived at particular times determined in advance, adding that,
while they were speaking, she could now see him coming. The
prior asked, "Where is he standing, what is he doing, where
has he come from, and which companion has he brought?"
The girl responded that the prior should move to the side, for
he had almost stepped on the ghost's foot. While the girl was
asking him the prior's questions, she noticed that with each inquiry the ghost looked back over his shoulder as though ex-
pecting a response from an adviser, whom she could not see.
With this hidden prompting, the ghost responded that he was
suffering a cleansing in the air, but it was not as harsh as usual;
he had an angel as his companion. And when the prior asked
that he show the angel to the girl and she requested to see it, he
quickly brought forth from his right-hand side a man dressed
all in white, enfolded in wings, his face shining with incomparable brightness, whose name, he said, was Michael, the
guardian of his soul and many others as well.

Then the girl asked of her own accord what it meant that on
the day before he had appeared so deprived and dressed in tat-
tered rags, but today, on the contrary, he was dressed in his
usual clothes. He responded that these clothes were his own,
which the mother of the girl had given to the poor. He could
not wear them before now, for they could provide him with no
benefit until they had been given away. He added that he was
suffering pain on account of a belt that he had not returned to
a citizen of Apt, saying that he would be released from a belt
of fire if that borrowed belt, which he had left in a chest, was
restored to its rightful owner, and this was done.

The prior asked what he had done upon his arrival at the
town of Beaucaire. The ghost responded that when wine had
been offered in the home of the teacher William Bedoch, the
prior had the first drink after he and his companions had argued for a long time about who should drink first. The prior
then asked if he had accomplished any good. The ghost replied
that the prior had brought him great relief by virtue of the
masses sung on his behalf. The prior asked what was the greatest help to the dead. The ghost responded, "The sacrifice of

the Mass." The prior then asked how he knew what was happening here among the living. He replied that a spirit can see everything and nothing can block its sight; for this reason, indecent deeds should be avoided at all costs because they happen under the gaze of innumerable spirits, while modesty is confirmed by the testimony of a legion of witnesses.

The prior asked if the ghost could see God and the blessed Virgin and the saints and the souls of the good and the wicked. He responded that he could not see God and he was in sight of the blessed Virgin, but he expected to see God more clearly when his time in purgatory was done and after the Day of Judgment he would hold Him in eternal regard with even greater clarity. In fact, the Eater has written that in their homeland, the saints and the angels behold God as he is, that is, in the manner that is granted to them, because no creature sees him nor will ever see him just as he is, that is, just as he really is, because the Trinity is an untouchable light that no creature can approach.[14]

The prior asked further questions through the girl in secret concerning his own life and behavior. The ghost replied that it was not advantageous to the prior for him to explain what his conscience already knew intimately to its own shame.

On another day, when the ghost was standing in sight of the girl, he reported that his friend William d'Agen had departed from this world and was crossing over to the next surrounded by wicked companions. And when she was asked if his friend would immediately enter the next world for purification, he replied that those who depart from this world sometimes do not arrive at their appointed place for three or four days. To weigh the truth of his statement, someone hastened to William's house, which was nearby, and discovered that the man mentioned by the ghost had indeed just died.

When asked by learned men through the girl if there was a milder word that they should use for *death* since the dead detest that word, the ghost replied, "Departing from this world."

When asked about the location of Gehenna, the ghost replied that hell is a gloomy place under the earth, a disgusting and horrifying pit, where no one goes until after the Day of

Judgment. For the damned stay in other places of punishment, awaiting in eternal pain their damnation, a much harsher sentence. Likewise, the bosom of Abraham is a pleasant and tranquil place where the souls of the good find rest until paradise is granted to those who deserve glory. Purgatory, he said, is in the air. But Gregory writes thus in his *Dialogues*, "The psalmist says, 'You have freed my soul from the lower hell.'"[15] So it seems that there is an upper hell on earth and a lower hell under the earth. And if it is for this reason that we call it hell (*infernus*) because it lies beneath us (*inferius*), then hell should be as far beneath the earth as the earth is beneath heaven.

When asked many times concerning events happening in this world or what was going to happen in the future, the ghost replied with reluctance, saying that one should not inquire concerning base and transitory things of this kind. He said that he was allowed to answer questions concerning spiritual matters and not those concerning worldly matters, except in their proper turn. And whenever he was asked a question, he would turn to his adviser, looking over his shoulder as though awaiting an answer.

When asked if all material things are burdensome to him, he replied that even the lightest straw could not be held by a spirit.

When asked if it was permitted for him to speak with living people in this way for a long time, he replied that he was allowed to do so, so long as the girl remained a virgin. Certainly when his time in purgatory was complete, there would be no more contact for him with people of this world.

When asked by whose permission he was appearing to this girl and from whom it had been granted, he replied that he had loved this girl more than any other female relative in our world and during the anguish of his sad death, she made him swear an oath that if he could return to her by any means possible, he would tell her about his condition. "Bound by this oath and receiving permission from God, I have come to her. But this girl, eager to learn more about my condition and other novelties and marvels about which she knows nothing, makes me swear by my affection at the end of every day to return to her. Truly though, the reason for my return is to convert the faithlessness of the unbelievers to faith by my words and to kindle the faith of true believers for the better."

Gregory concurs with this in his *Dialogues*, saying, "As much as the present world approaches its end, so too the world to come makes itself felt in its close proximity and reveals itself through unmistakable signs. Just as, when the night begins to end and the day begins to dawn, just before the rising of the sun, the darkness combines with the light in a certain way, until the vestiges of departing night turn completely into the light of the coming day, thus the end of this world now mingles with the dawn of the world to come, and the permeation of spiritual elements brightens the darkness of what remains, for we see these things in the twilight of the mind as though before the rising of the sun."[16]

So much for that. I turn now to the hidden secrets of divine counsel. There was a priest, a learned man, good, devout, and God-fearing. When news about this apparition began to spread, this man did not fully believe what was being said, but he approached the girl and carried a message to the ghost through her. He asked the girl to entreat the ghost if he would speak directly to the priest when he appeared, if it was possible, so that the water should not have to flow through a channel to the gardens, as it does now, but that the priest himself might hear his responses without an intermediary. What more can I say? She made the request and after a short time it was granted. Coming to a designated place, the priest tarried long into the night with questions about hidden things. And because he is a dear and close friend of mine, he posed questions from me for the ghost to answer as well. I have written this account by repeating what I heard from his own lips on his testimony and with the Divine Name as his witness.

When asked, the dead youth replied that upon his death he was terrified beyond measure and that good as well as wicked angels appeared to him. The good ones prevailed and escorted him to purgatory. He added that no torment is equal or comparable to death and that the slightest pain of purgatory is harsher than any pain experienced by a living body.

When asked, the dead youth responded that all of the souls

destined for salvation enter purgatory except for the souls of the saints, which immediately enter their own heaven, because they have already cleansed themselves of sin in their mortal bodies. Furthermore, those destined for damnation do not enter purgatory, nor do they enter the nether hell until the Day of Judgment, but they endure infernal punishments in the air without any respite. But the duration and severity of purgatory are in accordance with the seriousness of the sins that have been committed. There is truly a kind of heaven in the air where the saints reside, nowhere near purgatory, and there all of the saints rejoice and sing praises to the Lord. When asked what praises they sing, he replied, "The one that the angels sung, 'Glory to God in the highest,' and sometimes they offer prayers for the living."[17] He also said that some souls in purgatory sing this song and some of them, seeing the approach of their salvation, even rejoice amid the pains of purgatory, in hope of the fatherland or the glory to which they are striving.

When asked, the ghost replied that he could see all of the souls in purgatory and he could hear the groans of some of them and the rejoicing of others who had completed their time there. And he knew who some of them were; others who he had not known in this world were unrecognizable to him in purgatory. He could also see the suffering of the damned, but he did not know where they were.

Gregory says in his *Dialogues*, however, that it is clear from the parable of the rich man and Lazarus that good souls recognize other good souls, while bad souls recognize the bad. In this recognition, the sum of their respective rewards emerges and increases.[18] For not only do the good recognize those who they had known here in this world, but they also recognize those who they had never met before. Since everyone there looks upon God with clarity, what ignorance could they possibly have in that place where they know the one who knows everything? Also, a soul about to depart from this world usually recognizes those with whom it will share a single dwelling in the next world due to their shared faults or merits.

Also in the same book of the *Dialogues*, Gregory says that the souls of the completely just are received in the heavenly realm as soon as they depart from the prison of the flesh.[19] And so the Truth says, "Wherever the body will be, there also are the eagles," and Paul, "I desire to be dissolved and to be with Christ."[20] If, then, Christ is in heaven, then Paul is also in heaven. And the apostle says, "We know that if our earthly house of this habitation is destroyed, we have a dwelling place from God, a house not made by hand, but eternal in heaven."[21] What more do they gain on the Day of Judgment? I answer that they will then enjoy most fully the blessedness of the body. Likewise, the souls of the impious dwell in hell after death, but in which heaven the good reside and in which hell the wicked abide before the judgment, Gregory provides no answer. But I am in firm agreement that the ghost is more of an expert on these matters, for he can see heaven and hell as he lives within sight of both, and from this close proximity he can observe in detail the joy of the just and the misery of the lost. In fact, when souls depart from the body, he can see them coming and he can see where they go; he does not recognize them, however, because he does not know the people whose souls they are.

When asked where he lives, the dead youth replied that his abode is closer to Jerusalem than to the place where he used to dwell when he was alive.[22]

When asked if all of the saints enjoy the fullness of glory, he responded that certain souls enjoy as much glory as they can before the Day of Judgment, but others less so. For example, Saint Bernard suffered a great diminishment of his glory because he did not agree with those who wanted to celebrate the feast of the Conception of the Blessed Virgin.[23] Concerning this, Gregory says in his *Dialogues*, "The souls of some of the just are held back from the celestial kingdom in certain dwellings because they have fallen short of perfect justice."[24]

When asked if the souls in purgatory ever rest, he replied that every week from Saturday evening until Sunday evening they are granted relief from their torments, and when the sacrifice of the mass is offered for them all together, they all find peace. But when a mass is sung for one soul in particular, that soul enjoys complete relief while it lasts, while the others find some benefit from their participation in the general kindness, but not the full measure of it.

When asked, he responded that alms offered for the reverence and memory of the Father and the Son and the Holy Spirit and the blessed Virgin and the apostles Peter and Paul are especially helpful.

When asked, he replied that Michael was indeed his guardian. When one day he was asked if Michael could offer his blessing to the girl and the priest with whom he had spoken, he responded that the blessed Michael agreed, and when Michael reached out his hand to bless them, such a great flash of light struck the girl that she was not able to look at it directly or to endure the sight of it without losing her reason.

When asked, he replied that he could see both good and wicked angels and he saw both kinds of angels attending to their respective duties. And he added that every Christian had a good angel as their guardian, so long as he is without mortal sin. For, when a Christian commits a mortal sin, the good angel departs from him and suffers shame as though on his behalf. Once he has done penance, the angel returns to watch over him.

When asked, he responded that the image of his body that he presented was in fact a body made of air, asserting that it was unable to feel any pain, though his spirit could; nor could it endure any burden, even the lightest. As a result, it happened that when the priest placed his stole on the ghost, he was grateful, but he could not endure the weight that pressed down upon him, asserting that the priestly stole is the chain of the Devil.[25]

When asked if there was night in purgatory, or everlasting day, he replied that day and night alternate, but the night is not so dark as here in this world.

When asked, he responded that the utmost good in this world, after the sacrifice of the mass and the giving of alms, is to avoid lying.

When asked if John the Baptist, who was sanctified by the Lord in the womb and reacted by leaping for joy and was the true forerunner and prophet of the Lord, really doubted whether Jesus was the Christ when he sent his disciples to him to ask him, "Who are you?" the ghost replied that John had no doubts, but had sent his disciples to Jesus to take away their doubt.[26]

When asked if the death and slaughter of the Albigensian heretics pleased God, he responded that nothing else done in that region had ever pleased God so much and he added that God wants the good to be separated from the wicked in his judgment.[27] For even the good who have not stained their faith with heresy have committed a sin if they tolerate it; truly, those who burn in the body here in this world burn even more harshly in the spirit after their deaths.

Let me add an especially wondrous and memorable episode to our story. The ghost had a strong desire to meet with William, the most holy bishop of Orange, but the bishop could not come as he was about to depart for the meeting of the Cistercian chapter.[28] William did, however, send a list of questions in writing to the priest I mentioned above, which he had devised as much to test the authenticity of the ghost as to gain instruction from him. Therefore, one day, when our friend the priest was listening to his responses to various questions, the ghost said to those in attendance, "Behold, the bishop of Orange sends a list of questions and seeks from me the answers. His messenger has just arrived at the door!" And when he was asked about the topics on which the questions dwelt, in response he revealed the questions in order. And while he was doing this, the messenger entered and placed the list of questions in the hand of our priest. Everyone marveled at the ghost's foreknowledge, and while they pondered the capability of the spirit, they tethered their amazement with wisdom, asked their questions, and received their answers in turn. If you want to know the questions and their answers, go back and read what we have written above, from the sentence beginning, "When asked by whose permission, etc."

When asked once more whether Michael was the only angel who looked after all good souls, the ghost replied that Michael was the name of the office and not the individual, not of one angel, but of many, for truly all of the angels that look after souls have this name. When asked why on the evening before the feast of Saint Michael he asked for permission to depart more urgently than usual, even though the priest delayed him with further questions, the ghost responded that he wanted to hurry to the approaching celebration of Saint Michael. He said that all of the angels observed this feast in heaven and that all of the archangels gave glory and praises to God for the victory of this day. Moreover, he said that on this day all of the souls suffering in purgatory find relief and offer praises to Michael, their guardian angel.

What more can I say? When asked many questions about the future, he replied consistently, but I have decided not to include his answers in the context of our book, lest we should seem to anticipate God's decree with this information or to present an opportunity to those who plot against us. But I am sending you by a faithful courier, my most tranquil prince, a letter for your eyes only describing the ways that you please God and conversely the ways that you do not, just as I received it from the ghost. My intention is to kindle your gratitude for God's goodwill toward you and your desire to cultivate a penitential mindfulness concerning his displeasure, so that, while you strive to perfect yourself in goodness, you also hasten to guard against or correct your bad habits.

THE GHOSTS OF
BYLAND ABBEY[1]

*On the other end of the social spectrum from Gervase of Til-
bury's tales for the entertainment and edification of the emperor and his courtiers were the local yarns about unruly
ghosts in the Yorkshire countryside recorded around the year
1400 by a Cistercian monk of Byland Abbey. Montague
Rhodes James, who was equally authoritative as a medieval
scholar and an author of modern ghost stories, brought this
modest collection of tales to light in 1922. He described them
as "strong in local colour, and though occasionally confused,
incoherent, and unduly compressed, [they] evidently represent
the words of the narrators with some approach to fidelity."
Nearly all of these tales described supernatural encounters that
happened to normal people: rural laborers, artisans, and pilgrims, both men and women alike. The ghosts themselves are
eclectic in their appearance and unpredictable in their behavior
until the living "conjured" them, which forced them to reveal
their identity and the reason for their return.*

Concerning the ghost of a man-for-hire from Rievaulx, who
helped a man to carry beans.

A man was riding on a horse that carried upon its back a
measure of beans. The horse stumbled on the road and broke
its leg. When this became apparent, the man carried the beans
on his own back. And as he made his way down the road, he
saw something that looked like a horse standing on its hind
legs with its front legs raised up in the air. Terrified, he kept
the horse at bay in the name of Jesus Christ so that it would

not hurt him. Once he had done this, it went with him just like a horse, and after a little while it appeared in the shape of a bale of rolled hay and there was a light in the middle of it. The living man said to it, "God forbid that you do me any harm." After he had said this, it appeared in the form of a man and he conjured it. Then the spirit revealed its name to him and the reason for its unrest and the remedy it sought and added, "Allow me to carry your beans and to help you." And it did so, all the way down to the river, but it did not wish to cross over. And the living man did not know how the sack of beans came to be placed once more on his back. And afterward he had the ghost absolved and had masses sung for it and the ghost found the aid that it required.

Concerning the astounding confrontation between a ghost and a living man in the time of King Richard II.[2]

It is said that a certain tailor by the name of Snowball returned one night on horseback to his house in Ampleforth from Gilling East, and on the way he heard a sound like ducks bathing in a stream and a little while later he saw something like a raven flying around his head and then landing on the ground, its wings beating the earth as though it was about to die. The tailor dismounted from his horse to seize the raven and he saw sparks of fire scattering from its sides. Then he made the sign of the cross and forbade it for God's sake to inflict any harm upon him at that time. The crow flew with a great cry about the length of a thrown stone. Then the tailor mounted his horse once again and a little while later the crow opposed him in its flight and struck him in the side and threw the tailor to the ground as he was riding on his horse. Thrown to the ground in this way, the tailor lay prone as though in amazement or dismay, for he was overcome with fear. At length, rising and remaining steadfast in his faith, he fought with the crow, sword in hand, until he became exhausted and it seemed to him as though he struck the turf of the moor and he warded the crow off and he forbade the bird for God's sake, saying, "God forbid that you have the power to harm me at this time; instead, depart!" Once more it flew away with a terrible cry about the length of an arrow-flight. In truth, it appeared for a third time to the same tailor, who was holding the hilt of his sword like a cross over his chest out of fear and it blocked his way in the form of a chained dog. When he saw this, the tailor pondered his situation, courageous in his faith. "What will happen to me? I will command it in the name of the Trinity and by the power of the blood of Jesus Christ from the five wounds" so that the crow might speak to him and do him no harm, but rather stand without moving and respond to his questions and tell him its name and the reason for its punishment with a fitting remedy. And he did just that.

Once the ghost was conjured, sighing frightfully and moaning [it said], "Such and such have I done and I was excommunicated for this deed. Therefore, go to the priest seeking absolution for me. And it is necessary to complete twenty masses that should be celebrated on my behalf on nine occasions and from these two options you may choose one. You must either return to me alone on such a night, bringing back a response concerning these things that I asked of you and I will teach you how you can be healed [from the injury inflicted by the ghost in the form of a crow] and in the meantime you should not fear the sight of any man-made fire. Or [if you refuse] your flesh will rot and before long your skin will wither and peel from you. Therefore, know that I was able to hinder you just now because today you have not heard the Mass nor the Gospel of John, namely, 'In the beginning,' nor did you witness the consecration of the body and blood of the Lord; otherwise, I would not fully possess the power to appear to you." And while the ghost was speaking to him, it was as though it was made of fire and the tailor could see its insides through its mouth and the ghost formed its words in its guts and did not speak with its tongue. Then the tailor sought permission from the spirit to be able to have another companion return with him. The ghost responded, "No, but you should carry the four Gospels of the Evangelists and the title of triumph, namely, 'Jesus of Nazareth,' because two other phantoms linger in this place.[3] One of them cannot speak when conjured and takes the form of a fire or a thornbush and the other assumes the form of a hunter. They are both very dangerous to encounter. You must further swear on this stone that you will not defame my bones except to the priests celebrating Mass for me, and to any others you consult on my behalf who can help me." The tailor swore on the stone to keep this secret exactly as expressed above. At length, he commanded the ghost to go all the way to Hodge Beck until his return. It wailed in response, "No! No! No!" The tailor replied, "Then go to Brink Hill." The ghost was pleased and this came to pass.

Indeed, the tailor was sick for several days and once his strength returned, he went to York to the priest, who had formerly excommunicated the ghost, to seek absolution for him. The priest refused to absolve him and summoned another priest to confer on the matter. But this man summoned yet another priest, a third one to consult concerning this absolution. The tailor said to the first priest, "Lord, you know the proofs that I have offered for you to hear." He responded, "Yes, son." Finally, after much discussion between them, the tailor satisfied them and paid five shillings and received a letter of absolution written on a small sheaf of paper, having sworn that he would not defame the dead man, but he would bury the letter in his tomb in secret near to his head.

Once it had been settled, the tailor went to a brother named Richard of Pickering, a respected confessor, to inquire if this absolution would be sufficient and legal. He said that it was. Then the tailor went to all of the orders of the monks of York and had nearly all of the masses celebrated over two or three days. Then, returning home, he buried the letter of absolution in the tomb, just as he had been ordered to do. Truly, once all of these things had been completed in accordance with religious custom, he came home and a presumptuous neighbor, hearing that he was supposed to report to the ghost the things that had happened in York on some night or other, implored him, saying, "God forbid that you go to the spirit unless you warn me in advance concerning the day and the hour of your departure." Thus, bound to do so lest he should displease God, the tailor warned him in advance of his departure, rousing him from sleep, and said, "I am going now. If you want to come with me, let us go, and I will give you some of my books, which I am carrying with me because of my fears of the night." The other man responded, "Do you want me to come with you?" The tailor answered, "Decide for yourself. I do not want to tell you what to do." Then, at last, the other man said, "Go, then, in the name of the Lord and may God help you in all that you do."

Once these words had been spoken, the tailor came to the designated place and made a great circle [on the ground] with a cross [inside of it] and carried with him the four Gospels and other holy writings, and he stood in the middle of the circle, placing four reliquaries in the shape of a cross on the border of the circle. Salvific words had been written on these reliquaries, namely, Jesus of Nazareth, etc. Then, the tailor awaited the arrival of the ghost. At length the ghost came in the form of a she goat and went around the circle three times saying "Ah! Ah! Ah!" Once it was conjured, it fell over on the ground and rose up in the form of a man of great stature, both fearful and gaunt, in the likeness of a dead king. And when the tailor asked if his efforts had been fruitful, the ghost responded to him, "Let God be praised, yes! And I stood behind you at the ninth hour when you buried my absolution in the tomb and you were afraid. No wonder, for three devils were present there, who were punishing me with all manner of torments after you conjured me the first time until my absolution, suspecting that they would have me in their clutches to punish for only a short time longer. Therefore, know that next Monday with thirty other spirits I will enter into joy everlasting. Now go to the river and find a flat stone. Lift it up and under that stone you will find a piece of sandstone. Wash your entire body with water and rub it with the sandstone and you will be cured in a few days' time."

When asked concerning the names of the two other phantoms, the ghost responded, "I cannot tell you their names." Asked once more concerning their social standing, he declared, "One of them was a violent layman and he was not from this country. He killed a pregnant woman and he will not find salvation before the Day of Judgment, and you will see him in the form of a calf without a mouth and eyes and ears and, when it is conjured, you will not be able to speak to it. And the other was a devout man [who appears] in the form of a hunter with the horn of a bull and he will have salvation and he can be conjured through a certain little boy who has not yet reached puberty, if the Lord so disposes." Afterward the tailor asked the ghost concerning his own condition. It responded to him, "You are wrongfully in possession of a cloak and a gown that once belonged to a friend, who was your companion in war across the sea. For this reason, you should make amends to him or else you will suffer terribly." The tailor replied, "I do not know where he is." The ghost said to him, "He lives in such and such village near the castle of Alnwick." When asked further, "What is my gravest sin?" the ghost responded, "Your gravest sin is due to me." The living man asked, "How and in what way is this the case?" "Because the people are sinning because of you, speaking falsely and offending the other dead and saying, 'Either this man is the dead man who was conjured or that one or that other one.'" And he asked the same spirit, "What, therefore, should be done? I will have to reveal your name." The ghost answered, "No, but if you remain in such and such a place you will be rich and in such and such a place you will be poor, and you will have some enemies." Finally, the ghost said, "I cannot stay much longer and speak to you." When they departed from each other, a deaf and mute and blind calf followed the tailor all the way to the village of Ampleforth. He conjured it by every means he knew, but it could not speak to him at all. But the other ghost, who had been helped by him, advised him to put his most powerful amulets at his head while he slept and [said], "You should not say more or less than what I ordered you, and you should keep your eyes down and not look at a man-made fire on this night at least." When he returned home, the tailor became very sick for several days.

Concerning the ghost of Robert, son of Robert from Bolteby in Kilburn, who was seized in a cemetery.

Remember that the aforesaid Robert—the younger one—died and was buried in the cemetery, but he was in the habit of leaving his tomb at night and disturbing and frightening the villagers and the hounds of the village followed him and barked loudly. At length, the young men of the village were talking among themselves, proposing to capture him if in some way they could, and they set out together to the cemetery. But when the ghost appeared, everyone fled except for two of them, one of whom—Robert Foxton by name—seized the ghost as he was leaving the cemetery and pinned him to the church stile, while the other shouted bravely, "You hold him tight until I come to you!"⁴ His companion responded to him, "Go quickly and fetch the parish priest, so that the ghost may be conjured, because—God willing—whatever I am holding I will clutch it firmly until the priest arrives." Indeed, this parish priest hastened quickly and conjured the ghost in the name of the Holy Trinity and in the power of Jesus Christ until the ghost answered the questions he was asked. Once he had been conjured, the ghost spoke from deep inside its body and not with its tongue, but as though in an empty cask, and confessed his many crimes. When the ghost had made these things known, the priest absolved him but burdened the men who captured him so that they would not in any way reveal his confession, and as for the ghost, he rested in peace, according to God's will.

It is said, however, that before his absolution, the ghost would stand in the doorways and windows of a house and under walls and ramparts as though listening. Perhaps he was waiting to see if someone would come and conjure him in his need for help. Others say that he aided and abetted the murder of a certain man and committed other evil deeds concerning which no one is allowed to speak to the present day.

In turn, old folks have passed down the story that a certain man, Jacob Tankerley by name, formerly rector of Cold Kirby, was buried in front of the chapter house at Byland and he was in the habit of wandering at night as far as Cold Kirby and one night he blew on the eye of his mistress there and it is said that the abbot and the community had his body dug up from its grave with its coffin and they urged Roger Wayneman to haul it all the way to Lake Gormire and when he cast the coffin into the water, the oxen were nearly drowned in their fear. God forbid that, in committing it to writing in this way, I am in any danger, because just as I have heard this story from my elders, thus have I written it down. May the All-Powerful have mercy on him, if in fact he was numbered among those who merit salvation.

Likewise, what I write is astounding to relate. It is said that a certain woman seized a ghost and carried it into a particular house over her back in the presence of some people, one of whom reported that he saw the hands of the woman sinking deeply in the ghost's flesh, as though the ghost's flesh was decayed and not solid, but imaginary.

Concerning a certain canon from Newburg seized after his death whom [blank] apprehended.

It happened that this man was talking together with the steward and walking in a field. And suddenly the steward fled, having suffered a terrible fright, and the other man was wrestling with some ghost, which tore shamelessly at his clothes. But finally he was victorious and conjured him. The conjured ghost confessed that he was a canon from Newburg and had been excommunicated because of the matter of some silver spoons that he had hidden in a certain place. For this reason, he begged the living man to go to that place and retrieve the spoons in order to bring them to his prior and to seek absolution for his soul. He did just that and found the silver spoons in the place the ghost mentioned. Once he was absolved, the ghost then rested in peace. Nevertheless, the man fell ill and grew weak over the course of many days and he affirmed that the ghost appeared to him in the habit worn by canons.

Concerning a certain ghost conjured elsewhere who said that he was being punished severely, for he was the hired man of a master and he had stolen some sheaves of wheat that belonged to that man, which he gave to his own oxen so that they would appear fat. And another thing that weighed upon him even more, that he did not plow his own land deeply, but only with shallow furrows, in the hope that his oxen would stay fat. And he said that there were fifteen spirits being punished severely in one place for the crimes they had committed. For this reason, he pleaded that he might petition his master for an indulgence and forgiveness, so that he could obtain an appropriate remedy.

Likewise concerning another ghost following William of Bradeforth and crying out "How! How! How!" three times over three nights. It happened that on the fourth night around the middle of the night William went back to a new place from the village of Ampleforth. And while he was returning on the road he heard a fearful voice shouting a long way off and echoing as though on a mountain. And shortly thereafter the voice cried out again, but closer. And a third time it cried out on the road a short way ahead of him. And finally he saw a pale horse and his dog barked a little, but then became very frightened and hid itself between William's legs. Once this had happened, William restrained the same ghost in the name of the Lord and in the power of the blood of Jesus Christ so that he would depart and not block his way. When he heard this, the ghost withdrew in the likeness of a sheet with its four corners unfurled and rolled away. From this we gather that the ghost had a great desire to be conjured and to be helped effectively.

Likewise concerning the ghost of a man from Ayton in Cleveland. It is said that he followed a man for eighty miles in the hope that he would conjure him and give him aid. Once the ghost was conjured, he confessed that he had been excommunicated for a matter involving six pennies, but after he received absolution and reparation, he rested in peace. In all of these things God showed himself to be a bestower of just rewards since nothing evil goes unpunished and conversely nothing good goes unrewarded.

It is said that the same ghost, before he was conjured, threw the living man over a hedge and caught him on his way down on the other side. Once he was conjured, he said, "If you had done so in the first place, I would not have hurt you [and as a result] you were frightened in places like this and I caused it."

How a repentant thief vanished after his confession from the sight of a demon.

It happened once in Exeter that a digger, a hard worker with a big appetite, resided in a small room in a large house, which had many small rooms divided by walls and [above which was] a separate dwelling. When he was hungry the digger often used to climb up a certain ladder into the house and cut away meat hung there and he cooked it and then ate it, even during Lent. For this reason, the lord of the house, seeing his meat tampered with in this manner, asked his servants what had happened. After they all denied their guilt and purged themselves by oaths, the lord threatened that he would go to a sorcerer, a certain necromancer, and inquire through him about this strange happening. When he heard this, the digger feared greatly and went to the monks and confessed his crime in secret and was absolved by the sacrament. Indeed, the lord of the house, as he had threatened, went to the necromancer, and this man anointed the fingernail of a little boy and through his incantations asked him what he saw. The boy responded, "I see a groom with his hair shorn." The necromancer said to him, "You should conjure him to appear to you in the most beautiful form that he can." And the boy did so. And the boy affirmed, "Behold, I see a very beautiful horse." And after that he saw a man in the likeness of the digger climbing a ladder and cutting the meat while the horse followed as well. And the priest asked, "What are the man and the horse doing now?"5 And the child responded, "Behold, he cooks and eats the meat." And the priest inquired further, "And what is he doing now?" And the boy said, "They are going together to the church of the monks. But the horse waits outside the gates and the man enters and on bent knees he speaks with a certain monk, who puts his hand upon his head." Once again, the priest asked the boy, "What are they doing now?" The boy responded, "They have both vanished from my sight at the same time and I can see them no longer and I do not know for certain where they are."

Concerning a wondrous work of God, who calls forth things that do not exist so as to make them exist, and who can do so whenever and with whatever he wishes, and concerning a certain marvel.

It is commended to memory that a certain man from Cleveland by the name of Richard Roundtree, leaving behind his pregnant wife, went on pilgrimage to the tomb of Saint James with many others.[6] One evening they all spent the night in a forest near the royal road. Here it was that some of them kept watch through the evening because of their fear of the night, and the rest slept more securely. It happened that in that part of the night during which Richard was on guard as a watchman, he heard the loud sound of people traveling along the royal road. And some were sitting and riding on horses, sheep, and oxen, and some upon other animals and all manner of cattle, which had been their own mortuaries when they died.[7] At last, he discerned something that looked like a small child rolling upon the ground in a sock. And he conjured it, "Who could it be and why does it roll in this manner?" It responded, "It is not right that you have conjured me. For you are my father and I am your son, miscarried without baptism and buried without a name." When he heard this, the pilgrim took off his shirt and dressed his little boy, giving it a name in the name of the holy Trinity and he carried that old sock with him as evidence of this event. Indeed, once the infant had been named in this way, it leapt about excitedly and then walked standing upright on its own feet, when before it could only roll on the ground. Truly, once he had returned home from his pilgrimage, Richard held a feast with his neighbors and asked his wife for his socks. She found one sock, but could not find the other. Then her husband showed her the sock, in which the child had been wrapped, and she marveled at this. When the midwives confessed the truth concerning the death and burial of the child in the sock, the husband divorced his wife because he was the godfather of his own son, who had been miscarried. But I believe that this divorce was very displeasing to God.

Concerning the sister of old Adam of Lond, seized after her death according to a story that old folks tell.

It should be remembered that this woman was buried in the

cemetery at Ampleforth and within a short time after her death she was caught by the elder William Trower and, once she was conjured, she confessed that she traveled her own way in the night because of certain property deeds that she handed over unlawfully to her brother Adam. This happened long ago when a disagreement arose between her husband and herself. To the detriment of her husband and her own sons, she gave the property deeds to her brother. Thus it happened that after her death, her brother evicted her husband with violence from her property, namely from one homestead and field with all lands pertaining to it in Ampleforth and in Heslerton a piece of pasture with everything pertaining to it. For this reason, she begged William that he would advise this same brother that she wished to give the property deeds back to her husband and sons, and to restore her property to them. In no other way could she rest in peace before the day of Judgment. Indeed, William gave this advice to Adam according to her request, but he refused to return the property deeds, saying, "I do not believe these things you have said." William said to him, "My story is completely true. With God's help, you will soon hear your sister speaking to you concerning this matter." And on the next night, William seized her again and brought her to Adam's chamber, and she spoke with him. According to witnesses, her stubborn brother responded to her, "Even if you should wander about forever, I do not want to return the property deeds." Groaning, she replied to him, "May God judge between you and me in this case. You should know, therefore, that I will hardly rest until the time of your death, but after your death you will wander in my place." Furthermore, she said that his right hand would hang down and turn completely black. And when he was asked why this was the case, she responded that he often used that hand when fighting or making a false oath. Finally, she was conjured to another place because of the fear of the night and the terror of the inhabitants of the village. Yet, I beg pardon if perhaps I have offended by writing something contrary to the truth. It is said, however, that the younger Adam of Lond did in fact return some of his inheritance after the death of his father, Adam senior.

THE REFORMATION
OF THE WRAITHS

On October 31, 1517, a monk named Martin Luther issued a public protest against traditional Christian doctrines, especially the sale of indulgences to free souls from otherworldly torment. The religious revolution known as the Protestant Reformation began when Luther nailed The Ninety-Five Theses, his short, incisive critique of the medieval traditions of the Catholic Church, on the doors of All Saints' Church in Wittenberg, Germany. Luther's writings kindled the anger of traditional Catholics and inspired the enthusiasm of a new generation of Protestant Christians, forever fracturing the unity of doctrine and tradition that characterized the history of Christianity during the European Middle Ages.

Protestants were firm in their belief that purgatory was an invention of the human imagination rather than a divine truth because they could find no testimony of it in the Holy Scriptures. Moreover, they believed that it was presumptuous to assume that living people had any agency to help the souls of the dead, whose fate was determined by the inscrutable judgment of God. Since Protestants held that the souls of the dead went either directly to heaven or directly to hell, they did not believe in ghosts. But the centuries-old tradition of supernatural contact between the living and the dead proved hard to jettison completely. Protestant Christians were at pains, for instance, to explain one of the most well-known ghost stories from the ancient world: the conjuring of the soul of King Samuel by the witch of Endor (see pp. 29–30, above).

For their part, Catholic authors responded quickly to the Protestant attack on the existence of ghosts by marshaling long lists of examples of supernatural encounters from antiquity and the Middle Ages in their attempt to show that the sinful dead benefitted from suffrages offered by the living on their behalf.

OF GHOSTES AND SPIRITES
WALKING BY NYGHT[1]

*One of the earliest and most strident of the Protestant attacks
on the existence of ghosts was Ludwig Lavater's (1527–1586)
Latin treatise,* De spectris, lemuribus et magnis atque insolitis
fragoribus *(1569), which was translated into English in 1572
under the title* Of Ghostes and Spirites Walking by Nyght. *A
Protestant theologian who lived in Zurich, Lavater was the
author of numerous books in support of the Protestant faith,
but his refutation of the Catholic belief in ghosts was by far
his most enduring work. It remained in print throughout the
early modern period and was translated into French, German,
English, and Italian. Throughout this treatise, Lavater set out
to undermine the credibility of medieval ghost stories by at-
tributing them to the false perceptions of impressionable people or to frauds perpetuated by duplicitous monks and priests.
But Lavater could not deny that "many honest and credible
persons" had, in fact, encountered apparitions of one kind or
another. Following the authority of Saint Augustine (see pp.
49–54, above), he argued that these apparitions were not the
souls of dead Christians, but rather the disguise of good angels sent by God or, more often, bad angels in the service of
Satan. In the final part of his treatise, Lavater offered advice
to individuals who encountered such apparitions. It was best
to remain silent until its intentions were revealed. If the spirit
was malign, a statement of faith was the best protection
against its evil machinations.*

The first part of this book, concerning spirits walking by night, wherein it is declared that spirits and sights do appear and that sundry strange and monstrous things do happen.

Daily experience teaches us that spirits do appear to men.

To all of the premises before handled, this also is to be added, which no man can deny, but yet many honest and credible persons of both kinds, as well men and women, of whom some are living and some already departed, which have and do affirm, that they have sometimes in the day and sometimes in the night seen and heard spirits. Some man walked alone in his house and, behold, a spirit appeared in his sight, yea and sometimes the dogs also perceive them and fall down at their master's feet and will by no means depart from them, for they are sorely afraid themselves, too. Some man went to bed and laid down to rest and by and by there is something pinching him or pulling off the bedclothes. Sometimes it sat on him or lay down in the bed with him, and many times it walked up and down in the chamber. There have been many times men seen walking on foot or riding on horseback, being of a fiery shape, known unto diverse men, and such as died not long before. And it has come to pass likewise that some, either slain in the wars or otherwise dead naturally, have called unto their acquaintance being alive and have been known by their voice.

Many times in the night season, there have been certain spirits heard softly going or spitting or groaning, who being asked what they were have made answer that they were the souls of this or that man and that they now endure extreme torments. If, by chance, any man did ask of them, by what means they might be delivered out of those tortures, they have answered that in cases a certain number of masses were sung for them or pilgrimages vowed to some saint or some other such like deeds done for their sake, that then surely they should be delivered. Afterward, appearing in great light and glory, they have said that they were delivered and have therefore rendered great thanks to their good benefactors and have in like manner promised that they will make intercession to God and our Lady for them. And hereby it may be well proved that they were not always priests or other bold and wicked men, which have feigned themselves to be souls of men deceased, as I have said before. Insomuch that even in those men's chambers, when they have been shut, there have appeared such things, when they have with a candle diligently searched before, whether anything has lurked in some corner or no. Many used at this day to search and sift every corner of the house before they go to bed that they may sleep more soundly and yet nevertheless they hear some crying out and making a lamentable noise, etc.

It has many times chanced that those of the house have verily thought that somebody had overthrown the pots, platters, tables, and trenchers and tumbled down the stairs, but after it waxed day they have found all things orderly set in their places again.

It is reported that some spirits have thrown the door off from the hooks and have troubled and set all things in the house out of order, never setting them in their due place again, and that they have marvelously disquieted men with rumbling and making a great noise.

Sometimes there is heard a great noise in abbeys and in other solitary places, as if it were coopers hooping and stopping up wine vessels or some other handicraft men occupied about their labor, when it is most certain that all in the house are gone to bed and have betaken themselves to rest.

When houses are in building, the neighbors many times hear the carpenters, masons, and other artificers handling all things in such sort, as if they were busily laboring in the daytime. And this strange wonder is joyfully received as a sure token of good luck.

There be some that judge it came to pass naturally, that we suppose we hear these things in the night, which we heard before in the daytime. Which question I leave to be discussed of better learned than myself.

Pioneers or diggers for metal do affirm that in many mines there appear strange shapes and spirits, who are appareled like unto other laborers in the pit. These wander up and down in caves and underminings and seem to bestir themselves in all kinds of labor, as to dig after the vein, to carry together ore, to put it into baskets, and to turn the winding wheel to draw it up, when in very deed they do nothing less. They very seldom hurt the laborers (as they say) except they provoke them by laughing and railing at them, for then they threw gravel stones at them or hurt them by some other means. These are especially haunting the pits, where metal most abounds.

A certain godly and learned man wrote once unto me of a silver mine at Davos in the Alps, upon which Peter Buol, a noble man, the overseer of the same place (whom they call Landammanus), had bestowed great cost a few years before, and had gathered thereby good store of riches.[2] In the same mine was a spirit or devil of the mountain, who when the laborers filled the stuff they had dug into their vessels, he seemed, for the most part, every Friday, to be very busy, pouring metals of his own accord out of one basket into another. Wherewith the overseer was not offended and when he would either descend into the pit or come up again, blessing himself with the sign of the cross, he never received hurt. It chanced on a time that while the spirit was too busy intermeddling himself with everything, one of the miners being offended therewith, began to rail him very bitterly and with terrible cursing words bid him get him back thence in the Devil's name. But the spirit caught him by the pate and so writhed his neck about that his face stood behind his back, yet notwithstanding he was not slain, but lived a long time after, well known unto diverse of his familiar friends, which yet live at this day, how be it he died within a few years after.

Gregorius Agricola, whose learned works that he wrote of metals, be yet extant in the end of his book of creatures living under the earth, he made two kinds of devils haunting in certain mines abroad.[3] For he said, there are some cruel and terrible to behold, which for the most part do very much annoy and hurt the laborers digging for metal. Such a one was he who was called Annebergius, who only with his breath destroyed about twelve laborers at once in a cave called Corona Rosacea. The wind wherewith he slew them he let fly out of his mouth, for he appeared in the similitude and likeness of a horse. Such another was Snebergius, who wearing a black roll about his neck, took up a laborer aloft from the ground and set him on the brink of a certain exceedingly deep place, where there had sometime been a great store of silver, not without grievous bruising of his body.

And again he said there be some very mild and gentle, whom some of the Germans call *Cobali*, as the Grecians do, because they be as it were apes and counterfeiters of men, for they leaping and skipping for joy do laugh and seem as though they did many things, when in very deed they do nothing. And some others call them elves or dwarfs of the mountains, thereby noting their small stature, wherein they commonly appear. They seem to be *hoare*, wearing apparel like the metal refiners, that is, in a petticoat laced and an apron of leather about their loins. These hurt not the laborers, unless they misuse them, but do imitate them in all their doings. And he said, they are not much unlike unto those whom the Germans call *Guteli*, because they seem to bear good affection toward men, for they keep horses and do other necessary business. They are also like unto them whom they call *Trulli*, who taking on them the feigned shapes of men and women, do serve as it is said like servants both among other nations and specifically among the Suetians.

That there happen strange wonders and prognostications and that sudden noises and cracks and such like are heard before the death of men, before battle, and before some notable alterations or changes.

It happened many times that when men lie sick of some deadly disease, there is something heard going in the chamber, like as sick men were wont, when they were in good health, yea and the sick parties themselves do many hear the same and by and by guess what will come to pass. Oftentimes, a little before they yield up the ghost and sometime a little after their death or a good while after, either their own shapes or some other shadows of men are apparently seen. And diverse times it came to pass that when some of our acquaintance or friends lie dying, albeit many miles off, yet there are some great stirrings or noises heard. Sometimes we think the house will fall on our heads or that some heavy and weighty thing fell down throughout all the house, rendering and making a disordered noise, and shortly within a few months after we understand that those things happened the very same hour that our friends departed in. There be some men, of whose stock none do die, but that they observe and mark some signs and tokens going before, as that they hear the doors and windows open and shut, that something ran up the stairs or walked up and down the house or did someone or other such like thing.

But here I cannot pass this in silence that there are many superstitious men, which vainly persuade themselves that this cousin and this or that friend of theirs will shortly die. For in the end the falling out of the matter itself showed it was a vain and foolish persuasion that they understood such things by any signs.

Cardanus in his book *Concerning the Truth of Things* wrote that there was a certain noble family at Parma in Italy out of which so often as anyone died, there was seen an old woman in the chimney corner.[4] On a certain time she appeared, when a maiden of the same family lay very sick, and therefore they greatly despaired of her life, but soon after she recovered again, and in the meanwhile another, who was then in good health, suddenly died.

There was a certain parish priest, a very honest and godly man, whom I knew well, who in the plague time could tell beforehand, when any of his parish should die. For in the night time, he heard a noise over his bed, like as if one had thrown down a sack full of corn from his shoulders, which when he heard, he would say, "Now another has bid me farewell." After it was day, he used to inquire who died that night or who was taken with the plague to the end that he might comfort and strengthen them according to the duty of a good pastor.

It has been often observed in guildhalls where aldermen sit, that when one of those aldermen was at the point of death, there was heard some rattling about his seat or some other certain sign of death. The same thing happened beside pews and stalls in churches or in other places, where men are often conversant and accustomed to occupy their handy labor.

In abbeys, the monks, servants, or any other falling sick, many have heard in the night preparation of chests for them, in such sort as coffin makers did afterward prepare in deed.

In some country villages, when one is at Death's door, many times there are some heard in the evening or in the night digging a grave in the churchyard and the same the next day is so found dug, as these men did hear before.

There have been seen some in the night when the moon shone, going solemnly with the corpse, according to the custom of the people, or standing before the doors, as if some body were to be carried to the church to burying. Many suppose they see their own image or, as they say, their own soul and of them diverse are verily persuaded that except they die shortly after they have seen themselves, they shall live a very great time after. But these things are superstitious. Let every man so prepare himself, as if he should die tomorrow, lest by being too secure he purchase himself harm.

———

In the second part of this book, we have to consider what those things be that (as we have already shown) are both heard and seen in the daytime and the night, whether they be the souls of dead men or no. Also what the old writers have judged of them, and what the Holy Scriptures do teach us herein.

That the true Samuel did not appear to the witch in Endor.

Now touching the examples by them commonly alleged, which do think that the souls of men do return again unto the living upon the earth, I will first entreat of Samuel's apparition, of which matter nowadays there is great contention and reasoning.[5] And (as I trust) I shall prove by strong arguments that very Samuel himself did not appear in soul and body, neither that his body was raised up by the sorceress, which perchance then was rotten and consumed unto dust in the earth, neither yet his soul was called up, but rather some devilish spirit. First, the author of the two books of Samuel said that Saul did ask counsel of the Lord and that he would not answer him, neither by visions nor by Urim nor by his prophets.[6] Wherefore if God disdained by his prophets yet living and other ordinary ways to give answer unto him, whom he had already rejected, we may easily conjecture that he would much less have raised a dead prophet to make him answer. And the rather, for that as we have a little before said, the law of God has severely by a great threatening forbidden to learn ought of the dead and would not have us to search for the truth of them nor that any man should use divination by spirits, and such other devilish arts.

Secondly, if very Samuel indeed appeared, that must of necessity have come to pass either by the will of God or by the work of magical art. But God's will was not that Samuel should return. For he had condemned necromancy and would not have us to ask counsel at the dead and that the spirit of God did that which was contrary hereunto or did permit the saints to do it or was present with them that did ought contrary thereto, it may not be granted. And that those things were done by the force and operation of magical art, we cannot affirm. For the wicked spirit has no rule or power over the souls of the faithful to bring them out of their places when he wanted, if they be in the hand of God and the bosom of Abraham, nay (which is less) he has no power over filthy and unclean swine, for he was driven (as we read in the seventh chapter of Matthew) to beg leave before he could enter into the herd of swine.[7] And how then should he have any power over the soul of man? Yet can it not be denied that God sometimes for certain causes does give the Devil and his servants, magicians and necromancers, power to do many things, as to hurt and lame man and beast and to work other strange things? But that God does give the Devil leave to raise dead bodies, or to call, bring forth, or drive away souls, especially out of heaven, it has no ground at all in Scripture, neither can there be any reasonable cause alleged, wherefore God would or should give the Devil license to do these things contrary to the usual and common order, yea and against his own express commandment. For vain and childish is the cause hereof that is given of some men that Samuel should appear to certify and astonish Saul, as if God could not have feared him by other ways and means. Was he not before utterly abashed and dismayed?

Thirdly, if Samuel were brought back, the same was done either by his will and consent, or without the same, but that he did freely and of his own accord obey the sorceress, no man I think is so blind to imagine. For that were utterly repugnant to the law of God that he should confirm witchcraft and sorcery by his example. If the witch had called for Samuel while he lived, doubtless he would not have approached her. And how then can we believe that he came to her after his death? We may not so say that the witch compelled him to resort to her against his will, for the Devil has no power over the souls of the godly, and magic itself is of no force. Heathen superstition no doubt it is that words uttered by magicians after their peculiar manner or figures drawn should have such a secret and hidden operation . . .

———

The third part of this book, in which is shown why or to what end God suffers spirits to appear and other strange things to happen, as also how men ought to behave themselves when they meet with any such things.

God by the appearing of spirits does exercise the faithful and punish the unbelievers.

It follows now hereafter to be entreated of why God suffers spirits, ghosts, and horrible sights to appear, etc. and also why he does permit other strange and miraculous things to happen. And furthermore how men ought to behave themselves when they see any such things.

God does suffer spirits to appear unto his elect unto a good end, but unto the reprobate they appear as a punishment. And as all other things turn to the best unto the faithful, even so do these also, for if they be good spirits, which appear unto men, warning and defending them, thereby do they gather the care, providence, and fatherly affection of God toward them. But in case they be evil spirits (as for the most part they are), the faithful are moved by occasion of them unto true repentance. They look diligently unto themselves so long as they live, lest the enemy of mankind, who lies always in wait, should bring them into mischief and take further advantage to vex and hurt them. God also by these means does exercise and try their faith and patience, to the end they continue in his word and receive nothing contrary to the same, have it never so fair to show nor do any manner of thing against his word, although those spirits do not straightaway cease to vex them. God does also suffer them to be exercised with haunting of spirits, for this cause, that they should be more humble and lowly.

How Christian men ought to behave themselves when they see spirits and first that they ought to have a good courage and to be steadfast in faith.

How Christian men ought to behave themselves in this behalf, it is fully and amply declared in the Holy Scriptures, in like manner as all other things are, which pertain unto our salvation. To wit, that first we ought to be of good courage without fear, being assured and constant in true faith. For if they be good angels that show themselves unto us, then are they sent unto us from God to a good end and purpose. But if they be wicked and evil, they can do us no harm be they never so desirous, except God gives them leave thereto. If it be nothing but a vain imagination that we have, or an idle sight objected unto our eyes, surely it is great folly to be anything afraid. Indeed, it is natural unto us to be amazed with fear when we see such things, for very godly men, as we read both in the Old and New Testament, were stricken with exceeding fear when they saw good angels, but yet a man must pull up his heart again. When Christ's disciples saw their master walking on water and approaching near the ship, they thought they saw a spirit and they were astonished and cried out through fear.[8] But the Lord said unto them, be of good comfort, it is I, be not afraid . . .

But if it please God to exercise you by the Devil for a certain time, as he did sometime Job, you must patiently suffer all things that he lays upon you, and that willingly for God's commandments' sake.[9] And know you well that he cannot thus much hurt neither your goods, nor body, nor soul without the permission and sufferance of Almighty God. If God give him leave to plague your body, think with yourself howsoever it be done, that God has so done for your profit and commodity, who also sends grievous sicknesses upon other men, but other means and instruments, or else does exercise them with other kinds of calamities. Be therefore strong and constant in faith, yet let everyone beware of boldness, temerity, and heady rashness.

WHEN NIGHT DRAWS
SWIFTLY DARKLING ON[1]

Catholic authors were not slow to respond to the claims of Protestant theologians that ghosts were not dead souls, but good or bad angels in disguise. Only a few years after the publication of Lavater's book, a Capuchin monk named Noel Taillepied defended the traditional Catholic teaching on apparitions in the work called A Treatise of Ghosts, *which appeared in 1588. Taillepied rehearsed a long litany of examples drawn from the Bible as well as from ancient and medieval authorities, both pagan and Christian, to prove that the dead have always interacted with the living for the benefit of both parties. Despite their opposing theological stances, there are some striking parallels between the treatises of the Protestant Lavater and the Catholic Taillepied. For example, both works offered advice for conversing with spirits and warned that the Devil and his minions could appear in the guise of recently dead people in an effort to deceive and mislead the faithful.*

To Whom, When, and in What Places Spirits are wont to Appear, as also concerning their Business.

It is true that some classes of persons may be considered to be more aptly in the way of seeing ghosts: travelers, for example, who have to pass through lonely and remote districts; sentinels; shepherds; seamen who are on the ocean all day and all night for long periods; those engaged in rustic pursuits, who pass their days in the fields, in valleys, and among the mountains; folk, in a word, who are brought face-to-face with unspoiled Nature.

There are some men who have never seen, or perhaps could never see a ghost; there are others to whose lot it falls to have many such supernatural experiences.

In the same way some travelers meet with frequent strange and marvelous adventures, whilst others encounter nothing extraordinary.

It is commonly believed that children who are born on the first day of the Ember Seasons are able to see and hear spirits, and, indeed, it may well be that in God's providence those who come into the world at certain seasons of the year should be thus gifted.[2]

An angel, being a messenger of God, will address indifferently a man who leads a saintly life or a heinous sinner, a believer or an atheist. Thus the angel appeared to Saint Peter as well as to the centurion Cornelius, and in each case he faithfully performed the service appointed him by God.[3]

A ghost will naturally, if it is possible, appear to the person whom he has most loved whilst on earth, since this person will be the readiest to carry out any behest or fulfill any wish then communicated by the departed.

In all ages throughout history has it been recorded that disembodied spirits have appeared, as well by day as night, but more often about midnight when a man wakes from his first sleep, and the senses are alert, having taken some repose. Moreover, they frequently appear on a Friday or a Saturday, and on fasting days, when we are disciplining ourselves and are (so to speak) less in touch with the world, secluding ourselves in prayer and meditation, examining our spiritual progress and repenting our sins. As to the places where Spirits manifest themselves, there are not particular spots. They have been seen and heard in every circumstance. Chiefly, I ween, do they appear in places where in times past there have been horrid deeds, assassinations, riot and rape, or on battlefields, and again on spots where foul midnight murder has been done, by lonely gallows, in woods, and not unseldom even in churches and cloisters, near sepulchers and in graveyards, in prisons, old manor houses and castles, sometimes, too, in the shadow of stately palaces, such as are Gentilly, near Paris, and the house in the Palace Vauvert, where the Carthusians have their monastery, Notre Dame de Vauvert.

Saint Bonaventure, in his *Life of the Holy Franciscan Fathers*, says that the saint desired his brethren to repair and pray in abandoned and forsaken churches, so that the evil spirits might not be able to foregather in these holy but derelict shrines.[4]

The philosopher Pythagoras, in his *Symbols*, advises that on rising from sleep one should cover the bed with the quilt or blanket.[5] He does not give any precise reason for this, but the commentators say that it is done in order that no unclean spirit may lie down and rest in the warm bed a man has just quit, for incubi delight in occupying places where men have been.

This is alluded to and indeed proven by the Holy Scriptures. In the thirteenth chapter of Isaiah, God reveals the burden of Babylon, and he declares by the mouth of his prophet that fauns, satyrs, and the hairy ones shall dance in their palaces.[6] In the thirty-fourth chapter the prophet, announcing the general judgment of the wicked and the destruction of the Gentiles, says that Syim and Iym shall meet in their palaces, their strongholds and pleasure houses; that the hairy ones shall cry out one to another, and there shall Lamia lie down and find rest for herself.[7] Thus God permits that those places where heinous sinners have dwelled in the offense of heaven should be plagued and haunted by evil spirits.

Now these spirits appear in very many forms and shapes, as is amply shown by the instances already given. Sometimes they even appear under the likeness of some individual who can at once be recognized, a man either still living, or it may be long since dead. Sometimes they appear in the likeness of a man, but a stranger.

Several times spirits have appeared as women, tempting men to lust and venery. They also appear as four-footed animals, dogs, pigs, horses, goats, cats, hares, or again as birds, ravens, horned owls, or creeping beasts, such as snakes and serpents, which infest the dwellings of dwellers in tropical climes and are even worshipped and adored by the besotted natives.

———

Disembodied spirits, however, more often manifest themselves in their own proper mortal likeness than under any hideous or horrible aspect. Sometimes they are encountered on a high road as walking or riding. It is true that it has been recorded that a ghost will appear in a flame of fire, very ghastly; or all covered with wounds and blood; or again horribly mangled with the bowels gushing out and ripped from the belly. Sometimes only a hand appears, or a shadowy form, or it may be some sign or token, some object dear to the departed, is indicated. Sometimes, indeed, the apparition seems like a bundle of blazing straw; or, again, merely a muffled voice is heard.

Ten years ago, more or less, at the friary of the Franciscans of the Strict Observance at Nice in Provence, certain supernatural events occurred when one of the community, Father Gabriel (whom I had myself known intimately while I was a member of that house) appeared to several fathers of the house. His voice was plaintive and broken, almost a murmur and a sigh, muffled, as though he were speaking from a great distance. He said that he had not paid in full for the cloth of his habit, which had been bought from a merchant of Marseilles who had given him credit, and that he could not rest until what was due was discharged. He was asked why, before his actual appearance, he had made so hideous a din and hubbub through the corridors, and he explained that it was not he, but an evil spirit who had tried to prevent him from appearing, and wished to hinder him from communicating with his brethren on earth.

It is not at all surprising that this convent should be haunted, for it is built on the site of a very ancient house where Cemelenum once stood, the old city.[8] Spirits have indeed been heard walking up and down the corridors, turning over the leaves of books, seemingly the great elephant folios in the library, counting over money that rattled and chinked, moving tables and furniture about as though dusting the rooms.[9] Not unseldom in houses great noises like sudden claps of thunder or the roar of distant artillery are heard, and this is not without danger, for some spirits have the power to clutch persons by the dress or by the arm, nay even to deal blows and tug men by the hair. Some have even been seriously injured and lamed owing to these manifestations.

There resides in a country house about two leagues from Boulogne-sur-Mer, a lady, the natural daughter of the Sieur de la Meronnière. This lady was actually assaulted and struck by a spirit who screeched out, "I am your stepmother!" When she paid no heed at all to these manifestations, the spirit even snatched up her child, swaddling clothes and all, and cast him into the fire, in order to compel her to ask what it sought. The lady, however, persevered in ignoring these visitations, for she was convinced that it was a lying demon endeavoring to get in touch with her and entrap her, for the wife of her father, the Sieur de la Meronnière, had drowned herself in a creek of the sea. The lady then feared that the suicide must be lost, and she knew that spirits do not thus return from perdition. But the spirit, after many months of commotion and disturbance, revealed that she was of a verity the stepmother, who was not lost, inasmuch as she had taken her life when she was of unsound mind, and at the time she drowned herself she was distraught and not responsible. She entreated her relatives to go on certain pilgrimages for the benefit of her soul. This was done, since when all noises and manifestations have ceased.

Saint John Chrysostom, in his Eighth Homily to the people of Antioch, paints the dangers of darkness.[10] Night with her veil of gloom covers and conceals the face of the earth, shrouding from our eyes all that is lovely and fair in the golden sunshine, the beauty and thousand comely forms of Nature, which speak joy to the heart and mind of man. Nay, goblin fears are brought in her train, for those very objects in which we have taken pleasure and delight often assume such strange and unwonted shapes in the murk that our very hair rises on our heads. In the half-light a man seeing a writhen cord may take it for an envenomed snake; he may suppose his most intimate friend coming upon him suddenly to be his mortal foe, and often if he hears the least noise, even the rustling of a leaf, he shivers with fear when all is so mysterious and shadowed. Soothly we are by no means ill-advised when night draws swiftly darkling on, to be on our guard against unfamiliar sights and sounds.

It is well known that spirits often contrive to render a man's nights sick and sleepless by their malice. They will even so infest houses that those who dwell there are bound to leave, not without considerable loss in pocket and often injury to health as well. These demons or sprites will upset furniture, torment, nip, and thump persons, throwing stones and tiles at them; hold doors and jam them so fast that it is impossible to open them; maraud high and low throughout the whole house, damaging property and perilously molesting men and women, even sometimes (if so God permits) endangering life and limb.

Some ghosts of a particularly evil kind can wreak terrible hurt and harm, for they strike those who see them with a blast of pestilential wind, and then these unfortunate folk find that their lips crack and swell, their faces puff out all aghast and bloated, and it has been known that they are driven frantic with fear. Sometimes, too, the night-fiends or *pookas* torment and beset cattle grazing in the fields, and drive them helter-skelter in vain, headlong panic.

It was superfluous to tell at length the tale of their mischiefs and malice, since there is nobody who either has not by experience tasted, or else from others heard something of, their devilments.

HAUNTING THE
WINGS

*Protestant Christianity was firmly established in England be-
fore the birth of William Shakespeare in 1564. The publication of the Thirty-Nine Articles of Religion in 1563 provided
a clear definition of the teaching of the Church of England,
which declared that "the Romanish doctrine concerning Purgatory, Pardons, Worshipping, and Adoration, as well of Images as of Reliques, and also invocation of Saints, is a fond
thing, vainly invented, and grounded upon no warranty of
Scripture, but rather repugnant to the word of God." With the
abandonment of purgatory as a doctrine of the Church of
England, Elizabethans were no longer taught to believe that
ghostly apparitions were the souls of the returning dead, but
rather angels in disguise or, more frequently, devils masquer-
ading as the dead in order to tempt the living. The last safe
haven for ghosts in early modern England was the stage.*

THE TORMENTS OF
TANTALUS[1]

*The publication in 1581 of an English translation of the Latin
tragedies of the Roman philosopher, moralist, and playwright,
Seneca the Younger (c. 4 BCE—65 CE) had a profound influence on the function and depiction of ghosts in Elizabethan
theater. Drawing on a tradition of Greek tragedy dating back
to Aeschylus (c. 525–455 BCE) and Euripides (480–406
BCE), Seneca deployed ghosts in the prologues of his plays
Thyestes and Agamemnon. Due to their classical ancestry, the
ghosts of the Senecan tragedies evaded the scrutiny of Protestant critics, who never considered them to be agents of papal
propaganda in favor of the doctrine of purgatory. They were
correct, for characters like the ghost of Tantalus in the first act
of Seneca's Thyestes had little in common with the Catholic
ghosts of the Middle Ages. Doomed to perpetual hunger and
thirst in dark Acheron for murdering his son Pelops and feed-
ing him to the gods, Tantalus was compelled to return to the
world of the living as the agent of a fury to infect his ancestral
house with his loathsome presence and thereby incite his
grandsons Atreus and Thyestes to violence, as they vied
against one another for the throne of Argos.*

ACT I

*Before the royal palace of Argos. The time is just before dawn.
[TANTALUS'S ghost enters from a trapdoor in the floor]*

GHOST OF TANTALUS: Who, who has fetched me from my cursed seat in hell, where I was grasping for food that flees from my starving mouth? Who with malice in his heart shows to Tantalus once again these skies and the hateful mansions of the gods in heaven? Has some punishment been found that is worse than parching thirst amid pools of water? Worse than a hungry mouth always gaping for food? Am I to bear Sisyphus's slippery rock on my shoulders? Will Ixion's swiftly whirling wheel wrench my limbs? Will I suffer the punishment of Tityus, who lies stretched out in a vast cavern and feeds dark birds his mangled innards, growing back at night what they consume during the day, fresh fodder for those monstrous beasts when they return anew? To what new torture am I assigned?

O harsh judge of souls, whoever you are who dole out new punishments to the dead, invent some new form of torture, add it to your list! Devise something terrifying, something that would make the guardian of hell's grim dungeon tremble, send shivers through gloomy Acheron, and cause even me to quake in fear. From my seed there arises a new brood that will outdo its ancestors in crime and make me look innocent. They will do what no one has dared to do before. [*The* FURY *rises from the trapdoor behind* TANTALUS] If there is any empty space left in the region reserved for the wicked, *I* will fill it. So long as Pelops's line remains, Minos will never have rest.

FURY: [*cracking a whip with menace*] Go on, you damned ghost! Start tormenting your wicked family with madness! Make your descendants fight using every sort of crime and continually draw their swords in retaliation. Let there be no limit to their hatred, nor any shame. Let blinding rage incite their minds. Let parents' madness linger and let their long cycle of crimes be passed on to their children. Allow them no time to feel resentment for an old crime—no, let a new crime always arise on its heels, and not just an eye for an eye, but while an old crime is avenged let the new one grow greater.

Haughty brothers will lose their kingdoms, then be recalled from exile to rule again. The destiny of their house will swing violently back and forth between short-lived kings; the powerful will become humble, the humble powerful. Fortune will carry the kingship on a constant wave of uncertainty. When god restores to their country those exiled because of their crimes, they will return only to commit more. Everyone else will hate them as much as they hate each other. In their anger they will consider nothing off limits: brother will fear brother, father son, son father. Children will suffer wicked deaths but be born out of even greater wickedness. A hostile wife will plot against her husband. But in this wicked house adultery will be the most trivial of crimes. Righteousness, Faith, Law—all will perish. Wars will be carried across the seas; every land will be irrigated by bloodshed. Lust will exult victoriously over the mighty leaders of nations. Not even heaven will be exempt from your wickedness! Why do stars still shine in heaven's vault? Why do their flames still feel obliged to offer their splendor to the world? No! Let there be deep night! Let day retreat from the sky! Embroil your household! Summon Hatred, Slaughter, and Death! Fill the whole house with your contagion, fill it with the essence of Tantalus. Let the lofty columns and doors be festooned with lush laurel, and let a fire worthy of your advent blaze brightly. Let the Thracian crime be reenacted here—but in greater number.

Why is the uncle's hand idle? Will he ever raise it? It is time: let fires be lit, cauldrons be brought to a boil, and flesh be cut into pieces and thrown in. Let blood stain the ancestral hearth and the feast be laid out. You, Tantalus, you will come to this feast, a guest of a crime all too familiar to you. I have given you a day of freedom; I release you from your hunger to attend this banquet. Break your fast, satisfy your ravenous appetite! Look on, while wine mixed with blood is drunk! [TANTALUS *backs away, turns and runs*] Have I found a meal which even *you* would flee? Stop! Where do you think you're running off to?

GHOST OF TANTALUS: To the pools, the streams, the receding waters—even the fruit-laden tree that flees from my very lips! Please, I beg you, let me return to my dark prison cell! If you do not think that I suffer enough, then move me to a different river: let me be left in the middle of your stream, Phlegethon, surrounded by your fiery waters! Hear me, all of you who are sentenced to punishments doled out by the law of the Fates, you who lie within hollow caves and cower in fear of mountain walls threatening to collapse, you who are bound and tremble before the fierce maw of ravenous lions and the dread ranks of the Furies, and you who, already half-burned, try to hold off the onslaught of torches—hear the voice of Tantalus as he hurtles toward you! Trust me as one who knows: be thankful for the punishments you have! [*To the* FURY] When will you allow me to leave the world of the living?

FURY: After you have thrown your house into turmoil, after you have filled it with war and sword-lust, an evil to kings, and driven uncontrollable madness into their bestial hearts.

GHOST OF TANTALUS: I should *endure* punishments, not *be* one. Am I dispatched as some poisonous vapor from the earth's fissures? Or some pestilence to spread a baleful plague among my people? Will I lead my grandchildren into unspeakable evil? [*Holding up his hands*] Great parent of the gods, and mine, too, however much it may shame you! Even though my tongue may be assessed a heavy penalty and tortured for speaking out, I will yet voice this warning, too: descendants of Tantalus, do not defile your hands with accursed slaughter or stain the altars with the bloodshed of mad revenge! I will stand my ground. I will thwart this crime. [*The* FURY *rises up to her full height and threatens to lash* TANTALUS] Why do you threaten me with lashes and terrorize me with writhing snakes, rekindling that hunger residing in my deepest marrow? It burns, how my heart burns with thirst, and the flames of hunger flare up inside my burning belly! [*Relenting*] I'll comply.

FURY: [*cracking her whip*] Spread this, yes *this* madness throughout your house. Let your descendants be carried away, blinded by fury, and with hostility in their hearts thirst for each other's blood. Ah, the whole house senses your entrance, shuddering mightily at your wicked touch. Good, you have done more than enough. Now go back to the caverns of hell and the streams you know so well. Already the grieving earth revolts beneath your feet. See how the springs disappear, driven back underground? How the riverbeds grow dry? How few clouds are borne along by the scorching winds? Look, all the trees wither, their fruits gone, their branches barren. The Isthmus, once echoing with the roar of neighboring waters, once dividing neighboring shoals with a slender slip of land, now stretches wide, the distant sounds of the opposing seas now but a murmur. Lerna's spring has retreated into the ground. Inachus's channels lie hidden. The Alpheus no longer issues forth its sacred waters. No part of Cithaeron's peaks is white with fallen snow. Noble Argos fears the return of its primeval drought. Look! The Sun-god himself wonders whether he should pull on the reins and compel the day that is destined to perish to continue on its path!

[TANTALUS *and the* FURY *leave through the trapdoor*]

HAMLET, REMEMBER ME[1]

The influence of Seneca's tragedies on William Shakespeare's
The Tragedy of Hamlet, Prince of Denmark *(c. 1599–1602) is
unmistakable, but it was the genius of Shakespeare to blend
classical and Catholic traditions in his depiction of the ghost
of Hamlet's father. Like the specters of Senecan tragedy, this
ghost appeared in the opening act of the play and called for
vengeance in response to a murder in the family. But Shakespeare presented his audience with a "dreaded sight" that
challenged the prevailing notion that ghosts were, in the words
of Sir Thomas Browne "not the wandering souls of men, but
the unquiet walks of Devils, prompting and suggesting us
unto mischief, blood and villainy." The apparition of Hamlet's dead father haunting the ramparts of his castle frightened
and confounded Horatio and his companions, who could only
understand the specter in Protestant terms, as an evil spirit
that "usurp'st this time of night / Together with that fair and
warlike form / In which the majesty of buried Denmark / Did
sometimes march." It is only when Hamlet confronted the
ghost himself and recognized it as his father's genuine soul,
and not a "goblin damn'd," that Shakespeare's invitation to
his audience to consider this spirit in Catholic terms becomes
clear. The persuasive power of the ghost's plea for Hamlet not
only to avenge his "most foul, strange, and unnatural murder," but also to "Remember me" was contingent upon the
shared understanding that Hamlet was actually conversing
with the spirit of his beloved father, who was suffering in purgatory because he died before he could confess his sins. By*

depicting the ghost in this way, Shakespeare tapped into a
millennium-old tradition of medieval Catholic storytelling
that evoked profound feelings of empathy for the suffering of
others.

ACT I SCENE I

Elsinore. A platform before the castle.
[FRANCISCO at his post. Enter to him BERNARDO]
BERNARDO: Who's there?
FRANCISCO: Nay, answer me: stand, and unfold yourself.
BERNARDO: Long live the king!
FRANCISCO: Bernardo?
BERNARDO: He.
FRANCISCO: You come most carefully upon your hour.
BERNARDO: 'Tis now struck twelve; get thee to bed,
   Francisco.

FRANCISCO: For this relief much thanks: 'tis bitter cold,
And I am sick at heart.

BERNARDO: Have you had quiet guard?
FRANCISCO: Not a mouse stirring.   10

BERNARDO: Well, good night.
If you do meet Horatio and Marcellus,
The rivals of my watch, bid them make haste.

FRANCISCO: I think I hear them. Stand, ho! Who's there?

[Enter HORATIO and MARCELLUS]
HORATIO: Friends to this ground.
MARCELLUS: And liegemen to the Dane.
FRANCISCO: Give you good night.

MARCELLUS: O, farewell, honest soldier:
Who hath relieved you?

FRANCISCO: Bernardo has my place.
Give you good night.

                    [Exit]

MARCELLUS: Holla! Bernardo!

BERNARDO: Say,
What, is Horatio there?

HORATIO: A piece of him.
BERNARDO: Welcome, Horatio: welcome, good Marcellus.   20
MARCELLUS: What, has this thing appear'd again to-night?
BERNARDO: I have seen nothing.

MARCELLUS: Horatio says 'tis but our fantasy,
And will not let belief take hold of him
Touching this dreaded sight, twice seen of us:
Therefore I have entreated him along
With us to watch the minutes of this night;
That if again this apparition come,
He may approve our eyes and speak to it.

HORATIO: Tush, tush, 'twill not appear.

BERNARDO: Sit down awhile;   30
And let us once again assail your ears,
That are so fortified against our story
What we have two nights seen.

HORATIO: Well, sit we down,
And let us hear Bernardo speak of this.

BERNARDO: Last night of all,
When yond same star that's westward from the pole
Had made his course to illume that part of heaven
Where now it burns, Marcellus and myself,
The bell then beating one,—

[Enter GHOST*]*

MARCELLUS: Peace, break thee off; look, where it comes
  again!   40
BERNARDO: In the same figure, like the king that's dead.
MARCELLUS: Thou art a scholar; speak to it, Horatio.
BERNARDO: Looks it not like the king? Mark it, Horatio.
HORATIO: Most like: it harrows me with fear and wonder.
BERNARDO: It would be spoke to.
MARCELLUS: Question it, Horatio.

HORATIO: What art thou that usurp'st this time of night,
Together with that fair and warlike form
In which the majesty of buried Denmark
Did sometimes march? By heaven I charge thee, speak!

MARCELLUS: It is offended.
BERNARDO: See, it stalks away!   50
HORATIO: Stay! speak, speak! I charge thee, speak!
[Exit GHOST*]*
MARCELLUS: 'Tis gone, and will not answer.
BERNARDO: How now, Horatio! you tremble and look pale:
Is not this something more than fantasy?
What think you on't?

HORATIO: Before my God, I might not this believe
Without the sensible and true avouch
Of mine own eyes.

MARCELLUS: Is it not like the king?

HORATIO: As thou art to thyself:
Such was the very armor he had on   60
When he the ambitious Norway combated;
So frown'd he once, when, in an angry parley,
He smote the sledded Polacks on the ice.
'Tis strange.

MARCELLUS: Thus twice before, and jump at this dead hour,
With martial stalk hath he gone by our watch.

HORATIO: In what particular thought to work I know not;
But in the gross and scope of my opinion,
This bodes some strange eruption to our state.

MARCELLUS: Good now, sit down, and tell me, he that
    knows,   70
Why this same strict and most observant watch
So nightly toils the subject of the land,
And why such daily cast of brazen cannon,
And foreign mart for implements of war;
Why such impress of shipwrights, whose sore task
Does not divide the Sunday from the week;
What might be toward, that this sweaty haste
Doth make the night joint-laborer with the day:
Who is't that can inform me?

HORATIO: That can I;
At least, the whisper goes so. Our last king,   80
Whose image even but now appear'd to us,
Was, as you know, by Fortinbras of Norway,
Thereto prick'd on by a most emulate pride,
Dared to the combat; in which our valiant Hamlet—
For so this side of our known world esteem'd him—
Did slay this Fortinbras; who by a seal'd compact,
Well ratified by law and heraldry,
Did forfeit, with his life, all those his lands
Which he stood seized of, to the conqueror:
Against the which, a moiety competent   90
Was gaged by our king; which had return'd
To the inheritance of Fortinbras,
Had he been vanquisher; as, by the same covenant,
And carriage of the article design'd,
His fell to Hamlet. Now, sir, young Fortinbras,
Of unimproved mettle hot and full,

Hath in the skirts of Norway here and there
Shark'd up a list of lawless resolutes,
For food and diet, to some enterprise
That hath a stomach in't; which is no other—   100
As it doth well appear unto our state—
But to recover of us, by strong hand
And terms compulsatory, those foresaid lands
So by his father lost: and this, I take it,
Is the main motive of our preparations,
The source of this our watch and the chief head
Of this posthaste and romage in the land.

BERNARDO: I think it be no other but e'en so:
Well may it sort that this portentous figure
Comes armed through our watch; so like the king   110
That was and is the question of these wars.

HORATIO: A mote it is to trouble the mind's eye.
In the most high and palmy state of Rome,
A little ere the mightiest Julius fell,
The graves stood tenantless and the sheeted dead
Did squeak and gibber in the Roman streets:
As stars with trains of fire and dews of blood,
Disasters in the sun; and the moist star
Upon whose influence Neptune's empire stands
Was sick almost to doomsday with eclipse: 120
And even the like precurse of fierce events,
As harbingers preceding still the fates
And prologue to the omen coming on,
Have heaven and earth together demonstrated
Unto our climatures and countrymen.—
But soft, behold! lo, where it comes again!

                    [Re-enter GHOST]
I'll cross it, though it blast me. Stay, illusion!
If thou hast any sound, or use of voice,
Speak to me:

If there be any good thing to be done,   130
That may to thee do ease and grace to me,
Speak to me.

                    [Cock crows]
If thou art privy to thy country's fate,
Which, happily, foreknowing may avoid, O, speak!
Or if thou hast uphoarded in thy life
Extorted treasure in the womb of earth,
For which, they say, you spirits oft walk in death,
Speak of it: stay, and speak! Stop it, Marcellus.

MARCELLUS: Shall I strike at it with my partisan?   140
HORATIO: Do, if it will not stand.
BERNARDO: 'Tis here!
HORATIO: 'Tis here!
MARCELLUS: 'Tis gone!
                    [Exit GHOST]

We do it wrong, being so majestical,
To offer it the show of violence;
For it is, as the air, invulnerable,
And our vain blows malicious mockery.
BERNARDO: It was about to speak, when the cock crew.

HORATIO: And then it started like a guilty thing
Upon a fearful summons. I have heard,
The cock, that is the trumpet to the morn,   150
Doth with his lofty and shrill-sounding throat
Awake the god of day; and, at his warning,
Whether in sea or fire, in earth or air,
The extravagant and erring spirit hies
To his confine: and of the truth herein
This present object made probation.

MARCELLUS: It faded on the crowing of the cock.
Some say that ever 'gainst that season comes
Wherein our Saviour's birth is celebrated,

The bird of dawning singeth all night long: 160
And then, they say, no spirit dares stir abroad;
The nights are wholesome; then no planets strike,
No fairy takes, nor witch hath power to charm,
So hallow'd and so gracious is the time.

HORATIO: So have I heard and do in part believe it.
But, look, the morn, in russet mantle clad,
Walks o'er the dew of yon high eastward hill:
Break we our watch up; and by my advice,
Let us impart what we have seen to-night
Unto young Hamlet; for, upon my life,   170
This spirit, dumb to us, will speak to him.
Do you consent we shall acquaint him with it,
As needful in our loves, fitting our duty?

MARCELLUS: Let's do't, I pray; and I this morning know
Where we shall find him most conveniently.
                              [Exit]

ACT I SCENE II

A room of state in the castle.
[*Enter* KING CLAUDIUS, QUEEN GERTRUDE, HAMLET, POLONIUS,
    LAERTES, VOLTIMAND, CORNELIUS, Lords, and Attendants]
KING CLAUDIUS: Though yet of Hamlet our dear brother's death
The memory be green, and that it us befitted
To bear our hearts in grief and our whole kingdom
To be contracted in one brow of woe,
Yet so far hath discretion fought with nature   5
That we with wisest sorrow think on him,
Together with remembrance of ourselves.
Therefore our sometime sister, now our queen,
The imperial jointress to this warlike state,
Have we, as 'twere with a defeated joy,—   10
With an auspicious and a dropping eye,
With mirth in funeral and with dirge in marriage,

In equal scale weighing delight and dole,—
Taken to wife: nor have we herein barr'd
Your better wisdoms, which have freely gone   15
With this affair along. For all, our thanks.
Now follows, that you know, young Fortinbras,
Holding a weak supposal of our worth,
Or thinking by our late dear brother's death
Our state to be disjoint and out of frame,   20
Colleagued with the dream of his advantage,
He hath not fail'd to pester us with message,
Importing the surrender of those lands
Lost by his father, with all bonds of law,
To our most valiant brother. So much for him.   25
Now for ourself and for this time of meeting:
Thus much the business is: we have here writ
To Norway, uncle of young Fortinbras,—
Who, impotent and bed-rid, scarcely hears
Of this his nephew's purpose,—to suppress   30
His further gait herein; in that the levies,
The lists and full proportions, are all made
Out of his subject: and we here dispatch
You, good Cornelius, and you, Voltimand,
For bearers of this greeting to old Norway;   35
Giving to you no further personal power
To business with the king, more than the scope
Of these delated articles allow.
Farewell, and let your haste commend your duty.

VOLTIMAND and CORNELIUS: In that and all things will we
    show our duty.   40
KING CLAUDIUS: We doubt it nothing: heartily farewell.
        [*Exit* VOLTIMAND and CORNELIUS]

And now, Laertes, what's the news with you?
You told us of some suit; what is't, Laertes?
You cannot speak of reason to the Dane,
And lose your voice: what wouldst thou beg, Laertes,   45
That shall not be my offer, not thy asking?

The head is not more native to the heart,
The hand more instrumental to the mouth,
Than is the throne of Denmark to thy father.
What wouldst thou have, Laertes?   50

LAERTES: My dread lord,
Your leave and favor to return to France;
From whence though willingly I came to Denmark,
To show my duty in your coronation,
Yet now, I must confess, that duty done,   55
My thoughts and wishes bend again toward France
And bow them to your gracious leave and pardon.

KING CLAUDIUS: Have you your father's leave? What says
  Polonius?
LORD POLONIUS: He hath, my lord, wrung from me my slow
  leave
By labor some petition, and at last   60
Upon his will I seal'd my hard consent:
I do beseech you, give him leave to go.

KING CLAUDIUS: Take thy fair hour, Laertes; time be thine,
And thy best graces spend it at thy will!
But now, my cousin Hamlet, and my son,—   65

HAMLET: [*Aside*] A little more than kin, and less than kind.
KING CLAUDIUS: How is it that the clouds still hang on you?
HAMLET: Not so, my lord; I am too much in the sun.
QUEEN GERTRUDE: Good Hamlet, cast thy nighted color off,
And let thine eye look like a friend on Denmark.   70
Do not for ever with thy vailed lids
Seek for thy noble father in the dust:
Thou know'st 'tis common; all that lives must die,
Passing through nature to eternity.
HAMLET: Ay, madam, 'tis common.   75
QUEEN GERTRUDE: If it be,
Why seems it so particular with thee?

HAMLET: Seems, madam! nay it is; I know not 'seems.'
'Tis not alone my inky cloak, good mother,
Nor customary suits of solemn black,   80
Nor windy suspiration of forced breath,
No, nor the fruitful river in the eye,
Nor the dejected 'havior of the visage,
Together with all forms, modes, shapes of grief,
That can denote me truly: these indeed seem,
For they are actions that a man might play:
But I have that within which passeth show;
These but the trappings and the suits of woe.

KING CLAUDIUS: 'Tis sweet and commendable in your nature,
    Hamlet,
To give these mourning duties to your father:
But, you must know, your father lost a father;
That father lost, lost his, and the survivor bound   90
In filial obligation for some term
To do obsequious sorrow: but to persever
In obstinate condolement is a course
Of impious stubbornness; 'tis unmanly grief;
It shows a will most incorrect to heaven,
A heart unfortified, a mind impatient,
An understanding simple and unschool'd:
For what we know must be and is as common
As any the most vulgar thing to sense,
Why should we in our peevish opposition   100
Take it to heart? Fie! 'tis a fault to heaven,
A fault against the dead, a fault to nature,
To reason most absurd: whose common theme
Is death of fathers, and who still hath cried,
From the first corpse till he that died to-day,
'This must be so.' We pray you, throw to earth
This unprevailing woe, and think of us
As of a father: for let the world take note,
You are the most immediate to our throne;
And with no less nobility of love   110
Than that which dearest father bears his son,

Do I impart toward you. For your intent
In going back to school in Wittenberg,
It is most retrograde to our desire:
And we beseech you, bend you to remain
Here, in the cheer and comfort of our eye,
Our chiefest courtier, cousin, and our son.

QUEEN GERTRUDE: Let not thy mother lose her prayers, Hamlet:
I pray thee, stay with us; go not to Wittenberg.
HAMLET: I shall in all my best obey you, madam.   120
KING CLAUDIUS: Why, 'tis a loving and a fair reply:
Be as ourself in Denmark. Madam, come;
This gentle and unforced accord of Hamlet
Sits smiling to my heart: in grace whereof,
No jocund health that Denmark drinks to-day,
But the great cannon to the clouds shall tell,
And the king's rouse the heavens all bruit again,
Re-speaking earthly thunder. Come away.
                                   [*Exit all but* HAMLET]
HAMLET: O, that this too too solid flesh would melt
Thaw and resolve itself into a dew!   130
Or that the Everlasting had not fix'd
His canon 'gainst self-slaughter! O God! God!
How weary, stale, flat and unprofitable,
Seem to me all the uses of this world!
Fie on't! ah fie! 'tis an unweeded garden,
That grows to seed; things rank and gross in nature
Possess it merely. That it should come to this!
But two months dead: nay, not so much, not two:
So excellent a king; that was, to this,
Hyperion to a satyr; so loving to my mother   140
That he might not beteem the winds of heaven
Visit her face too roughly. Heaven and earth!
Must I remember? why, she would hang on him,
As if increase of appetite had grown
By what it fed on: and yet, within a month—
Let me not think on't—Frailty, thy name is woman!—
A little month, or ere those shoes were old

With which she follow'd my poor father's body,
Like Niobe, all tears:—why she, even she—
O, God! a beast, that wants discourse of reason,   150
Would have mourn'd longer—married with my uncle,
My father's brother, but no more like my father
Than I to Hercules: within a month:
Ere yet the salt of most unrighteous tears
Had left the flushing in her galled eyes,
She married. O, most wicked speed, to post
With such dexterity to incestuous sheets!
It is not nor it cannot come to good:
But break, my heart; for I must hold my tongue.

       [*Enter* HORATIO, MARCELLUS, *and* BERNARDO]
HORATIO: Hail to your lordship!
HAMLET: I am glad to see you well:
Horatio,—or I do forget myself.
HORATIO: The same, my lord, and your poor servant ever.   165
HAMLET: Sir, my good friend; I'll change that name with you:
And what make you from Wittenberg, Horatio? Marcellus?
MARCELLUS: My good lord—
HAMLET: I am very glad to see you. Good even, sir.
But what, in faith, make you from Wittenberg?
HORATIO: A truant disposition, good my lord.
HAMLET: I would not hear your enemy say so,   170
Nor shall you do mine ear that violence,
To make it truster of your own report
Against yourself: I know you are no truant.
But what is your affair in Elsinore?
We'll teach you to drink deep ere you depart.
HORATIO: My lord, I came to see your father's funeral.
HAMLET: I pray thee, do not mock me, fellow-student;
I think it was to see my mother's wedding.
HORATIO: Indeed, my lord, it follow'd hard upon.
HAMLET: Thrift, thrift, Horatio! the funeral baked meats
Did coldly furnish forth the marriage tables.   181
Would I had met my dearest foe in heaven
Or ever I had seen that day, Horatio!

My father!—methinks I see my father.
HORATIO: Where, my lord?
HAMLET: In my mind's eye, Horatio.
HORATIO: I saw him once; he was a goodly king.
HAMLET: He was a man, take him for all in all,
I shall not look upon his like again.
HORATIO: My lord, I think I saw him yesternight.
HAMLET: Saw? who?   190
HORATIO: My lord, the king your father.
HAMLET: The king my father!
HORATIO: Season your admiration for a while
With an attent ear, till I may deliver,
Upon the witness of these gentlemen,
This marvel to you.
HAMLET: For God's love, let me hear.
HORATIO: Two nights together had these gentlemen,
Marcellus and Bernardo, on their watch,
In the dead vast and middle of the night,
Been thus encounter'd. A figure like your father,
Armed at point exactly, cap-a-pe,
Appears before them, and with solemn march   200
Goes slow and stately by them: thrice he walk'd
By their oppress'd and fear-surprised eyes,
Within his truncheon's length; whilst they, distilled
Almost to jelly with the act of fear,
Stand dumb and speak not to him. This to me
In dreadful secrecy impart they did;
And I with them the third night kept the watch;
Where, as they had deliver'd, both in time,
Form of the thing, each word made true and good,   210
The apparition comes: I knew your father;
These hands are not more like.
HAMLET: But where was this?
MARCELLUS: My lord, upon the platform where we watch'd.
HAMLET: Did you not speak to it?
HORATIO: My lord, I did;
But answer made it none: yet once methought
It lifted up its head and did address

Itself to motion, like as it would speak;
But even then the morning cock crew loud,
And at the sound it shrunk in haste away,
And vanish'd from our sight.
HAMLET: 'Tis very strange.   220
HORATIO: As I do live, my honour'd lord, 'tis true;
And we did think it writ down in our duty
To let you know of it.

HAMLET: Indeed, indeed, sirs, but this troubles me.
Hold you the watch to-night?
BERNARDO: We do, my lord.
HAMLET: Arm'd, say you?
BERNARDO: Arm'd, my lord.
HAMLET: From top to toe?
BERNARDO: My lord, from head to foot.
HAMLET: Then saw you not his face?
HORATIO: O, yes, my lord; he wore his beaver up.
HAMLET: What, look'd he frowningly?
HORATIO: A countenance more in sorrow than in anger.   230
HAMLET: Pale or red?
HORATIO: Nay, very pale.
HAMLET: And fix'd his eyes upon you?
HORATIO: Most constantly.
HAMLET: I would I had been there.
HORATIO: It would have much amazed you.
HAMLET: Very like, very like. Stay'd it long?
HORATIO: While one with moderate haste might tell a hun
   dred.
BERNARDO: Longer, longer.
HORATIO: Not when I saw't.
HAMLET: His beard was grizzled—no?
HORATIO: It was, as I have seen it in his life,
A sable silver'd.

HAMLET: I will watch tonight;   240
Perchance 'twill walk again.
HORATIO: I warrant it will.

HAMLET: If it assume my noble father's person,
I'll speak to it, though hell itself should gape
And bid me hold my peace. I pray you all,
If you have hitherto conceal'd this sight,
Let it be tenable in your silence still;
And whatsoever else shall hap to-night,
Give it an understanding, but no tongue:
I will requite your loves. So, fare you well:
Upon the platform, 'twixt eleven and twelve,   250
I'll visit you.
ALL: Our duty to your honor.
HAMLET: Your loves, as mine to you: farewell.
                    [*Exit all but* HAMLET]
My father's spirit in arms! all is not well;
I doubt some foul play: would the night were come!
Till then sit still, my soul: foul deeds will rise,
Though all the earth o'erwhelm them, to men's eyes.
                    [*Exit*]

ACT I SCENE IV

The platform.
[*Enter* HAMLET, HORATIO, *and* MARCELLUS]
HAMLET: The air bites shrewdly; it is very cold.
HORATIO: It is a nipping and an eager air.
HAMLET: What hour now?
HORATIO: I think it lacks of twelve.
HAMLET: No, it is struck.
HORATIO: Indeed? I heard it not: then it draws near the season
Wherein the spirit held his wont to walk.

[*A flourish of trumpets, and ordnance shot off, within*]
What does this mean, my lord?
HAMLET: The king doth wake to-night and takes his rouse,
Keeps wassail, and the swaggering up-spring reels;
And, as he drains his draughts of Rhenish down,   10
The kettle-drum and trumpet thus bray out

The triumph of his pledge.
HORATIO: Is it a custom?
HAMLET: Ay, marry, is't:
But to my mind, though I am native here
And to the manner born, it is a custom
More honor'd in the breach than the observance.
This heavy-headed revel east and west
Makes us traduced and tax'd of other nations:
They clepe us drunkards, and with swinish phrase
Soil our addition; and indeed it takes   20
From our achievements, though perform'd at height,
The pith and marrow of our attribute.
So, oft it chances in particular men,
That for some vicious mole of nature in them,
As, in their birth—wherein they are not guilty,
Since nature cannot choose his origin—
By the o'ergrowth of some complexion,
Oft breaking down the pales and forts of reason,
Or by some habit that too much o'er-leavens
The form of plausive manners, that these men,   30
Carrying, I say, the stamp of one defect,
Being nature's livery, or fortune's star,—
Their virtues else—be they as pure as grace,
As infinite as man may undergo—
Shall in the general censure take corruption
From that particular fault: the dram of evil
Doth all the noble substance of a doubt
To his own scandal.
HORATIO: Look, my lord, it comes!
                    [Enter GHOST]
HAMLET: Angels and ministers of grace defend us!
Be thou a spirit of health or goblin damn'd,   40
Bring with thee airs from heaven or blasts from hell,
Be thy intents wicked or charitable,
Thou comest in such a questionable shape
That I will speak to thee: I'll call thee Hamlet,
King, father, royal Dane: O, answer me!

Let me not burst in ignorance; but tell
Why thy canonized bones, hearsed in death,
Have burst their cerements; why the sepulcher,
Wherein we saw thee quietly inurn'd,
Hath oped his ponderous and marble jaws,   50
To cast thee up again. What may this mean,
That thou, dead corpse, again in complete steel
Revisit'st thus the glimpses of the moon,
Making night hideous; and we fools of nature
So horridly to shake our disposition
With thoughts beyond the reaches of our souls?
Say, why is this? wherefore? what should we do?

[GHOST *beckons* HAMLET]

HORATIO: It beckons you to go away with it,
As if it some impartment did desire
To you alone.

MARCELLUS: Look, with what courteous action   60
It waves you to a more removed ground:
But do not go with it.
HORATIO: No, by no means.
HAMLET: It will not speak; then I will follow it.
HORATIO: Do not, my lord.
HAMLET: Why, what should be the fear?
I do not set my life in a pin's fee;
And for my soul, what can it do to that,
Being a thing immortal as itself?
It waves me forth again: I'll follow it.

HORATIO: What if it tempt you toward the flood, my lord,
Or to the dreadful summit of the cliff   70
That beetles o'er his base into the sea,
And there assume some other horrible form,
Which might deprive your sovereignty of reason
And draw you into madness? think of it:
The very place puts toys of desperation,

Without more motive, into every brain
That looks so many fathoms to the sea
And hears it roar beneath.

HAMLET: It waves me still.
Go on; I'll follow thee.
MARCELLUS: You shall not go, my lord.
HAMLET: Hold off your hands.   80
HORATIO: Be ruled; you shall not go.
HAMLET: My fate cries out,
And makes each petty artery in this body
As hardy as the Nemean lion's nerve.
Still am I call'd. Unhand me, gentlemen.
By heaven, I'll make a ghost of him that lets me!
I say, away! Go on; I'll follow thee.

[*Exit* GHOST *and* HAMLET]
HORATIO: He waxes desperate with imagination.
MARCELLUS: Let's follow; 'tis not fit thus to obey him.
HORATIO: Have after. To what issue will this come?
MARCELLUS: Something is rotten in the state of Denmark.   90
HORATIO: Heaven will direct it.
MARCELLUS: Nay, let's follow him.
[*Exit*]

ACT I SCENE V

Another part of the platform.
[*Enter* GHOST *and* HAMLET]
HAMLET: Where wilt thou lead me? speak; I'll go no further.
GHOST: Mark me.
HAMLET: I will.
GHOST: My hour is almost come,
When I to sulfurous and tormenting flames
Must render up myself.
HAMLET: Alas, poor ghost!
GHOST: Pity me not, but lend thy serious hearing

To what I shall unfold.
HAMLET: Speak; I am bound to hear.
GHOST: So art thou to revenge, when thou shalt hear.
HAMLET: What?
GHOST: I am thy father's spirit,
Doom'd for a certain term to walk the night,   10
And for the day confined to fast in fires,
Till the foul crimes done in my days of nature
Are burnt and purged away. But that I am forbid
To tell the secrets of my prison-house,
I could a tale unfold whose lightest word
Would harrow up thy soul, freeze thy young blood,
Make thy two eyes, like stars, start from their spheres,
Thy knotted and combined locks to part
And each particular hair to stand on end,
Like quills upon the fretful porpentine: 20
But this eternal blazon must not be
To ears of flesh and blood. List, list, O, list!
If thou didst ever thy dear father love—
HAMLET: O God!
GHOST: Revenge his foul and most unnatural murder.
HAMLET: Murder!
GHOST: Murder most foul, as in the best it is;
But this most foul, strange and unnatural.

HAMLET: Haste me to know't, that I, with wings as swift
As meditation or the thoughts of love,   30
May sweep to my revenge.

GHOST: I find thee apt;
And duller shouldst thou be than the fat weed
That roots itself in ease on Lethe wharf,
Wouldst thou not stir in this. Now, Hamlet, hear:
'Tis given out that, sleeping in my orchard,
A serpent stung me; so the whole ear of Denmark
Is by a forged process of my death
Rankly abused: but know, thou noble youth,
The serpent that did sting thy father's life

Now wears his crown.
HAMLET: O my prophetic soul! My uncle!   40
GHOST: Ay, that incestuous, that adulterate beast,
With witchcraft of his wit, with traitorous gifts,—
O wicked wit and gifts, that have the power
So to seduce!—won to his shameful lust
The will of my most seeming-virtuous queen:
O Hamlet, what a falling-off was there!
From me, whose love was of that dignity
That it went hand in hand even with the vow
I made to her in marriage, and to decline   50
Upon a wretch whose natural gifts were poor
To those of mine!
But virtue, as it never will be moved,
Though lewdness court it in a shape of heaven,
So lust, though to a radiant angel link'd,
Will sate itself in a celestial bed,
And prey on garbage.
But, soft! methinks I scent the morning air;
Brief let me be. Sleeping within my orchard,
My custom always of the afternoon,   60
Upon my secure hour thy uncle stole,
With juice of cursed hebenon in a vial,
And in the porches of my ears did pour
The leprous distilment; whose effect
Holds such an enmity with blood of man
That swift as quicksilver it courses through
The natural gates and alleys of the body,
And with a sudden vigor doth posset
And curd, like eager droppings into milk,
The thin and wholesome blood: so did it mine;   70
And a most instant tetter bark'd about,
Most lazar-like, with vile and loathsome crust,
All my smooth body.
Thus was I, sleeping, by a brother's hand
Of life, of crown, of queen, at once dispatch'd:
Cut off even in the blossoms of my sin,
Unhousel'd, disappointed, unanel'd,

No reckoning made, but sent to my account
With all my imperfections on my head:
O, horrible! O, horrible! most horrible! 80
If thou hast nature in thee, bear it not;
Let not the royal bed of Denmark be
A couch for luxury and damned incest.
But, howsoever thou pursuest this act,
Taint not thy mind, nor let thy soul contrive
Against thy mother aught: leave her to heaven
And to those thorns that in her bosom lodge,
To prick and sting her. Fare thee well at once!
The glow-worm shows the matin to be near,
And 'gins to pale his uneffectual fire: 90
Adieu, adieu! Hamlet, remember me.

[*Exit*]

HAMLET: O all you host of heaven! O earth! What else?
And shall I couple hell? O, fie! Hold, hold, my heart;
And you, my sinews, grow not instant old,
But bear me stiffly up. Remember thee!
Ay, thou poor ghost, while memory holds a seat
In this distracted globe. Remember thee!
Yea, from the table of my memory
I'll wipe away all trivial fond records,
All saws of books, all forms, all pressures past, 100
That youth and observation copied there;
And thy commandment all alone shall live
Within the book and volume of my brain,
Unmix'd with baser matter: yes, by heaven!
O most pernicious woman!
O villain, villain, smiling, damned villain!
My tables,—meet it is I set it down,
That one may smile, and smile, and be a villain;
At least I'm sure it may be so in Denmark:

[*Writing*]

So, uncle, there you are. Now to my word; 110
It is 'Adieu, adieu! remember me.'
I have sworn 't.

HORATIO: [*Within*] My lord, my lord,—
MARCELLUS: [*Within*] Lord Hamlet,—
HORATIO: [*Within*] Heaven secure him!
HAMLET: So be it!
HORATIO: [*Within*] Hillo, ho, ho, my lord!
HAMLET: Hillo, ho, ho, boy! come, bird, come.
            [*Enter* HORATIO *and* MARCELLUS]
MARCELLUS: How is't, my noble lord?
HORATIO: What news, my lord?
HAMLET: O, wonderful!
HORATIO: Good my lord, tell it.
HAMLET: No; you'll reveal it.
HORATIO: Not I, my lord, by heaven.
MARCELLUS: Nor I, my lord.   120

HAMLET: How say you, then; would heart of man once
    think it?
But you'll be secret?
MARCELLUS: Ay, by heaven, my lord.
HAMLET: There's ne'er a villain dwelling in all Denmark
But he's an arrant knave.

HORATIO: There needs no ghost, my lord, come from the
    grave
To tell us this.

HAMLET: Why, right; you are in the right;
And so, without more circumstance at all,
I hold it fit that we shake hands and part:
You, as your business and desire shall point you;
For every man has business and desire,   130
Such as it is; and for mine own poor part,
Look you, I'll go pray.
HORATIO: These are but wild and whirling words, my lord.
HAMLET: I'm sorry they offend you, heartily;
Yes, faith heartily.
HORATIO: There's no offense, my lord.
HAMLET: Yes, by Saint Patrick, but there is, Horatio,

And much offence, too. Touching this vision here,
It is an honest ghost, that let me tell you:
For your desire to know what is between us,
O'ermaster 't as you may. And now, good friends,   140
As you are friends, scholars, and soldiers,
Give me one poor request.

HORATIO: What is't, my lord? we will.
HAMLET: Never make known what you have seen tonight.
MARCELLUS: My lord, we will not.
HAMLET: Nay, but swear't.

HORATIO: In faith,
My lord, not I.

MARCELLUS: Nor I, my lord, in faith.
HAMLET: Upon my sword.
MARCELLUS: We have sworn, my lord, already.
HAMLET: Indeed, upon my sword, indeed.
GHOST: *[Beneath]* Swear.

HAMLET: Ah, ha, boy! say'st thou so? art thou there,
  truepenny?   150
Come on—you hear this fellow in the cellarage—
Consent to swear.

HORATIO: Propose the oath, my lord.
HAMLET: Never to speak of this that you have seen,
Swear by my sword.

GHOST: [*Beneath*] Swear.
HAMLET: *Hic et ubique*? then we'll shift our ground.
Come hither, gentlemen,
And lay your hands again upon my sword:
Never to speak of this that you have heard,
Swear by my sword.   160
GHOST: [*Beneath*] Swear.
HAMLET: Well said, old mole! Canst work i' the earth so fast?

A worthy pioner! Once more remove, good friends.
HORATIO: O day and night, but this is wondrous strange!
HAMLET: And therefore as a stranger give it welcome.
There are more things in heaven and earth, Horatio,
Than are dreamt of in your philosophy. But come;
Here, as before, never, so help you mercy,
How strange or odd soe'er I bear myself,   170
As I perchance hereafter shall think meet
To put an antic disposition on,
That you, at such times seeing me, never shall,
With arms encumber'd thus, or this headshake,
Or by pronouncing of some doubtful phrase,
As "Well, well, we know," or "We could, an if we would,"
Or "If we list to speak," or "There be, an if they might,"
Or such ambiguous giving out, to note
That you know aught of me: this not to do,
So grace and mercy at your most need help you, Swear.   180
GHOST: [*Beneath*] Swear.
HAMLET: Rest, rest, perturbed spirit!
                       [*They swear*]
So, gentlemen,
With all my love I do commend me to you:
And what so poor a man as Hamlet is
May do, to express his love and friending to you,
God willing, shall not lack. Let us go in together;
And still your fingers on your lips, I pray.
The time is out of joint: O cursed spite,
That ever I was born to set it right!   190
Nay, come, let's go together.
                       [*Exit*]

Notes

ODYSSEUS IN THE HOUSE OF DEATH

1. Homer, *The Odyssey* 11.13-256, trans. Robert Fagels (New York: Viking Penguin, 1996), pp. 250–256.
2. Erebus was the name of the place of darkness beneath the earth where the dead were thought to dwell.
3. Persephone was the daughter of Zeus and Demeter, who became queen of the underworld after her abduction by Hades.
4. Aeaea was the name of the island where Circe lived and where Elpenor still lay unburied after his accidental death.

PLINY CONTEMPLATES THE EXISTENCE OF GHOSTS

1. Pliny the Younger, *Letter* 7.27, in *The Letters of the Younger Pliny*, trans. Betty Radice (New York: Penguin Books, 1963), pp. 202–205 (slightly altered).
2. Curtius Rufus was a first-century magistrate of the senatorial rank, who may also have been the author of a history of Alexander the Great that proved to be very popular in the Middle Ages.
3. The veracity of the spirit's prediction indicated that she was a manifestation of the divine will (*numen*) rather than an empty hallucination.
4. Domitian was the emperor of Rome from 81 to 96.

A MISTRESS OF THE GRAVES

1. Lucan, *Civil War* 6.565-928, in *Lucan, Civil War*, trans. Matthew Fox (New York: Penguin Classics, 2012), pp. 164–175 (slightly altered).

2. Dis Pater is the Roman name for the god of the underworld, the equivalent of the Greek Hades.

3. Haemus refers to the Balkan mountain range, which is nowhere near Pharsalus, the town in ancient Greece, in the vicinity of which Caesar defeated Pompey in battle in 48 BCE. Lucan seems to be associating the name of the mountain with Haemonia, a poetic name for Thessaly.

4. Emathia is an ancient reference to Macedonia.

5. Rhodope is a mountain in western Thrace.

6. Avernus was the name of a crater located near Cuma in Italy. In the ancient period, it was believed to be an entrance to the underworld.

7. Taenarus was another entrance to the underworld in ancient lore. It was located on the southern tip of one of the peninsulas in the Peloponnese.

8. The Eumenides were the Furies, the Greek deities of vengeance. Cerberus was the great three-headed dog that guarded the gate to the underworld.

9. *Echenais* were small fish, whose name means "holds back ships" (Gr. *Echein naus*). In antiquity, they were a common ingredient in magical spells.

10. Elysium is the name of the isles of the blessed, the abode of dead heroes.

11. Tartarus and Orcus are synonyms for the underworld or the gods thereof.

12. Tisiphone and Megaera are the names of the Furies.

SPEAKING WITH THE DEAD IN THE HEBREW SCRIPTURES

1. Translated by Scott G. Bruce from the Latin Vulgate version of Deut. 18.9–14.

2. Translated by Scott G. Bruce from the Latin Vulgate version of 1 Sam. 28.1 and 3–25.

A GHOST UPON THE WATERS

1. Translated by Scott G. Bruce from the Latin Vulgate version of Matt. 14:22–33.

DREAMING OF THE DEAD

1. Translated by Scott G. Bruce from *Passio sanctarum Perpetuae et Felicitatis* 7-8, ed. H. Musurillo, in *The Acts of the Christian Martyrs* (Oxford: Oxford University Press, 1972), pp. 114 and 116.

THE DISCERNMENT OF THE SAINTS

1. Translated by Scott G. Bruce from Sulpicius Severus, *Vita sancti Martini* 11, ed. Jacques Fontaine, in *Sulpice Sévère, Vie de saint Martin*, 3 vols., Sources chrétiennes 133-135 (Paris: L'Éditions du Cerf, 1967–1968), vol. 1, p. 276.
2. Translated by Scott G. Bruce from Constantius, *Vita sancti Germani* 10, ed. René Borius, in *Constance de Lyon, Vie de saint Germain d'Auxerre*, Sources chrétiennes 112 (Paris: L'Éditions du Cerf, 1965), pp. 138, 140, and 142.
3. Recast in modern English from the translation of Whitley Stokes in *The Tripartite Life of Patrick with Other Documents Relating to that Saint* (London: Eyre and Spottiswoode, 1887), pp. 125 and 127.

EVODIUS'S INQUIRY: GOING FORTH FROM THE BODY, WHO ARE WE?

1. Translated by Scott G. Bruce from Augustine, *Epistolae* 158 and 159, ed. A. Goldbacher, Corpus Scriptorum Ecclesiasticorum Latinorum 44 (Vienna: F. Tempsky, 1904), pp. 488–496 and 498.
2. Phil. 1.23.
3. See Psalm 84.2; and Psalm 23.5, respectively.
4. See Rom. 8.37.
5. Compare Matt. 10.29.

AUGUSTINE'S REJECTION OF GHOSTS

1. Translated by Scott G. Bruce from Augustine, *De cura pro mortuis gerenda ad Paulinum* 12-15, ed. Joseph Zycha, Corpus Scriptorum Ecclesiasticorum Latinorum 41 (Vienna: F. Tempsky, 1900), pp. 639–646.
2 *Aeneid* 6.337-383.

POPE GREGORY THE GREAT: HOW CAN THE LIVING HELP THE DEAD?

1. Translated by Scott G. Bruce from Gregory the Great, *Dialogorum libri quattuor* 4.40, 4.47, 4.53, and 4.55, ed. J. P. Migne, in *Patrologiae Cursus Completus: Series Latina* 77 (Paris: Garnier Fratres, 1896), cols. 396–397, 408–409, 413, 416–417, and 420–421.
2. The dalmatic was a long tunic with wide sleeves worn by deacons during the celebration of the Mass.
3. See Acts 8.20.

THE VISION OF BARONTUS

1. Translated by Scott G. Bruce from *Visio Baronti monachi Longoretensis*, ed. W. Levison in Monumenta Germaniae Historica: Scriptorum rerum Merovingicarum 5 (Hannover and Leipzig, Germany: Impensis Bibliopolii Hahniani, 1910), pp. 373–394.
2. Saint-Pierre de Longoret in the diocese of Bourges, later renamed Saint-Cyran-du-Jambot.
3. Matins was the night office of the church, usually sung at midnight or in the early hours of the morning.
4. Presumably a reference to the liberation of the Israelites from slavery in Egypt through the agency of God working through his prophet Moses, as recounted in the Book of Exodus.
5. Modern Méobecq in central France.
6. Psalm 103.22.
7. Psalm 51.1.
8. See Gregory the Great, *Dialogues* 4.36.
9. Manuscript copies of the *Vision of Barontus* included illustrations depicting the keys of Saint Peter.
10. Psalm 51.1.
11. Matt. 19.21.
12. See Luke 16.22.
13. Gregory the Great, *Dialogues* 4.36. The quotation is from Matt. 13.30.
14. Gregory the Great, *Homilies on the Gospels* 12.5.
15. See Psalm 40.11.

DRYHTHELM RETURNS FROM THE DEAD

1. Translated by Scott G. Bruce from *Bede's Ecclesiastical History of the English People* 5.12, ed. Bertram Colgrave and R. A. B.

Mynors (Oxford: Clarendon Press, 1969), pp. 488, 490, 492, 494, 496, and 498.

IMPERIAL TORMENTS

1. Translated by Scott G. Bruce from *Annales Fuldenses*, *anno* 874, ed. F. Kurze, Monumenta Germaniae Historica: Scriptores rerum Germanicarum 7 (Hannover, Germany: Impensis Bibliopolii Hahniani, 1891), p. 82.

CLUNY AND THE FEAST OF ALL SOULS

1. Translated by Scott G. Bruce from Iotsald, *Vita Odilonis* 2.15, ed. Johannes Staub, in *Iotsald von Saint-Claude, Vita des Abtes Odilo von Cluny*, Monumenta Germaniae Historica: Scriptores Rerum Germanicarum in Usum Scholarum Separatim Editi 68 (Hannover, Germany: Hahnsche Buchhandlung, 1999), pp. 218–220.

A LESBIAN GHOST

1. Translated by Scott G. Bruce from Peter Damian, *Epistola* 168, ed. Kurt Reindel in *Die Briefe des Petrus Damiani*, Monumenta Germaniae Historica; Die Briefe der Deutschen Kaiserzeit, 4 vols. (Munich: Monumenta Germaniae Historica, 1983–1993), vol. 4, pp. 242–243.

THE HAUNTING OF THE CLOISTER

1. Translated by Scott G. Bruce from Peter the Venerable, *De miraculis libri duo* 1.9–11, ed. Denise Bouthillier, Corpus Christianorum, Continuatio Mediaeualis 83 (Turnhout, Belgium: Brepols, 1988), pp. 34–42.
2. Phil. 1.21.
3. Psalm 84.4.
4. Psalm 80.11.
5. The rules against mundane conversation were so strict at the abbey of Cluny that the monks developed a rudimentary form of sign language to communicate essential information to one another when speaking was forbidden. See Scott G. Bruce, *Silence and Sign Language in Medieval Monasticism: The Cluniac Tradition, c. 900–1200* (Cambridge: Cambridge University Press, 2007).

WARNINGS TO THE LIVING

1. Translated by Scott G. Bruce from Caesarius of Heisterbach, *Dialogus miraculorum* 12.18, 12.19, 12.24, 12.29, 12.36, and 12.41, ed. Horst Schneider, in *Caesarius von Heisterbach, Dialog über die Wunder*, 5 vols. (Turnhout, Belgium: Brepols, 2009), vol. 5, pp. 2214, 2216, 2218, 2236, 2238, 2248, 2250, 2252, 2262, 2264, 2266, 2278, and 2280.
2. Usury is the act of lending money at interest, which was forbidden among medieval Christians.
3. Wisdom 6.7.
4. See 1 Cor. 7.14.
5. This prayer serves as the offertory during the Mass on November 2, All Souls Day.
6. The Cisterican General Chapter was the annual gathering of Cistercian abbots at Cîteaux, the motherhouse of the entire order.
7. Lauds is the office of prayer that takes place at sunrise.
8. 1 Sam. 2.9.
9. *The Rule of Benedict* 7, trans. Caroline White (New York: Penguin Classics, 2008), p. 25.
10. Advent Day probably refers to Advent Sunday, the fourth Sunday before Christmas Day that marks the beginning of Advent, the first day of the liturgical year, and the start of Advent season, which culminates on Christmas Day. Since the date of this feast day changes every year, it is impossible to know the precise day when this miracle took place.
11. *Benedicte* means "Be blessed" in Latin; *Dominus* means "Lord."
12. *Cruselinum* is a rare Latin word for a small drinking cup.

SPIRITS OF MALICE

1. Translated by Scott G. Bruce from Thietmar of Merseburg, *Chronicon* 1.11-13, ed. Robert Moltzman, in *Monumenta Germanie Historica: Scriptores rerum Germanicarum*, n.s. 9 (Berlin: Apud Weidmannos, 1935), pp. 17–18.
2. Matins was the night office of the church, usually sung at midnight or in the early hours of the morning.
3. The invitatory is the name given to any of the psalms that signal the beginning of Nocturns, which are part of the office of matins.
4. See Rom. 12.3.

THE BLACKENED HEARTS OF
STAPENHILL

1. Translated by Scott G. Bruce from Geoffrey of Burton, *Life and Miracles of St. Modwenna*, ed. Robert Bartlett (Oxford: Clarendon Press, 2002), pp. 192, 194, 196, 198.

THE EVIL WELSHMAN

1. Translated by Scott G. Bruce from Walter Map, *De nugis curialium: Courtiers' Trifles* 2.27, ed. M. R. James, rev. ed. Christopher N. L. Brooke and Roger A. B. Mynors (Oxford: Clarendon Press, 1982), pp. 202 and 204.

RAMPAGING REVENANTS

1. Translated by Scott G. Bruce from William of Newburgh, *Historia rerum Anglicarum* 5.22-24, in *Chronicles of the Reigns of Stephen, Henry II, and Richard I*, ed. Richard Howlett, Rolls Series 82, 2 vols. (London: Longman, 1884–85), vol. 2, pp. 474–482.
2. The Feast of the Ascension, also known as Holy Thursday, was a moveable feast day in the liturgical calendar commemorating the bodily ascension of Jesus into heaven. It took place on the fortieth day after Easter, a Thursday.
3. Commemorating the entry of Jesus into Jerusalem, Palm Sunday is a moveable feast day in the liturgical calendar that always falls on the Sunday before Easter Sunday.

TERROR IN TONNERRE

1. Translated by Scott G. Bruce from Rodulphus Glaber, *Historiarum libri quinque* 5.6, ed. John France in *Rodulphus Glaber: The Five Books of Histories and the Life of St. William* (Oxford: Clarendon Press, 1989), p. 222.

HELLEQUIN'S HORDE

1. Translated by Scott G. Bruce from Walter Map, *De nugis curialium: Courtiers' Trifles* 1.11, ed. M. R. James, rev. ed. Christopher N. L. Brooke and Roger A. B. Mynors (Oxford: Clarendon Press, 1982), pp. 26, 28, and 30.

2. Pan, the Greek god of shepherds and flocks, likewise had the legs and hooves of a goat.
3. Ovid, *Metamorphoses*, 2.1–30.
4. Henry II was crowned at Westminster on December 19, 1154.
5. Translated by Scott G. Bruce from Orderic Vitalis, *Historia ecclesiastica* 8.17, ed. Marjorie Chibnall, in *The Ecclesiastical History of Orderic Vitalis*, 6 vols. (Oxford: Clarendon Press, 1968-1980), vol. 4, pp. 236, 238, 240, 242, 244, 246, 248, and 250.
6. Biers are wooden frames commonly used to transport corpses or coffins.
7. A cubit is an ancient unit of measurement that takes its name from the Latin word for elbow (*cubitum*) because its length is the distance between the tip of the middle finger and the elbow.
8. The Mont Saint-Michel is a small island off the coast of Normandy crowned with a church and monastery dedicated to the archangel Michael.

AN ARMY WHITE AS SNOW

1. Translated by Christopher A. Jones from MS Valenciennes, Bibliothèque municipale 516, fols. 109rb-110vb, dating from the thirteenth or fourteenth century. An edition of the Latin text will appear as Appendix A in Christopher A. Jones and Scott G. Bruce, *The* Relatio metrica de duobus ducibus: *A Twelfth-Century Cluniac Poem on Prayer for the Dead*, Publications of the Journal of Medieval Latin 10 (Turnhout: Brepols, 2017).
2. For what follows, see 2 Kings 6:8-18.

THE RAVENOUS DEAD

1. Translated by Scott G. Bruce from Saxo Grammaticus, *Gesta Danorum, The History of the Danes*, ed. Karsten Friis-Jensen and trans. Peter Fisher, 2 vols. (Oxford: Clarendeon Press, 2015), vol. 1, pp. 336 and 338.
2. *Seven Viking Romances*, trans. Hermann Pálsson and Paul Edwards (New York: Penguin Books, 1985), pp. 236–238.

OLD GHOSTS, NEW LAWS

1. *Eyrbyggja Saga*, trans. Hermann Pálsson and Paul Edwards (New York: Penguin Books, 1989), pp. 93–95 and 129–141.

2. In medieval Scandinavia, door-courts were *ad hoc* courts that convened at the door of the house of the defendant.

RECREATION FOR AN EMPEROR

1. Translated by Scott G. Bruce from Gervase of Tilbury, *Otia Imperialia* 1.20, 3.17, 3.99, and 3.103, ed. S. E. Banks and J. W. Binns, in *Gervase of Tilbury, Otia Imperialia, Recreation for an Emperor,* Oxford Medieval Texts (Oxford: Clarendon Press, 2002), pp. 112, 114, 588, 590, 752, 754, 758, 760, 762, 764, 766, 768, 770, 772, 774, 776, and 778.

2. See Matt. 26.26–30; Mark 14.22–26; Luke 22.14–20; and I Cor. 11.23–25.

3. St. Ruf was an Augustinian priory that was transferred to Valence in 1158. Pope Adrian IV (1154–1159) had been prior there from its founding in 1139 until 1148/49 and as pope had sanctioned its removal to Valence.

4. That is, the cellarer swapped out the much longer Psalm 51 for the much shorter Psalm 117.

5. John II, who was bishop of Pozzuoli around 1135.

6. Avernus was the name of a dormant volcano near Cuma, Italy, widely believed since the Roman period to be an entrance to the underworld. Gervase is using the term here as a synonym for purgatory.

7. Compare John 11.17: "Now when Jesus came, he found that Lazarus had already been in the tomb four days."

8. Compare 2 Cor. 12.2–4.

9. Lazarus's account of hell was made known in the Middle Ages through an apocryphal text called the *Vision of Lazarus* (*Visio Lazari*).

10. *Viaticum* (Latin for "provisions for a journey") is the name given to the Mass when it is administered to a dying person. It is a key component to the last rites performed when death is imminent.

11. Saint-Michel de Frigolet was a Benedictine priory situated between Tarascon and Avignon.

12. Gregory the Great, *Dialogues* 4.30.

13. Gregory the Great, *Dialogues* 4.45–46.

14. "The Eater" is a reference to Peter Comestor ("Peter the Eater"), a twelfth-century theologian and scholar whose voracious appetite for knowledge earned him his nickname.

15. Gregory the Great, *Dialogues* 4.44, quoting Psalm 86.13.

16. Gregory the Great, *Dialogues* 4.43.

17. Luke 2.14.
18. Gregory the Great, *Dialogues* 4.34 and 36.
19. Gregory the Great, *Dialogues* 4.26.
20. Matt. 24.28 and Luke 17.37; and Phil. 1.23.
21. 2 Cor. 5.1.
22. The medieval understanding of Jerusalem as the center of the world, the scene of the crucifixion, and the image of the heavenly city all play a role in its significance to the ghost.
23. In the thirteenth century, it was widely believed that Bernard of Clairvaux had rejected the celebration of the feast of the Immaculate Conception because the feast had not been formally recognized by the pope.
24. Gregory the Great, *Dialogues* 4.26.
25. That is, that the priest had the power to bind the Devil with his stole.
26. John the Baptist leaping for joy in the womb: Luke 1.41 and 1.44; sending his disciples to inquire about Jesus' identity: Matt. 11.2-3 and Luke 7.19-20.
27. Pope Innocent III launched a crusade against the Albigensian heretics of Languedoc in 1209.
28. The prelate in question was the Cistercian monk William Hélie, who was bishop of Orange from c. 1205 to 1221. On the Cistercian General Chapter, see p. 278, n.6, above.

THE GHOSTS OF BYLAND ABBEY

1. Translated by Scott G. Bruce from the Latin edition of M. R. James in "Twelve Medieval Ghost Stories," *English Historical Review* 37 (1922): 413-422.
2. Richard II was King of England from 1377 to 1399.
3. The title of triumph is probably a reference to the title posted on the cross above Jesus, when he was crucified: INRI, which stood for *Iesus Nazarenus, Rex Iudaeorum* ("Jesus of Nazareth, King of Jews"). See John 19.19-20. At the end of the Middle Ages, this title was commonly inscribed on protective amulets to ward off evil spirits.
4. The church stile is the entrace to the churchyard, in this instance presumably a gate.
5. No priest has been mentioned up to this point in the story. Either the priest has been present at the necromancer's ritual and silent until now or, more probably, the necromancer also happens to be a priest.

6. The shrine of Saint James in Santiago de Compostela in north-western Spain was one of the most popular pilgrimage destinations in the Middle Ages.

7. A mortuary was the name given to the customary offering by a recently deceased person to the parish priest of a farm animal in payment for any tithes still owed to the church.

OF GHOSTES AND SPIRITES WALKING BY NYGHT

1. Rendered into idiomatic English by Scott G. Bruce from Lewes Lavater, *Of Ghostes and Spirites Walking by Nyght*, trans. Robert Harrison (London: Thomas Creede, 1596), pp. 1, 71–75; 77–79; 98, 127–129, 175–176, and 191–192.

2. Davos is a town high in the Swiss Alps located in the canton of Graubünden, Switzerland.

3. Gregorius Agricola (1494–1555) was a sixteenth-century German scientist most famous for his influential book on mineralogy, *De re metallica* (1556), from which Lavater has drawn the following anecdotes.

4. Gerolamo Cardano (1501–1576) was a sixteenth-century Italian polymath who wrote many books on mathematics, cosmology, and the natural world. His treatise *De rerum veritate* (*On the Truth of Things*) appeared in 1557.

5. See pp. 29–30, above.

6. The *Urim* was an unidentified item that resided in the breastplate of a high priest of ancient Israel and had some function related to divination.

7. Here Lavater seems to be confusing Matt. 7.6 ("Do not give dogs what is sacred; do not throw your pearls to pigs.") with the story related in Matt. 8.30–32, in which demons entreat Jesus to enter a herd of swine when he casts them out of the person they have possessed.

8. See p. 31, above.

9. In the Hebrew scriptures, the Book of Job recounts the hardships endured by God's servant Job and his eventual restoration. In the medieval tradition, Job became a symbol of patience.

WHEN NIGHT DRAWS SWIFTLY DARKLING ON

1. Noel Taillepied, *A Treatise of Ghosts*, trans. Montague Summers (London: Fortune Press, 1933), pp. 94–95, 97–99, and 101–107.
2. Ember seasons refers to Ember days, a set of three days (Wednesday, Friday, and Saturday) in the liturgical calendar set aside for fasting and prayer. Ember days are celebrated four times a year, during weeks known as Ember weeks.
3. The visions of Cornelius and Peter take place in Acts 10:3–4 and 10:10–11, respectively.
4. Bonaventure (1221–1274) was a thirteenth-century Franciscan theologian. The saint in question is Saint Francis (1181–1226), the founder of the Franciscan order.
5. Pythagoras of Samos (ca. 570–ca. 495 BCE) was an ancient Greek mathematician and philosopher.
6. Isa. 13.19–22.
7. Isa. 34.1–17.
8. Cimiez, a neighborhood in Nice, France, is the site of the ruins of the Roman settlement of Cemelenum.
9. Elephant folios are massive books up to 24 inches tall.
10. John Chrystostom (ca. 349–407) was a renowned preacher. He was born in the city of Antioch and frequently preached there before becoming archbishop of Constantinople in 397. Hundreds of his homilies have survived.

THE TORMENTS OF TANTALUS

1. Seneca, *Phaedra and Other Plays*, trans. R. Scott Smith (New York: Penguin Books, 2011), pp. 201–204.

HAMLET, REMEMBER ME

1. William Shakespeare, *Hamlet, Prince of Denmark*, ed. K. Deighton (London: MacMillan and Co., 1919), pp. 3–17 and 21–30.

Index